White Bound

White Bound

Nationalists, Antiracists,
and the Shared Meanings of Race

Matthew W. Hughey

Stanford University Press
Stanford, California

Stanford University Press
Stanford, California

Printed in the United States of America on acid-free, archival-quality paper

Library of Congress Cataloging-in-Publication Data
Hughey, Matthew W. (Matthew Windust), author.
    White bound : nationalists, antiracists, and the shared meanings of race / Matthew W.
Hughey.
        pages   cm
    Includes bibliographical references and index.
    ISBN 978-0-8047-7694-3 (cloth : alk. paper)—ISBN 978-0-8047-7695-0 (pbk. : alk. paper)
    1. White nationalism—United States. 2. Anti-racism—United States. 3. Race—Social
aspects—United States. 4. United States—Race relations. I. Title.
    E184.A1H84 2012
    305.800973—dc23
                                                                          2012001452

Typeset by Thompson Type in 10/14 Minion

Contents

Acknowledgments

IT TAKES A VILLAGE TO RAISE A BOOK. Through concerted and cooperative effort, many hands brought this project to fruition. Of primary import, the utmost thanks go to the members of both National Equality for All and Whites for Racial Justice. I am appreciative of the courageous and compassionate ways you opened your lives to sociological scrutiny. Although I am confident we will disagree over some of my analysis, we certainly do share a profound concern over the future of race relations and the possibilities of a world without racial conflict.

This text holds the voices of many others to whom I owe direct thanks. In particular, Ira Bashkow, Bethany Bryson, Krishan Kumar, and Jeffrey Olick directly mentored my sociological treatment of race and racial identity formation. In particular, Milton Vickerman provided pragmatic guidance, emotional support, and a keen knowledge of racial theory and history. His open door and academic acumen were always at the ready. Thank you, Milton.

Quite a few others lent their hand to this book's binding. Sharon Hays gave me a tool kit stocked with theory on cultural sociology, ethnography, and inequality. She reminded me that the "writing of people" is always an ethical and political project that deserves utmost care. Wende Marshall was kind enough to bring her erudite knowledge of cultural anthropology to bear on the problem of white supremacy. Corey D. B. Walker's mantra that theory works in the interests of certain people was a welcome specter that haunted my writing. Eduardo Bonilla-Silva, David Brunsma, Ashley "Woody" Doane, Joe Feagin, Grace Hale, Claudrena Harold, John Hartigan Jr., Kimberly Kelly,

Amanda Lewis, Allison Pugh, Josipa Roksa, and Donald Shaffer all dropped jewels of wisdom that now enrich this text. Tristan Bridges, Todne Thomas Chipumuro, Carey Sargent, and Hephzibah Strmic-Pawl provided strong collegiality and intellectual insight that carried me through both data collection and analysis.

I am especially indebted to the students in my "Sociological Perspectives on Whiteness" classes at the University of Virginia. The discussion and argumentation in those spaces proved essential. It was a blessing to simultaneously research, write, and teach on white racial identity. In this vein, I am thankful to Cynthia Hoehler-Fatton, then Interim Director of the Carter G. Woodson Institute for Afro-American and African Studies, for going to bat for such a course.

I would be remiss if I did not acknowledge the years of navigational support from Joan Snapp and Katherine Shiflett in the Department of Sociology at the University of Virginia. As the gatekeepers of departmental and institutional knowledge, they were lighthouses in the fog of bureaucracy. I remain thankful for the countless pep talks throughout the years.

Completing a book is not just a matter of cerebral inspiration but is also an endeavor of material pragmatism. My daily sustenance came from an array of sources. The Ford Foundation Fellowship honorable mention, the Phelps-Stokes Fellowship, Seven Society & Teaching Resource Center Fellowships, the Charles H. and Nancy E. Evans Fellowship, and the University of Virginia College of Arts and Sciences Society of Fellows Grant all helped cover the costs of living and time spent in the ethnographic field. Also, I am indebted to the Carter G. Woodson Institute for Afro-American and African Studies and the Departments of African American Studies, Media Studies, and Sociology at the University of Virginia for affording me affiliate faculty positions. Finally, landing a tenure track position at Mississippi State University (during a moment of economic catastrophe) allowed me to bring this project home.

Stanford University Press and its associates have been a windfall of support. From the insight supplied by the anonymous reviewers, the editorial board, the work of assistant editors Joa Suorez and Clementine Breslin, and the copyediting of Margaret Pinette, to the countless readings and suggestions—both large and small—of executive editor Kate Wahl, everyone at Stanford made this book all the better for their efforts. In short, their work has been outstanding.

Lastly, I offer thanks to my parents who, while enduring financial hardship, helped sustain me by providing a place to live and work in peace and quiet. Their material, emotional, and spiritual buttressing of this endeavor can never be sufficiently repaid. I remain eternally grateful for their unwavering support.

1 Racists versus Antiracists?

*White antiracists? Misguided folks, but I get them, I mean,
[long pause] they want to have equality and multiculturalism,
and so do we . . . In many ways, we are not all that different. In
fact, I consider myself one of them [laughing]. I don't use your
language, but yeah, I'm a white antiracist!*

—Robert, National Equality for All

*The white nationalist movement today, they are using our
rhetoric, our ideas . . . because they feel threatened. I guess
on some level they want to be respected as individual human
beings, just like we want all people to be respected as human
beings. That's similar . . . in a strange sort of way.*

—Philip, Whites for Racial Justice

A LARGE OAK TABLE WITH PAPERS, books, and several coffee cups strewn about oc-
cupies the middle of the room. Numerous people sit in bulky, inflexible chairs.
Some type on laptops, several busy themselves with reading, and others jot
down notes on yellow legal pads. A few people scurry about the room, dive in
and out of file cabinets, briefly speak with colleagues, and wait for a turn at
one of the few computers to send an email or look up needed information. The
phone has been ringing incessantly for the past hour. Call after call is fielded,
schedules double-checked, and appointments made. People are a bit on edge.
Still, most manage to smile and remain courteous to one another. In less than
a week, it will be the anniversary of Dr. Martin Luther King Jr.'s birthday—a
U.S. federal holiday since 1986. People are readying their commemoration of
the day by preparing press packets about the life and legacy of Dr. King to dis-
seminate to radio, tv, and blogs. Derek, a thirty-four-year-old advertising and
marketing agent, sits down beside me. Seemingly exhausted, he slumps into
the chair with a deep sigh. He removes his glasses with his left hand, holding
them unfolded in his outstretched arm. With his right hand he loosens his
tie and undoes the top button of his shirt. For more than a few moments he
slowly rubs his forehead as if trying to massage away a deadening headache.
After some time he slowly replaces his glasses, looks down at the floor, and
says in a low tone: "It's hard to fight all the disinformation out there . . ." his
voice trailing off as he speaks. "But!" he asserts emphatically as he turns to
look at me, placing his hand on my shoulder. "We've got to get the truth out

there to people. This is one of the few times each year when people will really listen." Derek smiles and rises from his seat to greet a colleague who has
entered the room. "I think the big selling point we have," says Derek, looking
back at me as his colleague walks up to greet him with a handshake, "is that
King was against affirmative action, we're not saying anything different. . . .
We as white people must protect our racial heritage and separate. That is the
key to our self-determination." This is "The Office," the unofficial moniker for
the national headquarters of "National Equality for All," a white nationalist
organization located in a metropolitan area on the East Coast of the United
States.

"Whites for Racial Justice" is also located on the outskirts of a city on the
East Coast of the United States. It is the headquarters of a nationwide white
antiracist organization and is no more than a few hours' drive from the headquarters of National Equality for All. The group meets in the basement of a
member's house, but it is not the stereotypical dark and dimly lit space. A few
years ago, the members pitched in and finished it with drywall, wall-to-wall
carpeting, and modern wood furnishings. Bookshelves are everywhere in the
room. Many volumes end up in large piles several feet tall, stacked next to the
walls. There are history books on the civil rights era, the speeches of Frederick Douglass, John Howard Griffin's *Black Like Me*, and the heavily used
and dog-eared pages of *Whites Confront Racism* by sociologist Eileen O'Brien.
On this day, like many others before it, members slowly trickle in for the biweekly gathering. The theme for today's meeting is "Everyday Insurrections,"
or what white people can do on a daily basis to fight racism. Malcolm, one
of the official "coordinators" of the organization, enters the room, greeting
every person individually. After enjoining everyone to take his or her seat and
begin, Malcolm introduces a supplement to the day's agenda: "I think what we
need to do, as conscious, thinking, aware human beings who have decided to
take a stand against racism, is what we can, or rather, *need* [emphasizing the
word] to do to stop racism in our own lives as well as take a stand against it
structurally, is . . . well . . . to constantly ask ourselves, 'How can I become less
"white"?'" His fingers make the motion of air quotes around the word *white* as
he speaks. Smiling nods and looks of sincere appreciation greet his commen-
tary. This is a typical meeting of Whites for Racial Justice.

For a little over one year—from May 2006 through June 2007—I spent
at least one day a week with members of the white nationalist organization
National Equality for All (NEA) and the white antiracist organization Whites

for Racial Justice (WRJ). I attended their meetings, analyzed their literature, interviewed their members, and informally spent time with those members in a variety of settings: from long stays in organizations' offices and members' homes to quick trips to the post office and supermarket. I hung out with their friends and listened to their life stories. I shared meals with them in their homes. I met the elder members of their families, and I played with many of their children.

I came to NEA and WRJ with the interest of comparing how these two groups make meaning of white racial identity. In many ways, these two organizations are everything one would expect. They act, talk, and look quite different. They are near-perfect examples of how white racial identity can be marshaled toward antagonistic political projects. While they may seem strange and radical to many observers, they both appeal to fairly normative and logical arguments to shield their activism. They both spend a great deal of time defending who they are and what they do from outsiders. They detest jokes about their activism, they work very hard to be taken seriously, and they both worry about the future of race relations and white people in the United States, if not across the globe.

Like many whites today, both white nationalists and white antiracists see themselves as autonomous individuals making independent choices that reflect their authentic desires and true selves. Yet these choices, desires, and selves are anchored to racial categories and meanings that structure how they negotiate the world. It is important to recognize, then, that these actors do not engage in their activism in isolation. Both the white nationalists and white antiracists craft their understandings of the world, and who they are as white people in that world, out of available meanings and shared expectations. The members of both organizations use the dominant understandings of race today to continually re-create and re-form both their individual and collective white racial identities. They then use those identities as potent resources and rationales for how they should marshal their activism toward the world's problems.

I neither defend nor demonize either group or its members in this book. Rather, I present a comparative examination of how the members of both groups make meaning of race, particularly whiteness, in social situations of meaningful interaction. In coming to address this focus, I found something quite unexpected. Located just a short distance from one another on the East Coast of the United States, the members of these two groups inhabit incredibly different social worlds. Yet they rely on similar racial and cultural meanings to interpret and navigate those worlds. And while I document many of the differences between these two groups in the pages that follow, I concentrate on how they make meaning of whiteness in strikingly similar ways. This is a book about the racialized ideals that are held in common between white nationalists and white antiracists—and how such commonality relates to the reproduction of both racism and white racial identity. Several dimensions of this white ideal—what I call "hegemonic whiteness"—will be discussed in the chapters that follow. But before we embark on that journey, it is necessary to lay a foundation.

The Project of White Racial Identity

Making the argument that important and crucial similarities exist between white nationalists and white antiracists is rife with the potential to agitate. My point is not to provoke but rather to draw attention to how whites come to construct their own identities in ways that are simultaneously distinct *and* surprisingly similar. Whereas a great deal of scholarship views the vast landscape of different white racial identities as the result of antagonistic political ideologies and stratified material resources, I focus instead on how actors negotiate, contest, and reform the dominant *meanings* of white racial identity in everyday social relations. My goal is not to refute the standard arguments about the power of political ideals and material resources. This line of inquiry and reasoning has led to important insights. My concern centers on the ways that racialized meanings propel whites' interpersonal social relations and how white racial identity is enacted through these social relations. By social relations, I mean situations in which actors create or rely on a sense of who they think they are (here, white racial identity) in relation to real and/or imagined others in the situation or expected situations.[1]

Racial identity—as categories arranged in relational hierarchy—serves as a convenient and "commonsense" system for organizing social action and order across an array of social contexts. The meanings associated with race do not evaporate with the passing of one social relation to the next but structure our activities and identities across time and space. I will show how the dominant meanings of race organize our social relations and how this social order works to reproduce racist schema and racial inequality through the mundane activities of everyday life. To examine white racial identity, we must examine it as an ongoing process, as a meaningful accomplishment, and as a kind of "project." Omi and Winant argue that racial projects "connect what race *means* in a particular discursive practice and the ways in which both social structures and everyday experiences are racially *organized*, based upon that meaning."[2] I follow suit to examine whiteness neither as a biological fact nor as an illusion but as a real social classification that supplies a meaningful worldview and set of strategies to those who embody that category. To empirically access these meanings and strategies, I focus on the symbolic boundaries and shared narratives that make up white social relations.

"Symbolic boundaries" are the conceptual divisions that people make between objects, between themselves and other people, and between practices. These meaningful distinctions operate as a "system of rules that guide interaction by affecting who comes together to engage in what social act."[3] Applied to race, these boundaries then constitute, and often justify or naturalize, a system of classification that defines hierarchy and moral worth between and within racial groups. Such "boundary work" involves the construction of a collective white identity by drawing on supposedly common traits, experiences, and a shared sense of belonging.[4] Regarding "shared narratives," the key idea is that people interpret their lives as a set of recognizable stories that contain causally linked sequences of events. Shared narratives are central to how we construct racial identities because they link the social world together; stories provide accounts of how individuals view themselves in relation to others. Narratives affect behavior because people often choose actions that are consistent with the meaningful expectations of their racial identities. Together, symbolic boundaries illuminate the meanings and cultural basis of racial categories, and narratives order the links between categories in a recognizable story. Only when these categories and stories are "widely agreed upon can they take on a constraining character and pattern social interaction in important ways . . . [as] identifiable patterns of social exclusion."[5]

People are bound to meaningful categories and stories to establish group membership, to cope with their lives, and to provide strategies for resisting and reproducing aspects of society they find troubling and pleasing. For the white activists covered in this book, the already established meanings of race were used to construct stable, knowable, and respected white racial identities. In thinking about white racial identities as strategic and usable things, I certainly do not imply that the white nationalists and white antiracists studied herein always made rational and conscious decisions through a sort of "cost/benefit" approach to life. Rather, these white racial activists employed the cultural resources of symbolic boundaries and shared narratives in intelligent, creative, savvy, and emotional ways. And at the same time, these strategies held unconscious, unforeseen, and unintended results; sometimes the actors even reproduced the very dilemmas they sought to displace. And while I consider white racial identity to be an ongoing act of accomplishment that gains significance in social interaction, I note the importance that these activists place on portraying coherent and firm identities that seem anything but in flux.

In the chapters that follow, I argue that these white racial activists are fastened to the dominant expectations of white racial identity and are in search of idealized forms of that identity; thus the double entendre of _White Bound_ as a sense of *attachment and trajectory*. Each chapter demonstrates how the shared meanings of race and whiteness—and the strategies derived from those meanings—affect NEA's and WRJ's antithetical goals in strikingly similar ways. On the whole, this book throws theoretical speculation about the supposed bifurcation of white racial identity into relief against the realities of two groups never before directly compared. In a recent study of white identity, sociologist Paul Croll wrote, "There is a significant relationship between boundary maintenance and claiming a strong white racial identity . . . By and large, scholars have either focused their research on racist organizations or on anti-racism activities, rarely have they looked at both."[6] By examining seemingly antithetical white groups, we can begin to see not just a plurality of white racial identities but also the strategies that recreate the dominant ways of being white.

Rethinking Racial Dichotomies

We love things that come in pairs. Whether male/female, nature/nurture, fact/opinion, mind/body, reason/emotion, winners/losers, or good/bad, binaries are a cornerstone of social structure and a road map for our navigation of everyday life. The lumping and splitting of our culture into distinct and polarized categories is a meaningful enterprise.[7] After all, particular descriptions of reality are quite arbitrary, and categorization does not merely sort our experiences but helps to infuse everyday life with specific meanings. And when the controversial topics of racism and racial identity are introduced, binaries become extremely useful frameworks for making agreed-on meaning out of racial chaos, controversy, and conflict.

Consequently, North Americans generally discuss racism along the lines of "racists and antiracists." This is not a new phenomenon. The categories "racist" and "antiracist" are deeply historical. The historian Herbert Aptheker documented white racist and white antiracist activism from the 1600s to the 1860s. He effectively challenged the notion that whites universally accepted racism until the outbreak of the Civil War, bringing to light a neglected, but vibrant, white antiracist history.[8] Yet, as amateur historians, we tend to examine such tales through a bifurcated lens. Driven by this paradigm, "white racists" become the originators and protectors of slavery, the cause of Jim Crow segregation, the supporters of eugenics, and the keepers of hidden prejudices toward immigrants. Conversely, the "white antiracists" are the enlightened; a group that somehow escaped the disgrace of supporting "Manifest Destiny" against Native Americans, decried the internment camps for the Japanese during World War II, and traversed the U.S. South on "Freedom Rides" in the 1960s. While some of this story is certainly true, such a view is dangerously reductive and violently oversimplified for understanding the link between racism and white racial identity.[9]

One could argue that the continued reverence for this bifurcated understanding of whiteness enables an articulation of two static versions of whiteness. One account is a tale of heroic whites untainted by the ugly spectacles of bigotry, violence, and hypocrisy, while another narrative describes whites that were simply the "bad apples" that fell prey to hate. To put it bluntly, a simple and sanitary tale of innocence and guilt is seductive. Such seductions are what sociologists Joe Feagin and Hernán Vera call "sincere fictions":

> Usually unfeigned and genuine, the negative beliefs about and images of African Americans provide the make-believe foundation for white dominance and supremacy. Yet the sincere fictions of whites encompass more than negative images of the out-group; they also involve images of one's self and one's group. *The key to understanding white racism is to be found not only in what whites think of people of color but also in what whites think of themselves* [my emphasis].[10]

In examining what "whites think of people of color . . . [and] what whites think of themselves," it is tempting to assume that essential distinctions exist between these two "types" of white identity formations (racists and antiracists) and then proceed to study how the differences in their identity manifest in their understanding of the world.

For example, consider the tracking of hate groups undertaken by the Southern Poverty Law Center (SPLC), a group on which the Federal Bureau of Investigation (FBI), Bureau of Alcohol, Tobacco, Firearms, and Explosives (ATF), and other government agencies rely for information. After documenting the unprecedented rise in (predominantly white) hate groups—an increase of 300 to 1,002 between the years 1992 and 2010—the SPLC also began recording a rise in "people of goodwill." Presented in the form of a color-coded map, the United States is portrayed as a nation growing in racial polarization; blood-red dots signify hate groups while calming patches of chartreuse denote people "standing strong against hate."[11]

Such a view paints a polarized picture of mainstream white America. This picture implicitly enables our navigation of racial tempests. When we encounter an overtly racial action or statement, we can invoke the preset narrative. Consider the 2008–2010 Birther and Tea Party depictions of Barack Obama as a primate living in a watermelon-infested White House, the June 2009 Holocaust Museum shooter James von Brunn, or evolutionary psychologist Satoshi Kanazawa's May 2011 evaluation that black women are physically less attractive than women of other races.[12] We quickly frame such events as atypical and fringe "racism," labor to throw the racist rascal(s) out, and dispatch a few white antiracist warriors to guard against racism's return. Problem solved.

Or is it? Understandings of white racism and white antiracism as distinct polarities allow us to construct sanitary tales of political conflict. But what if the relationship between white racial identity and racism transcends politics and the singling out of the "bad apple" racists?[13] Can we understand white racial identity as something more than a reflection of abstract political disputes? How do we explain not only rampant racial segregation in housing, education, religion, and employment but also prejudicial and narrow beliefs amid *both* "racist" and "antiracist" white populations? What do we make of the continued legacy of white racial privilege that protects white "racists" and "antiracists" alike? How do we explain the vast heterogeneity of whiteness that exceeds, if not explodes, a politically bifurcated spectrum? And, most importantly, how do the white actors intimately engaged in these debates interpret and manage their lives? Do they frame their involvement in this struggle as an absolute battle between good and evil, as mundane decisions, or as something altogether different? The answers to these questions lie in a closer examination of peoples' lives within these polarized groups.

The Contemporary Meanings of Whiteness

The study of whiteness is far from new. White racial identity had been scrutinized by an array of intellectuals long before mainstream sociologists were interested in the topic. An explicit yet embryonic interest in whiteness stretches
back, at the least, to William J. Wilson's 1860 essay "What Shall We Do with
the White People?"[14] Since that time, there have been an array of influential
studies, from W. E. B. Du Bois's classic essay "The Souls of White Folk" in
Darkwater, to Langston Hughes's *The Ways of White Folks*, to James Baldwin's
simplistic, but no less astute, observation that "there are no white people, only
people who think they are white."[15] Given that whiteness has long been studied, it has traversed several stages of inquiry.

A large part of the early scholarship on whiteness explored the observation
that whites generally have a lower degree of self-awareness about race and
their own racial identity than do members of other racial groups.[16] In interviews with white respondents, various scholars found that when asked about
the meaning of whiteness, most replied along the lines of "I've never really
thought that much about it."[17] Such data bolstered scholars' assertions that
the power of whiteness stemmed from its mundane normality. As Richard
Dyer wrote in key essay on whiteness: "White power secures its dominance by
seeming not to be anything in particular."[18]
While the invisibility and normality of whiteness is an important insight,
it is crucial not to overemphasize white racial unconsciousness. In a study
of white college students, Charles Gallagher found that whites exhibit a high
degree of racial consciousness when they are the racial minority or if they
perceive themselves as a threatened group.[19] Other scholars demonstrate how
challenges to the status quo can result in a defensive white racial consciousness that takes the form of white nationalist groups like the Ku Klux Klan,
White Citizen's Councils, neo-Nazis, anti-immigration forces like the Minutemen, or factions of the newly made Tea Party.[20] Accordingly, such a trend
led Frankenberg to reject her earlier understanding of whiteness as simply an
invisible normality.[21]

While the invisibility factor in whiteness studies is a lesser trope of late,
the associations of whiteness with privilege are far more immune to challenges. Much of the recent work on whiteness bears on the methods by which
whites minimize or feel guilty about their privileged status.[22] This denial of
white privilege is the foundation of "color-blind racism." Sociologist Eduardo

Bonilla-Silva argues that many people—especially whites—now assert that the post–civil rights era in which we now live is racially egalitarian.[23] Under this logic, many whites argue we should be "color-blind." Any focus on race in terms of redressing the effects of past racism or current racial discrimination and racial inequality is reframed as an antiwhite form of "reverse racism."

Another approach to the study of whiteness centers on the white "backlash" against the advances born from the civil rights movement. From the passage of Proposition 209 in 1996, the Supreme Court *Bollinger* decisions in 2003, the passage of the Michigan Civil Rights Initiative (MCRI) in 2006, to the change in precedent set by *Brown v. Board* (1954) in the 2007 Supreme Court ruling of *Meredith v. Jefferson County Board of Education*, many argue that white backlashes against recent human rights legislation are increasing.[24] Accordingly, "many whites see themselves as victims of the multicultural, pc, feminist onslaught . . . [and this] would be laughable if it were not for the sense of mental crisis and the reactionary backlash that underpin these beliefs."[25] The white (and often male, middle-class, and heterosexual) identities once taken for granted as secure, stable, and in charge are now changing due to challenges from younger generations, the "browning of America," the civil rights movement, and fundamental crises in the neoliberal economy. Abby Ferber wrote, "Central to this backlash is a sense of confusion over the meanings of both masculinity and whiteness, triggered by the perceived loss of white, male privilege."[26] Whiteness becomes an overt topic of political discussion; most tend to frame whites, especially white men, as orchestrating a backlash against recent progress in gender and racial politics.

Despite the aforementioned organized and legal responses of the white backlash, I believe that the concept of "backlash" oversimplifies and obscures contemporary white struggles with the meanings of race. Today, whites are not just rebelling against civil rights gains or other "progressive" social programs; many are fighting to protect them. What whites should do and what it means to be white are highly contested questions. Accordingly, Howard Winant demonstrates how a neoconservative "backlash" does not solely characterize white identity but that white identity resembles a bifurcated political spectrum. Winant writes:

> Existing racial projects can be classified along a political spectrum, according to explicit criteria drawn from the meaning each project attaches to "white-

ness." . . . Focusing on five key racial projects, which I term, far right, new right, neoconservative, neoliberal, and new abolitionist.[27]

Winant maps a theory of white identity formation onto this bifurcated politics of progressive and conservative movements. Labeling this phenomenon "racial dualism as politics," Winant writes, "Today, the politics of white identity is undergoing a profound political *crisis* [my emphasis] . . . This volatility provides ongoing evidence of racial dualism among whites."[28] Under this rubric, whiteness is understood as a series of white racial reactions that resemble a political spectrum. Chief among these varied white formations are the white racist and the white antiracist movements. Winant writes that these two movements indicate "a *new politicization of whiteness* . . . that has taken shape particularly in the post-civil rights era . . . the significance of white identity was reinterpreted and repoliticized."[29]

Evidence that whiteness is politically polarizing is surely available in widely divergent registers, from the recent proliferation of "whiteness studies" of a particular leftist and antiracist stance to popular newsmagazine and television coverage of the anti-immigration Minutemen that constructs a picture of white America and white people as under attack from the brown masses of Central and South America. Whiteness appears to shift in response to changes in the social, political, and cultural terrain. Responses are often multiple and sometimes contradictory. This is especially true when considering a population as economically, religiously, and politically diverse as the white population in the United States.

The Changing Sameness of White Racial Identity

Given the heterogeneity of whiteness, there is great debate over who the white racists and white antiracists are in our society. Yet there is little disagreement that "racism and antiracism" exist as two, stable, divergent, and opposing sides. Alastair Bonnett writes that the story of racism and antiracism "is staged with melodrama, the characters presented as heroes and villains: pure anti-racists versus pure racists, good against evil."[30] So, also, sociologist Jack Niemonen remarks that we often "paint a picture of social reality in which battle lines are drawn, the enemy identified, and the victims sympathetically portrayed. . . . [distinguishing] between 'good' whites and 'bad' whites."[31] Eduardo Bonilla-Silva even makes the point that scholars interested in studying race can unintentionally impose a dichotomous framework on their data:

"Hunting for 'racists' is the sport of choice of those who practice the 'clinical approach' to race relations—the careful separation of good and bad, tolerant and intolerant Americans."[32] After the 2008 election of Barack Obama, racial dualism proved prevalent among many as they celebrated a white antiracist triumph over racism in the political mainstream. Journalist Tim Wise wrote: "While it may be tempting . . . to seek to create a dichotomy whereby the 'bad whites' are the ones who voted against the black guy, while the 'good whites' are the ones who voted for him, such a dualism is more than a little simplistic."[33]

In creating distance from this dichotomous framework, it is important to avoid either reducing whiteness to an aggregate of disconnected actors or painting whiteness as a one-dimensional category of uniform power and privilege. We can accomplish this task if we examine white nationalist and white antiracist identity as less of a thing and more of an ongoing process. Race is not a static event but a process of patterned events that demonstrate a larger cultural system that continually reracializes certain objects, habits, rituals, words, and people. Because white racial identity formation is a part of this process, the meaning of whiteness varies spatially (by location), temporally (by historical eras and within the individual life span), contextually (by the relative culture), differentially (by power), and intersectionally (by combination with class, gender, sexual orientation, and so on). Yet, at the same time, these varied forms of white identities are bound together as a singular dominant and racially privileged group. Sociologist Troy Duster writes that whiteness:

> can be *simultaneously* Janus-faced and multifac(et)ed—and also produce a singularly dominant social hierarchy. Indeed, if we make the fundamental mistake of reifying any one of those states as more real than another, we will lose basic insights into the nature and character of racial stratification in America.[34]

Hence, it is imperative to examine the cultural strategies that simultaneously splinter and bind the white formation process. If we approach white identity in this way, we can avoid reproducing the Manichean conflation of unquestionably different *political stances* as essentially different *racial identities*.

Ideal ("Hegemonic") Whiteness

Writing about racial interactions in his landmark book *Soul on Ice*, Eldridge Cleaver observed, "The ideal white man was one who knew how to use his head, who knew how to manage and control things and get things done. Those whites who were not in a position to perform these functions nevertheless aspired to them."[35] Cleaver's observation was an important one. While there is no question about the political differences and individual heterogeneity of white actors in an array of settings, it is important to recognize that certain forms of whiteness can become dominant and pursued as an ideal.

In any given setting or context an ideal of whiteness emerges alongside many other ways of "being white" that are complicit, subordinate, or marginalized in relation to that ideal. What may be an ideal in one context may not be at all ideal in other. For example, how a white male student in a majority black and urban high school is expected to perform his racial identity in ways that bring him status and respect from other whites—as described in Edward Morris's *An Unexpected Minority*—is much different from how white girls in middle-class suburbs are expected to behave if they too wish to gain admiration and standing from their peer groups—as portrayed in Lorraine Kenny's *Daughters of Suburbia*.[36]

However, people do not live in isolated vacuums. Different contexts and locales are not completely disconnected from one another. The racial expectations and assumptions in one area may overlap or envelop another. In so doing, a supraideal of whiteness may share the expectations from many different, even supposedly opposite, areas. Sociologist Amanda Lewis unpacks this nuance:

> Whiteness works in distinct ways for and is embodied quite differently by homeless white men, golf-club-membership-owning executives, suburban soccer moms, urban hillbillies, antiracist skinheads, and/or union-card-carrying factory workers . . . In any particular historical moment, however, certain forms of whiteness become dominant.[37]

For example, in both NEA and WRJ I found striking similarities in relation to how they understood white racial identity. In both groups, I recognized comparable taken-for-granted meanings, rules, and expectations that guided the interactions of members and their interpretations of whiteness. Members of both groups held a common understanding of what white racial identity *is*, and more importantly, what it *should be*.

These meanings were particularly dominant. They took on the status of "common sense." Throughout my research, members of WRJ and NEA often said to me: "Matthew, of course that's so, isn't it?" I argue that those "of course" statements were indicative of important moments in which systems of meaning were at work. Members were the least aware that they were using particular boundaries and narratives. Because these common interpretations were taken for granted, they became "hegemonic." Hegemony structures the activities of actors, both constraining and enabling attitudes, actions, and identities. However, hegemony is always contested and never complete.[38] It is always in process.

I found that both organizations hold similar commonsense ideals of what white identity should be. That ideal—what I call "hegemonic whiteness"—was found to extend beyond the overt political goals and racial agendas of both groups. Members of both groups valorized certain performances of whiteness that they strove to attain but of which many fell short. This resulted in a great deal of variation in white racial identities, but it was a variation cohesively bound by their shared understandings and expectations.

One-Dimensional Activists?

I do not paint these actors as one-dimensional activists.[39] Member of the anti-racist Whites for Racial Justice and the nationalist National Equality for All are far from "cultural dupes" who robotically pursue the white ideal because ideologies of white supremacy have implanted themselves in their minds.[40] If this were true, people would be active agents only as instruments of social structures and dominant ideology. Conversely, people are in complete control of neither the social world nor themselves. This "voluntarist" position would frame actors as romanticized "rational actors" completely unfettered by so-cially structured resources and relations.[41] This frame is antisociological and wholly abandons the social base of human action and order as if choices are objective realities outside of history and culture.[42]

Rather, I emphasize that the members of WRJ and NEA make choices that are not always intentional, conscious, and individual. Rather, they interpret, shun, and embrace choice through interactional activities that occur within a durable, patterned, and systemic culture that simultaneously enables and constrains those choices.[43] As actors sharing a culture, their behaviors are governed, but not overdetermined, by the culture that they share and remake together. These actors make meaning of race, and the pursuit of an ideal form of whiteness, within a white supremacist culture in which they live and with a white supremacist logic often thought normal, natural, and mundane. Their decisions are not predestined or foreordained but often reproduce the dominant meanings of race and expected racial interactions. Hence, the agency to act should not be romanticized or conflated with social change or counter-hegemony. Most agency is reproductive of culture and social structures. So, too, just because actors reproduce the social world, they should not be looked on as one-dimensional actors incapable of active meaning making. The following chapters show how these actors draw on the vast reservoir of racialized meanings and expectations and actively negotiate these meanings within unequal systems of social relations and consequences. While they do not always pursue the hegemonic ideal of whiteness, they do pursue this ideal with durable, layered, and patterned regularity.

Making the Familiar Strange

White Bound: Nationalists, Antiracists, and the Shared Meanings of Race takes an empirically grounded sociological approach to the similarities, differences, and ideals of whiteness that have, for too long, been left in the hands of journalists, activists, and political theorists. In head-on fashion, this book explores the contemporary meaning of whiteness and its relationship to racism by comparing two movements assumed mirror opposites. I approached this topic from the point of view that I should not attack or defend either movement. My role as a researcher was to take the familiar dichotomy that grounds the recognizable polarities of whiteness and, simply, make it strange. I attempted to accomplish this approach to whiteness as a disinterested, yet attentive and immersed, observer. I think this an efficacious method for encouraging distance from binary conceptions in order to contemplate the differences and similarities of whiteness anew. Doing so is a slippery task. Yet it is a necessary one if we are to understand the import of whiteness and white identity movements for those who organize their lives around them and for those who are affected by the actions of these people. It is not my intention to marginalize the very real differences between these two movements. Instead I wish to examine certain key assumptions and logics they share, especially in their understanding and performance of white identity and its connection to racism.

Design of the Study

From May 2006 through June 2007 I spent at least one day a week, often much more, with members of the white nationalist organization NEA and the white antiracist organization WRJ. The research was composed of: (1) ethnographic fieldwork, (2) semistructured in-depth interviews, and (3) content analysis inclusive of newsletter issues and textual information such as emails and office memos. While this account aims for accuracy, I maintain the anonymity of participants by changing names and potentially identifying information. I offer no blatant or hidden clues as to actual names and places referenced herein to protect my research subjects and the ethical soundness of the study (more information is available in Appendices A, B, and C).

The Cases in this Book

NEA is a nationwide "white nationalist" organization founded in the early 1980s. The headquarters is located in a mid-Atlantic city I call "Riverside." They report around twenty NEA chapters throughout the United States, and they boast a roll of over 500 dues-paying members. Their national newspaper—billed as a "manifesto of white rights"—supposedly circulates over 1,000 copies of each issue and is printed approximately four to six times a year. Their headquarters is composed of twenty-four regular, but part-time, volunteers. NEA members proudly identify as white and explicitly advocate a racial definition (or redefinition) of the nation-state; they desire official racial segregation in terms of social institutions and wish for limited interracial interactions. As one NEA member told me, "We believe that for a nation to be a nation, and not just an incoherent group of people, it must consist of people that share the same culture, language, history and aspirations . . . it must be people of the same race." Members do not believe that successful racial integration is intelligent or even possible. They argue that predisposed genetic and cultural differences among racial groups only serve as a catalyst for racial antagonism. Hence, other ideologies, policies, or arguments to the contrary (from multiculturalism to assimilation) are propaganda or misguided worldviews that only obfuscate the essential differences among racial groups. Separation, they believe, will be better for all races.

The headquarters for WRJ is located just a couple hours' drive from Riverside in another metropolitan area I call "Fairview." Founded in the 1970s, WRJ has developed into a nationwide organization of around thirty chapters with an approximate membership of 800. All twenty-one members of the headquarters chapter consider themselves white. The individual chapters are organized around teaching whites how they can end "racial oppression." On both the national and local levels, WRJ generates publications, gives workshops, and promotes media events about what white people can do to eliminate racism both from their daily lives and from the social structures that surround them (for example: education, religion, family, and work). WRJ supports a variety of political and social agendas: from theoretical indictments of the white supremacist underpinnings of capitalism, to the more active disruption of white nationalist events, to the more mainstream activities such as counseling and "diversity training." By making their organization all white, they believe they are making a "safe space" for whites to engage in the identification and isolation of racism in their own lives. Such an environment fosters, as many members told me, active consultation, emotional release regarding their frustrations and setbacks in trying to live an "antiracist life," and strategy building on how to live as "allies" of people of color.

Overview of the Book

I move carefully through the following chapters to consider the differential nuance of both NEA and WRJ while paying attention to important similarities. In both groups, the pursuit of an ideal whiteness is paramount, and while different strategies are used, these strategies often result from or draw on similar understandings of race. These actors' white racial identities are bound to the pursuit of the white ideal and the ideal itself; means and ends blur in their everyday lives.

In the next two chapters I afford the reader a detailed account of NEA and WRJ. These chapters stand together as my ethnographic "thick description." I attempt to paint a detailed picture of the everyday activities and patterned social dynamics in both settings—all with the aim that the reader should have a sense of being there and of how different these two groups are. I wish the reader to gain an appreciation for how NEA rationalizes and legitimates its use of "color-blind" logic (legitimating racial difference and inequality through appeals to nonracial dynamics such as the nature, biology, God, market dynamics, belief systems, work ethic, and the like), while WRJ uses a different "color-conscious" framework (racial distinctions and inequality are interpreted as the result of the racist intentions, ignorance, fear, and hate). This distinction is important because, as with any dialectic, there exists a unifying thread.

[handwritten margin note: Color Blind v. → Color Conscious]

This accord is explored in Chapters 4 through 8. I detail how both groups share in five key understandings of white racial identity. I investigate these similarities as the five dimensions of "hegemonic whiteness"—the idealized form of whiteness created and conditioned when whites make hard-and-fast distinctions between themselves and (1) people of color and (2) other whites thought inferior or lacking. My aim is to demonstrate how the shared meanings of white racial identity structure and guide members' actions just as much, if not more, than their overt political leanings.

I conclude in Chapter 9 by bringing the findings from previous chapters to bear on what may be the most important question relevant to whiteness: How do we conceptualize an understanding of white identity that accounts for the long-term staying power of white privilege and supremacy amid the varied and even oppositional forms of whiteness active today? The answer includes a theory centered on the relationship between meaning and identity. The similarities between the groups are not the product of simply bad or "racist" political views or by practicing antiracism "incorrectly."[44] Such similarities cannot simply be fixed through reeducating people or somehow magically "changing culture." I show that the dominant racial meanings from which both these groups draw—and on which their racial identity is based—are appealing, seductive, and normalized because those cultural forms are themselves structural and connected to material conditions of inequality.

2 Navigating White Nationalists

National Equality for All

*Yes there is still inequality . . . not because of racism though.
I can't support affirmative action when the overwhelming
majority of this inequality is because of, well, frankly, bad
values and choices among some [nonwhite] people . . . or
because whites prefer to be with whites and blacks with blacks.
That's completely natural; people just prefer to be in the
company of others like themselves . . . it's not a crime to love
your people more than others. Some people just don't mix.*

—**John, National Equality for All**

*Whereas Jim Crow racism explained blacks' social standing
as the result of their biological and moral inferiority, color-
blind racism avoids such facile arguments. Instead, whites
rationalize minorities' contemporary status as the product of
market dynamics, naturally occurring phenomena, and blacks'
imputed cultural limitations. . . . For instance, . . . 'Does a cat
and dog mix? I can't see it. You can't drink milk and scotch.
Certain mixes don't mix.'*

—**Eduardo Bonilla-Silva, *Racism Without Racists***[1]

My [Unintentional] Introduction to NEA

After vast trials and tribulations in securing a group of white nationalists to
study, my first visit to the headquarters of National Equality for All (NEA)
was quite involuntary. I contacted quite a few white nationalist groups along
the East Coast of the United States, but my attempts to reach them were rarely
recognized. Among the select few that acknowledged my request, many were
so distrustful and advanced so many preconditions that conducting an ethnographic study would have been functionally impossible.

The leadership of NEA was extremely skeptical of my intentions. One of
their leaders told me that a sociologist had, years prior, interviewed some of
their members only to "critically misrepresent us," so the deck was already
stacked against me. Rather than explicitly accepting or declining my request
to study their members and organization, they told me to attend a public meeting at a hotel whereby a couple members would speak on a panel about the
current state of race relations. After the talk, so they told me, members would
meet with me and decide whether they would consent to the study. I was less

than optimistic but readied myself and headed to the event. When I arrived at the hotel, I found a group of shouting antiracist protestors from a local university standing on the street by the hotel's entrance. They vowed to attend the event and shout down any NEA member who would attempt to "spread hate." I approached the entrance and looked for signs of NEA members. After about an hour of both standing around and checking the hotel's conference room for signs that a meeting would begin, I returned outside. After a few minutes, a young man in his twenties, whom I later came to know as Nick, approached me and asked in a hushed tone, "Are you Matthew?" After I nodded in the affirmative, he quickly blurted out, "Follow me to my car." He briskly spun on his heel and walked down the street.

I looked around and took in a deep breath as I began to follow him. Suddenly, I felt as if the entire scenario was an overdrawn cliché. My imagination transported me to a dramatic Cold War spy film in which I was tasked with smuggling someone out of East Berlin. I cautiously followed Nick away from the hotel. When I caught up to him, he told me that NEA was moving the event to their headquarters across town. He gave me directions and sent me on my way as he walked back toward the hotel to ensure no one else was "scared away by the crazy leftists and antiracist activists."

The drive to NEA's headquarters was an uneasy one. I was anxious to begin my research, but I failed to anticipate being so suddenly thrown into the heart of it. Here I was, on the way to the headquarters of a white nationalist organization. Before I knew it, I was parked outside of NEA's office. Gathering my notepad and audio recorder, I pulled myself together and headed inside.

I was the first guest to arrive. Evidently, Nick had called ahead and told his fellow members to expect me. As I entered the front door, a large man in his late forties approached me. "I'm Paul. Welcome to The Office," he said. After we exchanged brief pleasantries, Paul led me into a large room set up with folding chairs and told me to wait until the event began. Being left to myself, I sat down and took out my paper and pen. In trying to calm my nerves, I recounted the events that just transpired, but I only became more self-conscious. I noted the hum of the air conditioner reverberating in the vents above my head with a constant dull roar. The lighting from the florescent bulbs hidden behind the opaque ceiling panels gave the room an artificial, light-purplish tone. There was a light patter of raindrops on the windows. I opened up my pad of paper and set it on my lap, anxiously awaiting the beginning of the event. I began to think about the disruptions at the hotel and hoped that the meeting would still go off without a hitch. I then realized that such a disturbance might put the members on edge. Would this disruption lead them to decline my request to study them?

Suddenly, a middle-aged man burst into the room. Walking briskly to the back of the room, he slammed his briefcase on a chair and threw down his coat with disgust. After a few moments, he suddenly became aware of my presence and walked over to me. Sticking out his hand and introducing himself as a "six-year member of NEA," he told me that he was happy to see guests already at the event. After we exchanged formalities, he abruptly cut off the conversation and returned to the back of the room where he paced back and forth, mumbling to himself. His speech was almost indiscernible, but every so often his pitch grew louder and he lashed out in shrill, punctuated tones. I made out words and phrases like "serious trouble," "white solidarity," and "organizational focus." After a few minutes of his solitary machinations, people slowly trickled into the room, no doubt tardy because of the change of location. John fumbled with his briefcase, and after a few awkward moments he retrieved a stack of magazines and placed them on the table at the front of the room. Some of the magazine covers advertised articles entitled "Why Reparations for Slavery Are Racist" and "White Men: Victims of Political Correctness."

A man in an oversized suit rushed up to me and introduced himself as Charles. Eagerly telling me he was with NEA and that he was aware I was a sociologist, he told me that he would be sure to talk with me at the conclusion of the meeting. His pleasant and excited mood put me more at ease, but just then two other gentlemen entered the room and sat down next to me. One of the gentleman, sporting a confederate flag belt buckle, leaned in close to me and whispered, "Did you hear that they threatened us?" "Who did?" I replied, trying to imitate his hushed and excited tone. "I don't know!" he stated abruptly right on the heels of my sentence. After pausing for a couple seconds he said in matter-of-fact fashion, " But they did." He gave me a look of concern, fear, and anger, which I acknowledged with a sympathetic nod.

Soon the room was packed to capacity at nearly a hundred people. The seats were full, and wall space was claimed. Some still milled about, laughing, conversing, and greeting one another with smiles and hugs. On the table at the front of the room, people placed more NEA-friendly books and pamphlets. I noticed that there was only one person of color in the room, a black male panelist who would later speak from a "Southern Baptist perspective" on the dangers of both Darwinism and liberalism. There were almost no women in the room, only five by my count. The whites in attendance came in all ages, shapes, and styles of presentation. Most men were dressed in suits and ties, while a handful wore sneakers and blue jeans. Some looked like bankers and lawyers, while others looked like blue-collar, hourly wage workers.

Nearly an hour after I arrived, a short and stout middle-aged man walked to the front of the room with a microphone and urged everyone to take seats or places along the wall. He thanked everyone for attending and praised everyone's resolution in braving the rain, the dark, and the change of venue. Lastly, he thanked NEA for opening its doors for the event: "If not for their courtesy," he said, "we would have had to cancel tonight's talk. Let's please give them a big hand."

The first speaker, whom I later knew as Laurence, stood tall behind the podium in a pair of neatly pressed khakis and a button-up dress shirt. He began by praising everyone's commitment to talk openly about race: "This is not something easy to talk about. Race is woven into the very fabric of this nation, yet it is sometimes hard to talk about it honestly because of its volatility. It is high time we realized," his voice rising, leading the audience by his verbal crescendo, "that we as white people must do something about racism. It is destroying this county, it is destroying the people of this country—it is destroying us! . . . We must realize that this country has not and cannot move past race, that race is the primary axis of social relationships, that the majority of the country is stratified along racial lines. If there is to be peace, harmony, and accord, then we as white people must look out for our own. And, most importantly, at various times and place, we must separate ourselves so that we can maintain our own interests and self-determination."

Cheers erupted from nearly all in attendance. Laurence continued:

This is not an antiblack, anti-Hispanic, or an antianything position. We are not antianything. We are prowhite nationalists. The problem is that most blacks hate us; most everyone hates us; we are being victimized to such an extent that we are the only ones who can't have an explicitly *white organization*. If we do, then we are labeled racist. We're not racist. We are simply protecting our own. There is nothing ideological about that. If I love my own child more than someone else's, that doesn't mean I hate other children. It is natural and it is right. . . . There is no denying the truth.

As the speech wore on, Laurence reiterated how NEA's project was based on love, rather than hate. He made the point that whites should not take from other racial groups but should develop their own institutions, resources, and communities. He commented that white nationalism does not deny the rights of any racial group but concentrates on the development of self-sufficient white communities. To conclude he stated, "We have come to a point in which white love and white unity is a fundamental prerequisite of racial healing in this country. To disallow such action is to invite continued racial antagonism and conflict. Hands off of the white race . . . allow us our freedom, too."

After the other panelists spoke on topics ranging from British nationalism to religious fundamentalism, the meeting entered the question-and-answer portion. However, few questions were asked. Most people offered pro-NEA confirmations that revolved around Laurence's words being "not all that bad." It was during this time that I became aware of a group of several young university students who sat in the row behind me. They spoke in hushed voices to one another about whether to ask a question, what kind it would be, and toward what end. By their comments and tone, I could tell they were frustrated by Laurence and the event. They came looking to confront an overt hate-monger—a "white racist." They expected to hear arguments about how whites were biologically superior to nonwhites, how whites deserved to dominate people of color via the reinstitution of some sort of nouveau slavery system, or how black leaders were ignorant, lazy, and pathetic excuses for human beings. Hearing none of these explicit arguments, they found little with which to argue. After the meeting, I approached them and introduced myself as a sociologist. I asked them what they thought of the talk. A young white female remarked:

> It's frustrating . . . I know NEA is up to no good; they hide their racism. But what do you do when they say they want nothing but "white rights"? If you challenge them there, then they would just turn around and say "What? Black and brown people can have rights, but we can't? See, you're proving our point. It's an antiwhite, not antiblack, world." I mean, we don't want to do that, but how do you fight that logic? There's nothing wrong with having something of your own . . . white people deserve a place at the multicultural table, too. It's like that's all they were saying, but, at the same time, it seems like something more, like they are hiding what they *really* believe, you know? I just think there is something more, like this is a smart way of going about their agenda, because I agreed with a lot of their statements, but I refuse to believe that I agree with who they are.

"Who do you think they are?" I asked. She replied:

> Well, you know, it seems they want to have white businesses, white spaces, white areas, and I am just not for that; but, at the same time, I would advocate for black businesses, black spaces, etcetera, so that's a contradiction on my part. I don't know, it just seems weird. [long pause and heavy sigh]. Maybe they're not all that racist after all, but still, I just don't agree with them wanting to segregate because when blacks do it, it's not *segregation* [her emphasis] to me, it seems positive, but when they do it, it seems selfish, a step backwards. It just feels wrong.

This white antiracist activist's frustration seemed common. The new brand of white nationalism is carefully constructed around discourses of unity, acceptance, and multiculturalism and principles of abstract liberalism, fairness, and laissez-faire egalitarianism and individualism. For those opposed to a white nationalist agenda, combating their rhetoric of "color blindness," on which I will expand later in the chapter, is fraught with difficulty.

The construction of a "color-blind" white nationalism was a necessary adaptation for those who believe in the biological existence of race, that the races are naturally arranged in a hierarchy of intelligence and/or moral capacity, and that white people (especially white men) are coming under increasing unfair attack from a social order gone awry. Members of NEA, like many other white nationalist organizations, are distrustful of those who do not feel the same. Their care and concern for (dis)allowing access to an outsider like myself is warranted given their self-understanding as embattled victims. They are careful to speak of their agenda in terms with which it is hard to disagree: Their speaking points always returned to abstract principles in which *all* people, whites included, should have equality, liberty, and fraternity—the often highlighted tripartite principles of Westernized democratic nation-states.

As promised, I met with the NEA leadership after the event. Once they understood that my mission was not to study their particular racial and political ideology, but the "meaning" or "culture" of whiteness, they were both disarmed and slightly confused. In the former, I was no longer as potent a threat. Because I did not wish to malign their white nationalist ideology or agenda, possibly exposing them and their core beliefs in white separatism and superiority, I was immediately more palatable. In the latter, studying the "meaning of whiteness" seemed abstract and confusing. "What meaning?" one member asked me. "Whiteness is, or it isn't. People are white, or they are not. It's just a fact. Facts don't have meaning." Another member told me in a perplexed tone. "It's fine by me if that's what you want to study, but you won't find anything. If I were you, I'd be bored. We're just normal." In the end, the leadership hesitantly agreed to my study.

National Equality for All

At my time of study, the headquarters of NEA was located in an office building in a metropolitan area in the eastern United States that I call "Riverside." The city saw increased population growth and prosperity in the wake of the New Deal and the post–World War II economic boom. However, since the 1980s, many of Riverside's key industries have either relocated or dried up, the population and the tax base have declined, and the city's housing and educational institutions slowly resegregated.

NEA's place in the city is atypical. The area is in the midst of "urban revitalization" or what others simply call gentrification. New office buildings are mixed with old ones, indicating some economic growth in that area. The area is filled with an array of businesses, from banks and marketing firms to restaurants to newsstands. These stand against the backdrop of tall buildings and the sounds of beeping horns, revving bus engines, and the flutter of pigeons. There is an antiseptic aura to the building in which NEA is located: The adjoining sidewalks are clean, the shrubs are carefully manicured, rust is absent from metallic fixtures, and even the lines that mark parking spaces glow with a white sparkle against the dark asphalt.

Founded decades ago, NEA has gone through many changes in name, leadership, and tactics, so its history and manifestations are murky, perhaps intentionally. NEA was birthed from disaffected members of other white nationalist and supremacist organizations—from the most overt like the Ku Klux Klan and neo-Nazis to more "refined" conservative groups that eschew any formal linkages with white nationalism, such as Conservative Citizens Councils and the John Birch Society. These older members felt that the traditional hard-line approach was alienating and formed a new kind of organization. Such a move is common. Kathleen Blee notes that most white nationalist activists view "those who use overtly racist symbols in public or who adopt an exaggerated racist style as movement novices."[2] In dropping the odious discourse and the regalia of traditional racists, NEA repackaged their messages to encourage whites to adopt "identity politics" that align with the aforementioned abstract principles of equality and individualism. In pleading their case to a white mainstream, the leaders of NEA appropriate the language of the traditional left. For example, while proponents of multiculturalism argue that all groups should celebrate their unique cultural, ethnic, and racial heritage, NEA concludes that if such politics are good for people of color, then they must be good for whites as well. NEA leaders argue that white Americans are discriminated against. The remedy, in their eyes, is for whites to band together to protect their interests. While traditional white supremacy was kept in place by brutality, terror, and the laws and policies of the state, NEA argues for the preservation of "European" culture and values in the United States. In everyday practice, NEA is a hybrid think tank, consulting firm, educational institution, and public policy institute in which reactionary racial stances are mapped onto civic policies such as small government, social and fiscal conservatism, tough-on-crime stances, and other proxies for debating the future of race relations.

NEA and "The Office"

"The Office"—the name that members bestow on their meeting space—is fairly hidden. Located within a newly constructed office building, the multi-room space is advertised neither on the placard outside nor on its front door. Only a formal office number marks the location. Surrounded by a real estate brokerage and a travel agency, NEA keeps a low profile. On entering their office space, one is immediately struck by its clean simplicity. The rooms are neat and orderly. Furniture and file cabinets are arranged in linear fashion, potted plants guard the corners, and a water cooler with disposable plastic cups graces the lobby. Photos and paintings of white (almost exclusively male) leaders like Thomas Jefferson, Winston Churchill, and Strom Thurmond adorn the walls. Between and among these pictures hang matted and framed pictures with motivational quotations reminiscent of the cheap, mass-produced photos that adorn overachieving college student dorm rooms. For instance, one picture depicts a stone walkway leading up and away into a forest with the caption: "LEAD THE WAY. The lessons of the past provide the path to the future." Overall, The Office stands as a tribute to a Westernized sense of rationality, efficiency, and discipline.

The collective demeanor of the NEA members also contributes to this sense of order. Almost exclusively male, and all of them white, the members present themselves as though they are sales associates at an upscale clothing store. Speaking in soft monotone voices and walking at a brisk but not hurried pace, they present an aura of professionalism and address every question with a customer-service smile.

NEA members are drawn from the larger Riverside area, and most live in middle-class suburbs. Twenty-four members regularly volunteer at The Office. The amount of time an average member commits to NEA is close to fourteen hours a week, in spite of their responsibilities to their family and paid employment. Still, most of the twenty-four consider themselves "full time." Of those core members, all identify themselves as "white" or "European American." Half of the members describe themselves as "middle class," while the other half thought of themselves as "upper class" or "lower class." Yearly incomes have a wide range ($14,000 to $91,000), and the household average income among members is $62,000 per year. The members range in age from twenty to fifty-eight, with an average age of thirty-six and a median of thirty-five. All but one of the members is male. Most are single or divorced, hold college degrees, and have a Christian background. However, although most remarked that they have a connection to the morality of a Judeo-Christian tradition, many do not believe in either a higher power or an afterlife. The geographic areas in which they were born and raised extend from California to Florida, but most grew up in the mid-Atlantic region of the United States. Half of the members have no children. Thirteen members are politically "independent" or have no particular political affiliation, nine members are Republican, and two affiliate with the Democratic Party. Members are employed in a wide range of activities; they are schoolteachers, marketing agents, retail sales associates, and police officers. Three members are lawyers (see Tables 2.1 and 2.2).

For almost all NEA members there was, for all intents and purposes, a "uniform." The expected dress code mirrored that of a stereotypical white college fraternity trying to put its best foot forward. Khaki pants were the norm, some of which were starched so the front leg crease rarely lost its form. Religiously tucked into the belted khakis or occasional dress slacks, almost all members wore a button-up shirt covered by a navy-blue sports coat. Individuality was expressed through the wearing of unique ties. The lone woman of NEA, Lisa, generally wore a dark business suit deemed "appropriate" for her work as an executive secretary at another place of business.

Many members stated that they used to hold prejudices about white nationalism before joining. Had it not been for the friendships, nuanced worldview,

Table 2.1 NEA membership.

Pseudonym	Age	Occupation	Education	Politics	Membership (years)
Derek	34	Marketer	College degree	Republican	6
Erik	31	High school teacher	College degree	None	3
John	42	Consultant	Graduate degree	Republican	6
Nick	28	Elementary school teacher	College degree	None	4
Laurence	55	Lawyer	Law degree	None	6
Paul	49	Police officer	College degree	Republican	5
Lisa	36	Executive secretary	Some college	Democrat	2
Josh	20	Student	Some college	None	1
Joey	36	Retail sales	Some college	Republican	3
Chris	44	Business manager	College degree	Republican	4
George	38	Accountant	College degree	Republican	2
Tim	33	Counselor	PhD	Independent	4
Will	37	Real estate agent	College degree	Independent	6
Steven	28	Banker	College degree	None	4
Mason	30	Retail assistant manager	College degree	Republican	3
Albert	58	Plumber	Some college	None	6
Charles	25	Graduate student	College degree	None	3
David	33	Construction contractor	College degree	Republican	3
Franklin	37	Sales associate	College degree	Democrat	5
Daniel	32	Registered nurse	Some college	Independent	4
Joseph	41	Lawyer	College degree	none	1
Harry	39	Lawyer	Law degree	Republican	6
Adam	34	Consultant	Master's degree	Independent	6
Robert	34	Police officer	College Degree	Independent	5

and sense of racial empowerment that they developed, so the members told me, they would have never become part of such a group. Especially in regard to white racial pride, members told me that NEA was the first place they felt "good" about being white. NEA was not just an organization. It provided a sense of belonging. As NEA member Charles told me, "white nationalism provides *new guards for our future security.*" "Isn't that from the Declaration of Independence?" I asked. "Yes," Charles replied, "This is supposed to be a white nation, you know. Thomas Jefferson said it, as did Abraham Lincoln."[3] He continued citing, verbatim, from Lincoln: "There is a physical difference

Table 2.2 NEA descriptive statistics.

Mean years active in organization (median, SD)	3.29 (5, 2.77)
Mean age in years (median, SD)	37.18 (37, 8.19)
Age range in years	25–58
Gender (male, female)	(23, 1) (95.8%, 4.2%)
Religion	
Catholic	3 (12.5%)
Protestant	16 (66.6%)
Atheist	1 (4.2%)
Agnostic	2 (8.3%)
"Spiritual"/other	2 (8.3%)
Where primarily raised (geographic location)	
Midwest	6 (25%)
North	3 (12.5%)
South	14 (58.3%)
West	1 (4.2%)
Political orientation	
Democrat	2 (8.3%)
Independent	5 (20.8%)
Republican	9 (37.5%)
No affiliation	8 (33.3%)
Relationship status	
Single	10 (41.7%)
Married (mean length in years)	7 (8) (29.2%)
Divorced	7 (29.2%)
Mean number of children (median)	0.96 (0.5)
Highest level of education attained	
Some college	5 (20.8%)
College degree or equivalent	14 (58.3%)
Some graduate classes	0
Advanced degree (MA, PhD, JD, etc.)	5 (20.8%)
Occupational status	
Working	1 (4.2%)
Lower middle class	2 (8.3%)
Middle class	12 (50%)
Upper middle class	9 (37.5%)
Upper class	0
Yearly income	
<25,000	2 (8.3%)
25,000–49,999	9 (37.5%)
50,000–74,999	11 (45.8%)
75,000–99,999	2 (8.3%)
100,000>	0
Housing	
Own home	13 (54.2%)
Rent	11 (45.8%)

between the white and black races which I believe will forever forbid the two races living together on terms of social and political equality."

A Day in the Life

In the following pages I reconstruct a typical day in the life of a NEA member at The Office. Rather than condense every event or retell one singular day in specific, I aggregate various experiences from my fieldwork into a fictional "day." Linear chronology is sacrificed to illuminate patterned and repeated social relations.

Black Coffee, White Racism

After a couple months of regular visits, members were more lenient toward my requests to spend extended amounts of time in The Office. I was finally granted permission to "show up when you wish," and I seized this opportunity to take daylong observational field notes. After several early-morning arrivals before NEA opened up, I noticed that Joey and Lisa regularly started up daily operations of NEA.

Both Joey and Lisa were committed to NEA. Joey, raised in an almost all-white town in Pennsylvania, told me that when he moved to Riverside he was shocked by the abundance of people of color. He stated, "I never saw so many black people before. . . . so many immigrants that don't speak English . . . they all expect a job. . . . It's divisive." He joined NEA because of his view that racial and ethnic diversity is "dangerous and destructive for national unity" (NEA literature). "I don't hate black people, or Latinos, or whatever," Joey told me. "I just want a space for me and my future children to live where there won't be interracial hostility. . . . Helping out here, and doing the little things . . . makes me feel good." Lisa, born and raised in Baltimore, remarked of her commitment to NEA:

> . . . if I can give any help to the struggle. I mean, these guys are really working hard to keep us [whites] safe. I'm going to have children one day, and I don't want to worry about their safety like I had to in school. Blacks and whites were always fighting . . . even if it's as simple as coming in early, you know before I have to be into work, and making the coffee, that means a lot to me.

Members made clear that they earnestly believed in the goals and methods of NEA and felt that their service to the organization, no matter how seemingly trivial, was important. Yet, because the morning hours were dominated by low-status members like Joey and Lisa and filled with tasks like making coffee and reviewing a to-do list made by a leader from the previous evening, a feeling of resentment occasionally emerged. The "morning crew," as they jokingly called themselves, often consisted of four to six NEA members with less than four years of experience in the organization. For instance, Mason moved from Florida to "get away from all the Puerto Ricans." There was also Josh, David, Joseph, and the occasional appearance by Erik.

On days I arrived at The Office before it opened (between 7:00 and 7:30 am), I would sit down in the hallway and wait. It was mornings such as these that Joseph would round the corner to the hallway and joke that I was "more committed" than NEA members. As his work in real estate law was incredibly successful, he considered himself "semiretired" and, as a consequence, had a great deal of leisure time to devote to NEA. Joseph possessed a friendly demeanor and became accustomed to my intrusions. On one particular morning he brought two coffees instead of one, handing me the cup as he smiled and said, "I knew you'd be here."

Soon after opening, a handful of members slowly trickled in, politely interjecting a "good morning" while avoiding any significant interruption of already established morning conversation. On one particular morning, three members burst into the room already in the midst of heated dialogue. George, Derek, and Lisa conversed about a white supremacist in New Jersey who was imprisoned for the illegal sale of firearms.[4] "What case is this?" I interjected. As the members recounted the story, they expressed bitter distaste for the supremacist's actions. His behavior was coded as irresponsible and bad for "the movement." He made it harder to talk to others about white nationalism.

The members were also divided over the racial tone of the case. Some felt it was another case of white victimization. George stated, "The only reason he was sentenced so harshly was because he said he was a white supremacist. The judge or the jury or whoever really bit on that one. He was really stupid to say that." "I don't know," remarked Lisa, " . . . seemed fair to me; as far as I am concerned, he broke the law." Derek chimed in: "It's not about whether it's fair, or if it's not, or if it's because he said he was a white supremacist, that's missing the point." We all swung our attention to Derek, who seemed to instantly command deference when he spoke. "It is about a pattern of a sustained and continued marginalization of our people by the establishment," he said in a slow and measured tone. Derek continued:

Wow

I'm tired of having to feel like I have to apologize for being white and for sticking up for my people. We are superior to nonwhites; it's been proven, it's been proven, time and time again in these scientific studies that keep saying the same thing over and over. At what point can we just stop with all this bullshit and just tell it like it is? [said rhetorically] . . . It's like if you happen to be white and proud of your heritage and proud of just having white friends and family, then that's somehow wrong. [The others nodded their heads approvingly.] I know you're sick of having to apologize for being better than blacks. . . . I'm sick of it, and I know you are too [pointing in Lisa and George's direction].

He ended his statement with a sigh, dropped his head in exasperation as if he had just finished hours of debate, and grasped his cup of coffee with both hands as he slowly sipped from it.

While an adamant and heartfelt defense of the "color-blind" mission of NEA was frequently reiterated among NEA members, it became clear to me that this was far from a uniform feeling. Members were not robotically acting out the demands of this brand of white nationalism, and the "morning crew" frequently challenged such "color-blind" rhetoric. Early in the morning, while the coffee was being made, during the checking and returning of phone messages, throughout the crafting of email replies, and while items from the to-do list were being checked off, the most overt and traditional forms of racist white nationalism were exposed.

The members who dominated the morning hours were assigned activities that were deemed mundane or "necessary, but not ultimately important," as Laurence once told me. One morning, I passed by the door of one of the smaller rooms in which Charles, one of the youngest members of NEA, regularly sat. Charles was attending graduate school and was determined not to "struggle" like his working-class parents, whom he deemed "hardworking, but not critical thinkers." Not yet a member for three complete years, Charles held a quiet and shy persona; he generally spoke when spoken to and was rarely opinionated, and many treated him like a pushover. As I stopped at the door to say hello, Charles beckoned me to come in, and he began to laugh. Pointing to his computer screen, he was looking at an array of overtly racist cartoons. Assigned to conduct research for NEA's bimonthly publication, he was perusing a website maintained by another white nationalist organization called WAR (White Aryan Resistance). As he laughed, I asked why he thought the images were funny. He replied:

Well, okay, I guess because [long pause] I used to think that blacks were equal to me too, and I was an apologist for, you know, black deficiencies as well. But once I started reading [J. Phillip] Rushton, [E. O.] Wilson, and other studies from other racial realists like, well, you know the Pioneer Fund studies? So, I got that I didn't need to make excuses anymore. They are what they are. . . . Why be afraid of it, really? If it's offensive, so what? We should just step up to the plate and deal with it. . . . I mean, I'm not naive, I don't think it would be easy, especially with all the brainwashed whites out there, but [long pause] I guess I feel like the brutal honesty can save some of them [whites]. . . . Sometimes we [NEA] do too much tiptoeing around the truth. . . . If I can incorporate some of this perspective into [our publication], then obviously, that's a good thing.

As I left the room, Charles asked me not to tell anyone else in NEA that he was looking at the cartoons, concluding with that statement, "The style doesn't quite fit with what we do, you know?"

Charles was not alone in his adjustment to the direction of NEA's brand of white nationalism. It was not uncommon for these younger (both in age and in organizational longevity) to engage in gossip about the "misdirection" or relative lack of "potency" constitutive of NEA's color-blind approach. As David told me, "While it's work that's a little underappreciated, it is a nice time [the morning] to bond with the others. . . . We definitely use it to collectively complain a little [laughing], but that's good. [long pause] How else do we revise our mission but through self-criticism?" So also, George mentioned to me, "Maybe I just don't get it yet, but I feel like we blunt our message. Isn't it possible to just say what we mean?"

As the mornings wore on, the racial discourse took on more of an antagonistic tone. For instance, Daniel exhibited this unfettered racist ideology on more than one occasion. On every morning that Daniel arrived, he promptly marched over to a row of file cabinets to retrieve a stack of manila folders sandwiched in between green and brown hanging folders, tucked them under his arm, and walked over to his seat by a computer and phone where he carefully arranged them on his desk. Soon he was checking email, cradling a phone in his neck and scribbling notes on a pad of paper. He told me he was engaging in a "research project" on white voter disenfranchisement. "Is there a lot of that?" I asked. "You would be amazed," he replied. "But the problem is getting people to chime up about it. White people have a tendency to take abuses without complaining, and we need to be more vocal and awaken." I wanted to know more about his logic for getting whites to "awaken" and asked him to tell me how he got involved in this project:

> I didn't really know what to do as a new member of NEA. I mean, I came into The Office a couple times a week when I could and helped other people with what they were working on, but I didn't really feel connected. I didn't really feel like we were doing a whole lot. Then I heard about Ike Brown—he's a black democrat down in Mississippi that was sued by the feds last year for throwing away whites' ballots. . . . That really upset me, so I started looking for more instances of this kind of shit and couldn't find a lot, so now I'm trying to get the leadership to make this a local issue with a nearby NEA chapter down there. If we can get them to work with the CCC [Council for Conservative Citizens] down there that would be ideal. . . . Blacks will take any advantage that they can if you let them. . . . and these are good, hardworking people [whites] down there that might not even know they are being oppressed, or if they do, don't know how to respond to it . . . If this isn't proof that the niggers are starting to run things, then I don't know what is.[5]

Daniel's comments illustrate several dynamics seemingly endemic to the morning hours of The Office. First, many of the newer NEA members were in the process of learning the "polite" and "color-blind" form of white nationalism, and many were less than proficient in its articulation. Second, many of the newer members resented what they thought was menial work (such as cataloging research for other members or making the morning coffee). In this vein, some were challenging and/or resisting the agenda of NEA by not following through on their morning "assignments" or by trying to impress the leadership with what they thought was a better course of direction of the organization. Third, because of the overall feelings of resistance toward multiculturalism and politically correct understandings of race, many of the white members demonstrated a hostility toward both nonwhites and the white leadership of NEA whom they felt were somehow out of touch or even cowardly.

In this light, it is evident that the morning crew was making not just coffee but a particular type of white identity. As the structure of detailed tasks, particular members, and hostile attitudes combined in the morning hours of The Office, a specific culture of resistance and frustration melded with members' sense of self. They were navigating the tension between a type of white identity based on the overt expression of superiority and a polite and color-blind white nationalism in which arguments for white self-determination were couched within polite language and appeals to seemingly "natural" forms of superiority and separatism. Such a dynamic illustrates that NEA is not simply a monolithic white nationalist organization but is constituted by various cultural processes in which the "proper" white identity is constantly under negotiation and surveillance.

Afternoon Hours, Polite White Powers

As the sun reached its zenith, several members of the "morning crew" left for their paying jobs, for home, or for whatever daily errands demanded their attention. Usually one or two members remained at The Office to keep it open. These couple members continued working on seemingly unending research assignments, caught up with the gossip from their personal lives, and met any guests or newly arriving members of NEA with friendly salutations and small talk. It was on older members' arrival that the tone of The Office shifted. Older members seemed less concerned with socializing, catching up with others, or even sitting around to consult; their first few minutes consisted of hastily grabbing a cup of coffee, immediately asking for information that had been (supposedly) collected earlier that morning by the newer members, tasking people with new assignments, and then retiring in solitude to an empty office. Even among the unofficial activities, such as chatting around the water cooler, smoking on the sidewalk outside, or taking an occasional walk to the corner store, there was a clear expectation of white racial identity as calm, collected, and cooperative. Early afternoons in The Office were quiet, as the open debate of ideas and conversation was replaced by calm, measured, and even restrictive professionalism. During this time members seemed on guard.

The angry white supremacist invective of the morning all but completely disappeared and was replaced by talk of whites as victims. Racial invective gave way to NEA as a "human rights organization for whites." The newer members attempted to mirror the afternoon discourse. Sitting around a table of other NEA members, Charles (who had just hours before stated the aforementioned racist comments) ironically proclaimed, "There's no place for angry rhetoric in our movement." However, Erik, one of the relatively new members, reacted negatively to what he felt was a kind of surveillance on the part of older members:

It's not like we're idiots [referring to himself and many of the other younger members]. But when they [older NEA members] come around, it's [long pause] okay, don't take this out of context, but it's like we can't really be ourselves sometimes. . . . In many ways, it's not our fault, you know? We all came to [NEA] for different reasons, and it's like, well, I don't know, it's when we don't exactly conform to their brand of activism, it, uh, it just makes life around The Office a bit difficult. . . . Don't get me wrong, I love the organization and what it has done for me, everything I have learned. . . . I just don't feel like my ideas are appreciated [laughing] . . . *There are times when I think they don't think I'm the right type of white person for them* [my emphasis].

At this point, my time in The Office yielded a number of observations regarding NEA's organizational dynamics, one of those being the shift in the demeanor of members. Yet, Erik's last statement revealed something more—that such demands, surveillance, and pressure were felt on the level on their racial identity. I asked him what he meant when he said the "right type of white person." He responded:

Ah, you know, ha, I knew you were going to ask about that as soon as I said it [laughing] . . . I mean, you've noticed it, I'm sure . . . This whole ultraprofessional demand they place on things. . . . And I get it, I do, we're [whites] under attack these days, and it requires a new mode of thinking, I got it. . . . Look at some of the neo-Nazis out there; they're crazy, and people are laughing at them.

MWH: Like who?

Erik: You know, [Jeff] Schoep [of the neo-Nazi "National Socialist Movement] is a joke; he and his dress-up storm troopers. . . . They don't represent what most whites want or need. At the same time, they capture a lot of attention since we are too quiet. But if you say that around the wrong people, they might think you are just the wrong kind of white person for [NEA], I guess that is what I mean. . . . Meaning that your racial consciousness is just not in the right place.

Other observations seemed to confirm Erik's feelings. Through members' body language, the rolling of eyes when others' backs were turned, and abruptly abbreviated conversations when certain older members of NEA's leadership entered the room, it was evident that there was, at the least, a slight fracture in the organization. Newer members clearly worried that they would not be fully accepted as the right type of member and also worried about whether NEA's demure type of white nationalist was potent enough to effect the change they felt was needed. "Sometimes you just have to be more direct with the agenda than we are," said George.

On the other side of things, Will, one of the respected leaders of NEA, told me in rather nonchalant fashion, "The newer guys need a lot of guidance, we keep an eye on them. . . . It takes a while to really settle into our project, and how best to appeal to others. . . . Without some form of discipline they'd likely screw up." "What do you mean by 'discipline'?" I asked. Will replied:

> I don't mean like a parent over a child, but, in many ways it's obvious you have to shadow them and scrutinize what they are doing, give them small things to do and let them work up to the bigger things. . . . A new member is not going to screw this up for the rest of us. . . . I guess on an emotional level, I just don't want them to hurt the race.

Such "shadowing" and "scrutiny" of younger NEA members is embodied in the policies, procedures, and cultural practices of NEA; it provides the disciplinary backbone for NEA's variant of color-blind white nationalism.

Blind in the Dark: Color-Blind Racism in the Evening

Evenings in The Office usually meant closing up. Yet once or twice a week, the evening brought various activities: from closed-door meetings among the senior members, leadership seminars, the teaching of European and African history classes, think-tank/brainstorming sessions, quasi-academic panel discussions and lectures on immigration and race relations, and recruitment meetings for new members.

Despite such activism, the leadership of NEA felt it was best to keep a low profile and gave many of their programs anonymously, through cosponsorships with conservative organizations like the Council of Conservative Citizens or representatives of the British National Party or simply by crediting an individual member or friend of a member. During these evening events, NEA labored to articulate its brand of white nationalism as a "fact-only, undisputed examination of the racial truth, unfettered from the bonds of bias and liberalism." That is, NEA frames their race-as-biology belief systems, anti-immigration policies, desires for racial segregation, and convictions in white supremacy as an objective view of the world.

For example, one evening at The Office included a panel discussion on "Law and Race." The central topic of discussion was the then-recent University of Michigan affirmative action cases that had reached the Supreme Court in 2003—*Grutter v. Bollinger* and *Gratz v. Bollinger.* Sporting academic credentials, suits and ties, and friendly faces, the panel calmly explained that the court's decision was a clear indication of both a setback and victory for "human rights" in the United States. The speakers explained to the audience of about forty people that the 2003 decisions marked the first time the Court had "accurately examined" the use of race under the Equal Protection Clause of the Fourteenth Amendment. With a tone of heartfelt sadness and remorse, the panelists explained that *Grutter* upheld the University of Michigan Law School admissions policy that used racial diversity as a "compelling governmental interest" but that the Court showed "hope for our racial future" in regard to *Gratz.* They remarked that the Court was "courageous" enough to admit "white oppression and suffering" by striking down the University of Michigan's undergraduate admissions policy because it was "too narrowly focused" on providing "undeserved handouts to nonwhites." One of the panelists stated, reading from his prepared script:

> In a six-to-three decision, the Court ruled that the undergraduate admissions policy was unconstitutional because it did not provide individualized consideration of each applicant. . . . This is what we want. We are not un-American. We are patriots. We refuse to feel bad for having pride in white accomplishments or to be frightened into not defending white rights. White rights are human rights. White people are human beings, and to fail to defend a white person's rights, or any person's rights, is to stand against the God-given human rights to which each of us are entitled. Each individual must have their rights respected, and that includes white people. . . . We are just like any other group that is looking out for their own.

The panel illuminated NEA's utilization of color-blind ideology. In particular, NEA uses what sociologist Eduardo Bonilla-Silva calls the "frame of abstract liberalism" in which their claims to "white rights" can sound reasonable and moral even when the outcome of the analysis may serve to perpetuate de facto racial inequality and white supremacy.[6]

Through the lens of abstract liberalism, the goals of diversity pursued through race-conscious programs are framed as detrimental to individual liberty. Because NEA understood the University of Michigan case as an instance in which virtually every underrepresented nonwhite who applied was granted admission solely on account of his or her race, while every white who applied and was denied admission was done so on account of his or her race, they were able to make claims that race was put ahead of individual merit and intelligence. Instead of making an explicit appeal to a white takeover of the University of Michigan, NEA appeals to nonracialized individual rights and speaks of race consciousness (in terms of diversity) as a vice and white consciousness (in terms of defending white group interests) as a virtue.

Such abstract liberalism obfuscates the material reality of racism and white supremacy. While many whites believe (or want to believe) that the gap between whites and blacks in higher education has all but closed during the recent era of court-sanctioned affirmative action, the numbers continue to show a gap in access to colleges and universities between these two racial groups. According to the Department of Education, despite the fact that almost one-half of all whites believe that blacks have attained education levels equal to that of whites, only 16 percent of all black adults are college educated, as opposed to 28 percent of adult whites. Accordingly, the application of abstract liberalism to the affirmative action debate erroneously presupposes that nonwhites are on equal social ground with whites.[7]

Even when such seemingly confounded evidence is raised, it is reframed through the other three aspects of "color-blind racism": naturalization, cultural racism, and the minimization of racism.[8] First, racial segregation is portrayed as "natural": "It is natural for whites to desire to be in the company of other whites, just as it is natural to love one's own children more than someone else's," Laurence said to the crowd gathered at the "Race and Law" discussion. Second, black incarceration is framed as a result of cultural (and sometimes biological) deficiencies, as emphasized by another one of Laurence's statements, "Blacks and Latinos are inherently more lazy than whites. It's a part of their culture . . . They don't know how to stop having babies. Hyperreproduction is embedded in their DNA. . . . Genetics explains why so many blacks are in prison; they are more genetically predisposed to violence than whites and Asians." Third and finally, the significance of racism itself is downplayed. As a panelist responded to a question from the audience regarding antiblack racism:

> Sure blacks still suffer from racism. Everyone does. But it's not as bad as it used to be. I'm from Illinois, and we have a black senator [referencing Barack

Obama]. That could never have happened years ago. Whites suffer from just as much racism as blacks do . . . this is one of the reasons why the races should separate; interracial mixing just adds to racial hostility. If racism does get worse, it's going to be because of diversity initiatives. . . . If you let Michigan accept people on IQ scores, it would get a lot whiter and a lot more racially peaceful, less racist, than if you keep tinkering with social engineering.

As NEA's "Law and Race" panel discussion demonstrates, matters of racial inequality are rearticulated as nonracial in essence or as "color-blind." Such color-blind appeal allows NEA the ability to advocate and protect white privilege without calling it such. Color-blind white nationalism becomes an attractive mainstream proposition while facilitating the perpetuation of racial inequality.

Other evening activities further engrained the legitimacy of color-blind white nationalism within the minds of both members and visitors. In addition to public talks, NEA sponsored many two- and three-month-long "classes" on various aspects of history, biology, and social sciences. Paying a nominal fee, participants attended biweekly evening lectures on various topics. One such class was a seminar course on "Black Nationalism." As the syllabus of the class stated, "To understand and appreciate White Nationalism, you must become acquainted with the forms of racialized nationalism, especially black nationalism . . . [you must become] competent in comparing and contrasting them." Many current members of NEA were once enrolled in such classes. Speaking of one of those classes, David told me:

I wasn't too keen on the idea of hanging out with a bunch of nationalists . . . but after a few months, I learned that these guys weren't what I expected. There's no hate here. It's about white pride. If there's one thing I learned it's that if blacks can have black pride, then we can have white pride. There's no difference. . . . To each his own.

In my time with NEA, there was never a nonwhite student in attendance in their classes. Students were generally in their thirties, and most came to such classes with a certain apprehension and skepticism. Such trepidation was soon overpowered by NEA's firmly constructed color-blind rhetoric that facilitated a sense of students' whiteness (previously burdened by feelings of guilt, emptiness, or alienation) as wholesome, connected, and deserving of defense.

Believing that white Americans have been left out of the discourse and practice of "multiculturalism," members and guests sometimes fill NEA's evening hours by brainstorming white nationalist responses to immigration, a shrinking white population, and their perception of the inherent criminality of black and brown people. Compiling articles, papers, and briefs on these issues, NEA works to influence both the public through the mass media and the government through supplying lawmakers with their studies and findings. For example, NEA literature states:

> Through the guise of advocating for nonwhites, our country's laws, programs, and practices work to actively discriminate against whites, whether in employment, housing, business loans, college admission and a plethora of other social structures. These unfair policies are actively applied against all whites from across the nation, regardless of age or income, while nonwhites are simultaneously compensated. [NEA] provides the vital public policy analysis to fulfill its mission and our publicly available studies consider and critically dissect the legal, regulatory, and cultural questions that impact the interests of white, if not all, Americans. . . . We maintain a wide-ranging list of key policymakers and academics dedicated to our mission. We stand strong in the face of those that attack Western morality and white self-determination.

Home Life

I would be remiss if I failed to include a part of NEA members' lives that is an equally important window into the culture of white nationalism—their "private" home lives.[9] As not all members consented to my intrusions into their home, I cannot claim to have extrapolated the cultural meanings and impact of all members' home life on the white nationalist agenda of NEA. However, some "magnified moments" from certain members' home lives are particular illuminative of the dynamics of living NEA's particular brand of color-blind white nationalism.[10]

Members live in variety of settings: from suburban homes in all-white neighborhoods where a cadre of white children play in front yards, to urban apartment buildings in which their next door neighbors are black, Latino and Latina, and Asian. Members' living spaces run the gamut, generally reflective of the aesthetics associated with their socioeconomic class and employment status. As several members hold advanced degrees (from PhDs to JDs to master's degrees) and work in associated fields as lawyers, consultants, and bankers, their homes are decorated with all the trappings of their expected aesthetic tastes: from the display of fine china in hardwood cherry cabinets and expansive recessed bookshelves in the walls filled with the "Great Men" of canonized European writers to the collection of Victorian- and arts and crafts–style knickknacks on coffee tables that sit beside polished humidors filled with expensive cigars. Other members are blue-color workers such as plumbers, construction contractors, police officers, and teachers whose homes and apartments are filled less with books and more with VCR tapes and DVDs. Popular culture posters and pictures of friends and family adorn their walls, and the central family meeting places are Formica tables within or just off the kitchen, in which cigarettes, not fine cigars, are the norm.

I was allowed access to several members' homes after long days at The Office. Often invited at the last minute, I would arrive to different settings: from a cluttered apartment in which we ate cold pizza from the box, to pristine homes in which a member's wife seemed dutifully bound to provide a meal and then disappear into another area of the house while explaining to her children (as one wife did), "Let's go play. Let daddy talk with the man. . . . Men always have important business." In particular instances, I played with some members' children and met grandparents, aunts, and uncles. Many of the older generations instructed me not to misrepresent what was simply "white people looking out for themselves, just like we encourage any race to do." Much of the time I felt as if the evenings at members' homes were a continuation of evenings at The Office. Members avoided explicit talk of race at home, further lending to the dynamics of color blindness. When race was brought up, it was discussed in a manner akin to what some scholars call "race talk."[11] Race talk is the rhetorical strategy used to avoid being labeled as "racist." For example, "I'm not racist but . . ." and "Some of my best friends are black . . . ," which are almost immediately followed by negative assessments of the racial minority group in question.[12] I found that home life discursively reflects and reinforces this "color-blind" ideology through a resistance to recognizing racial inequalities for anyone other than whites, minimization of the existence of racism toward nonwhites, and attempts to explain nonwhites' lower social standings as the result of "socioeconomic," "cultural deficiency," or "meritocracy" issues.

While such color-blind rhetoric was a part of many of the adults' rhetorical strategies and cultural scripts, the children of these families were not yet proficient in discussing white nationalist worldviews without blatant offense. In this light, the racialized and racist underpinnings of a supposed "color-blind" and "egalitarian" white household fell into relief against the comments of one NEA member's child. A young white girl around the age of seven or eight came up to me one evening with a quizzical look on her face, staring at me for what seemed like several minutes, finally blurting out, "Do you like niggers?"

Shocked, I collected myself while everyone else in the room tranquilly watched the interaction. "That is a bad word," I said to her. "I like all people, it doesn't matter what color they are." After a couple of seconds of staring at the floor and twisting her foot back and forth, she turned her face up to me and said in as calm a tone as one could imagine: "No, you're wrong." She quickly turned and ran away into another room. I looked up to see her grandmother softly laughing and a couple of other family members whispering to another. Suddenly, the room seemed deathly quiet and unbearably hot. Embarrassed at the interaction, I picked at the food in front of my plate, took a bite (in order to compose myself), and looked at my host member of NEA. After a few seconds he spoke, "I guess when it comes down to it you have to draw your lines . . . She [referring to his daughter] knows what side she's on. . . . Doesn't matter if she says things you don't like, *she'll learn not to say those things* [my emphasis] . . ."[13] In another interaction at a different member's home I was summarily "kicked out" after I mentioned that I had dated a black woman. As I was shown to the front door, I was told, "Race mixers are not welcome here"; the member's wife ironically apologized for asking me to leave and stated that she couldn't understand why I saw "something wrong with good white women."

Constructing a Color-Blind White Identity

For members of NEA, white identity is in the midst of a social and political crisis. Their responses to this "crisis," while varied, demonstrate a unified belief in the solution of white nationalism. Yet it seems that anything short of a nation in which whites are understood as inherently moral and pure relative to the criminality and disorder of nonwhites will be not enough for NEA. Any thing less than that goal will enable the construction of an embattled and victimized white self. For these members, "being white" is built on several a priori assumptions: (1) Whites are inherently superior to nonwhites, (2) whites are not afforded their proper place atop a hierarchical society, and (3) whites are constantly attacked for simply being white. To them, the world is unfairly passing them by. And NEA members are not content to simply commiserate about their embattled status in their suburban office. They are vigorous and passionate activists. I often felt exhausted after spending time with them. Their organization is politically active as a kind of racial and immigration policy think tank. They are actively working with other groups and funding agencies to revive eugenics programs and outmoded immigration statutes and to reinstitute racialized segregation. White nationalism is not a pipe dream for these members. In their daily endeavors, they manifest a pragmatic optimism.

The cultural logic—or the particular meanings used to reason through everyday problems—of NEA is not found by simply examining their political activities and goals. A more complete understanding of NEA is evident in the members' ongoing meaning making of white racial identity. Given that point, how do members respond to the discourse of whites' inherent moral superiority alongside an unmerited victimization of white people? Their response, far from being a "natural recognition of the facts," is constructed from the logic of "color blindness." Members have learned how to keep their supremacist and nationalist agenda alive in an era in which such expression is, by and large, unfashionable. When NEA members do talk about their goals of racial segregation and white control of the United States, these narratives are couched within appeals to "science" (especially genetic biology), morality, individualism, economic theory, and even a kind of "multiculturalism" in which every racial group should have the "power to control its own destiny" (which several members repeated to me like a mantra). Rather than appearing as self-interested actors, they claim they are "color blind" to the extent that they let the "facts" guide them. If whites are on top of the social order, it is either by chance or by nature. "It's just a genetic fact," one member told me. In continuing, he said, "If blacks were the smartest, then they would get to run things, but they're not, so it's whites who are in charge. It's evolution. . . . It's not my fault I was born white."

While this is quite a savvy technique and rhetorical device, I did not think that most NEA members were feeding me a line to hide their true intentions. After more than a year of time spent with these activists in an array of contexts, I was certain they believed what they said. These white actors collectively held deeply embedded and structured sensibilities, temperaments, perceptions, tastes, and worldviews. These dispositions are constructed from the logic of color blindness in which white segregation, supremacy, and solidarity are interpreted not as "racial" effects per se, but as "normal" and "natural" consequences. The logic thus creates and conditions subjectively felt, and objectively shared, white racial identity through collective belonging, racial solidarity, and a sense of group position in relation to both (1) people of color and (2) whites thought lesser, lacking, or inauthentic.[14]

3 Everyday Activities with Antiracists
Whites for Racial Justice

*Being conscious of racism is ninety-nine percent of the battle . . .
I can't fight what I am not conscious of . . . I think that if whites
consciously put themselves in locations in which they have to
be uncomfortable and unlearn their racist tendencies then you
will see a retreat from racism in society as a whole. . . . Racism
exists in the mind and is manifested in what we do—if we root it
out here, then the possibilities for disrupting the mechanisms of
power in society that oppress nonwhites will be weakened.*
—**Mark, Whites for Racial Justice**

*Much of the whiteness literature originates in the school of
thought stemming from educational studies about "unlearning
racism." In this argument, racism and prejudice are seen
as being learned early in white experience but as being
"unlearned" if one reexamines one's part and denounces
earlier learned prejudices. This assumes that the problems of
racism can be solved by white people changing their minds.
Confronting one's own racial prejudice and race awareness
is no doubt a part of challenging the racial order, but, like
studying prejudice in the absence of racial stratification,
leaving things in the hands of "unlearning racism" is likely to
do little to unseat the apparatus of racial power.*
—**Margaret L. Andersen, *Whitewashing Race*[1]**

My First Visit to WRJ

After making contact with several of the leaders of Whites for Racial Justice, or "coordinators" (as they preferred to be called), I was invited to a small meeting to work out the details of my study. Unlike NEA, the members of WRJ seemed trusting, cooperative, and ready to give me the benefit of the doubt. To attend the meeting, I was given an address and time at which to arrive and even instructed not to eat beforehand, as they would happily serve dinner.

On my arrival at the address, I thought I was lost or that I had misheard their instructions over the phone. I found myself in a suburban residential neighborhood. As I stepped out of my car, a young African American boy rode past me in a tricycle and a Latina mail carrier smiled and said hello. I walked up a brick path to a large home with a covered front porch and knocked on the screen door.

I was greeted by the owner of the home and chief coordinator of WRJ, a young man I call "Malcolm" because of his affinity for the slain human rights leader Malcolm X. Malcolm held a look of jovial relaxation underpinned by his love of ice cream cones, which he frequently ate all throughout my study of WRJ. Greeting me with an infectous smile, he ushered me into his home and bade me sit on his living room couch. The son of a lawyer (his father worked in civil rights law) and counselor (his mother counseled victims of domestic abuse), Malcolm explained how his commitment to white antiracism was a synthesis of his parents' work:

> Dad worked with lots of black groups like the NAACP, CORE, and some with SNCC, I think. He was always happy to do pro bono work for those groups that he felt were doing the right thing. . . . My mother, she dedicated her life to helping women work through the traumas of abuse. I remember she would come home and just start crying, and my dad would comfort her and tell her about his day and the struggles and victories there. . . . So, this kind of work [referring to WRJ] was something engrained in me as a child, but it's a lifelong endeavor.

Malcolm's home can best be described as "organized clutter." Most of the house was clean, except for a few dusty shelves, but books were arranged in piles on the floor instead of on empty bookshelves right next to them. Stacks of paper lay all over various tables, which, while neat and tidy, disallowed use of the tables for anything but a horizontal filing system. Almost all the wall space in the house was covered by pictures of some sort—whether a local arts and crafts fair poster, a reproduction of Degas' *Blue Dancers*, or a photograph of a setting sun over the horizon of a calm body of water. The art was an eclectic mix of various odds and ends and seemed more for covering space than for an aesthetic theme.

After relating how he came to WRJ, Malcolm told me that other WRJ members would soon arrive and that we should go downstairs to "The Center" (the name that members used for their headquarters). He opened up a door to the basement, and we walked down to a very well-lit and carpeted basement. "Here we are," he said with a proud tone. "Welcome to The Center. This is where we do our work." The stairs descended into a large meeting room. The walls were all finished with drywall in an eggshell color. Bookshelves were everywhere in the room, and they were bowed with the weight of hundreds of books on race, immigration, human rights activism, psychology, and counseling techniques. Modern wooden chairs and a large oval table, capable of seating about a dozen people, took up most of the space in the middle of the room. A finished bathroom was just off the main room, and there was a door that opened to the outside—granting members access to the office without intruding into the upstairs. The basement was also divided into several smaller rooms used for offices. After the tour of the location, and with a sigh of accomplishment, Malcolm told me that he would be more than happy to open WRJ to my study under the condition that I visit as much as possible. "We're a committed group," he told me. "I think everyone will like you, and after your research, I think you'll come to think of yourself as one of us."

Whites for Racial Justice

The headquarters for WRJ is located just a couple hours drive from Riverside in a metropolitan area I call "Fairview." Unlike the neighborhood of the headquarters of NEA, the surrounding area of WRJ does not carry the loud reverberations of the city. A walk through the neighborhood resonates with the dull drone of slow-moving station wagons and the hum of lawn mowers in the summer and snow shovels scraping the sidewalks in the winter. The area is quiet and quaint, as children play in their lawns or at a nearby park. The neighborhood is filled with an abundance of younger, middle-class households and is racially mixed.

Fairview is also a racially mixed city composed of younger, working-class families. Until the 1970s, Fairview's wealthy class played a significant role in the city's most visible political and social institutions. Several streets became venues for the city's elite to engage in conspicuous consumption of high-dollar real estate. These neighborhoods are replete with manicured parks with elaborate fountains. The presence of "old money" in these areas now clashes with the influx of Latinos and African Americans. These traditionally elite and "all-white" areas are quickly diversifying—resulting in "white flight."

WRJ was founded in the 1980s and has since developed into a nationwide organization that claims approximately forty chapters and about 400 members. On both the national and local levels, WRJ generates publications, gives workshops, and promotes media events about what white people can do to eliminate racism both from their daily lives and from the social structures that surround them (education, religion, family, work, and so on). As Eileen O'Brien writes in her study *Whites Confront Racism*:

Antiracists, quite simply, are people who have committed themselves, in thought, action, and practices, to dismantling racism. In our culture, "I'm not a racist" rolls off the tongues of many people, often right before they make incredibly derogatory or racially stereotypic remarks, so it is important to distinguish between "nonracists" and "antiracists." . . . Nonracists try to deny that the prison exists. Antiracists work for the prison's eventual destruction.[2]

Accordingly, members make meaning of their decision to join WRJ as an all-encompassing choice—a dedication toward an antiracist lifestyle rather than just a part-time organizational endeavor.

WRJ's beginnings have roots in several majority white, liberal organizations during the civil rights movement of the 1960s and 1970s. Mirroring the Student Nonviolent Coordinating Committee (SNCC) decision to turn toward an almost all-black membership and embrace the ideology of black nationalism, many whites felt that they could be sufficient allies to the struggle if they created a white "safe space" in which they could theorize and plan pragmatic ways to oppose racism. Thus, WRJ was founded with the mission of "eliminating racism in our minds and communities. . . . [Such an activity] is a necessary for the progress of humankind. We are committed to working with other groups that share this vision." As a consequence, WRJ maintains ties to many human rights and racial activist groups but works primarily on its own. WRJ is growing, but at a snail's pace.

WRJ and "The Center"

There are many kinds of white antiracist activism in the contemporary United States. While they vary in their scope and intensity, a central tenet of most white antiracist praxis is to challenge white mind-sets. White antiracists often understand that challenging white prejudice is the first and crucial step toward the eradication of racism. Accordingly, WRJ members spoke to me with great pride that they were carrying out a long fight against racism. Samuel told me:

> Part of why I'm in WRJ is because I feel like I benefit unfairly from a undemo-
> cratic system because of my skin color, and those advantages don't come out
> of thin air but are reaped from someone else's opportunities. That hurts me
> on a fundamental level, I mean, let me clarify . . . I gain a material advantage,
> but that I am gaining those privileges in a way that is unearned, and that I
> recognize that, privilege—that recognition hurts. It goes to the core of me.

I can't say that I am for democracy and justice and not fight racism and racial inequality in this country. Seriously, if I didn't, I think I would be the biggest hypocrite ever.

Toward this end, WRJ holds meetings on a biweekly basis, organizes frequent public activities, and publishes a quarterly newsletter delivered to hundreds of U.S. addresses.

As The Center is located in the basement of a member's home in a residential neighborhood, their interactions with the public are limited. The decision to base their headquarters in such a personal mileau mirrors much of their organizational logic.

WRJ has a relaxed atmosphere. Whereas NEA had few markings of personal or individual expression, opting for marking their office with abstract qualities of leadership and white nationalist sentiment, WRJ exalts individual expression and rights as the pathway to antiracist action: from members being free to arrive late to meetings to the finger paintings and ceramic ashtrays made by members' children. Unlike the linear layout of NEA, the furniture arrangements of WRJ facilitate conversations rather than lectures. Chairs and desks are often set up in circles or in crescent moon fashion so that members may counsel one another on becoming a better "white antiracist."

The material arrangement of WRJ's center reflects a central tenet of WRJ membership: Everyone is born with tremendous intellectual potential, natural zest, and an inherent loving attitude toward others. Unlike the majority of NEA members who believe that human beings are inherently selfish and naturally gravitate toward members of their own racial group, WRJ assumes that people are taught racialized divisions, hate, and distrust. Such miseducation causes pain, distress, and the blockage of one's authentic emotional and cognitive expression. WRJ's meetings center on racism's effect on the individual white self—the emotional, mental, and psychological damage done to whites that perpetuate whites' racist actions. As WRJ member Duncan told me:

We can effectively wade through the hurt of racism and establish its psychological hold on the white mind by establishing a more loving environment. As that trust and mutual concern develops, we will be more effective in looking out for our own and others' [referring to nonwhites] interests and will be more capable of acting successfully against injustice. . . . Sometimes this is a slow process, but it is a necessary one . . . if we are going to be true to our calling of "white antiracism."

Most WRJ members happily consented to interviews and readily agreed to follow up at later dates when time ran out. Many saw my questions as vitally important to their process of becoming better white antiracists, as a music teacher named Jerry told me: "I think your expertise and alignment with our goals will help. . . . I always feel like your line of questioning makes me think more critically about myself. . . . It's better for my activism." WRJ members embodied Becky Thompson's argument in *A Promise and a Way of Life: White Antiracist Activism*: White antiracist culture is "a merging of people's political action and personal lives."[3] Members were giving with their resources, they traveled regularly to give seminars at distant locales, and they actively put themselves in uncomfortable racial situations.

WRJ members consider themselves part of a larger community of like-minded activists. As a young WRJ member named Colin told me, "I might have more knowledge, experience, or be a bit better at communicating than someone else, or even be more aware about particular racial issues than someone else, but [in WRJ] it doesn't make me higher up than the next person. . . . I think that is important to know." WRJ sees itself as incredibly meritocratic. Any role that someone holds is due to both ability and acceptance of responsibility, not because of age, experience, title, or prestige. Members are bound to this community through the singular goal of identifying the presence of prejudice in their own minds, analyzing its mechanisms and effects, and then working to interrupt its reproduction in both thought and action. Members of the WRJ community require no other activities or goals. Malcolm stated:

> WRJ is committed to reaching as many people as possible with our tools and theory. . . . We can reach the largest amount of people, and be the most diverse as possible, you know, among whites, if we require agreement only on this one point: that we take responsibility for our whiteness and work to fight racism. Unique manifestations of racism require unique strategies; anything more structured could easily backfire. . . . It's best to stay open with this as our point of agreement.

Members in all chapters across the country are expected to meet at least once or twice weekly to discuss such issues in ways that (1) alleviate, as Bret told me, "emotional baggage that clouds decision making"; (2) "rationally" illuminate instances of white prejudice; and (3) put in place actions that will attack the effects of that prejudice. WRJ holds various activities toward these ends, such as an annual conferences, workshops, publications, public lectures, classes, support groups, and book clubs. All twenty-one members of the head-quartered chapter of WRJ live within a radius of approximately thirty miles from the Fairview area. Members committed approximately twelve hours per week to the organization. All twenty-one members expressed to me that they considered themselves full-fledged members and take their membership and antiracist mission seriously, akin to a religious "calling."

All members identified as either "white" or "Caucasian." Most members were middle class, some differentiating among "middle middle class," "upper middle," and "lower middle." Yearly incomes ranged from just $9,000 to over $200,000, with a household average income of $39,000 per year. The age range of members was forty years (twenty-two to sixty-two) with an average age of thirty-seven and a median of thirty-five. All but two members were male, and most were single or divorced. All members attended some college, while some held baccalaureate degrees and others held advanced degrees like a master's or a doctorate. Most were of a Christian background, and they reported that their beliefs played a small to moderate role in their lives. Some connected their work as antiracists to a belief in the inherent spirituality of humans or remarked that racism is against the wishes of God or a higher power. Most members were raised in the southeastern and mid-Atlantic United States. Eight members have children. A slight majority rent an apartment or a room while the rest own their own home. Fifteen of the members are politically "independent" or have no particular political affiliation, while five are active Democrats, and one member agreed with Republican ideas but is not officially a party member. Members hailed from a variety of socioeconomic backgrounds: Their parents hold jobs such as chemists, lawyers, and architects as well as janitors, butchers, and teachers. Members showed a high degree of social mobility, as many of their parents came from lower-class or blue-collar working jobs; they reported a great deal of satisfaction with their present occupations (see Tables 3.1 and 3.2).

Many WRJ members reported that they joined WRJ because of a commitment to fight racism among other whites, not just to work against racism in an abstract or general sense. White antiracist activism is grounded in camaraderie and a sense of shared struggle. White antiracists tend to keep company with politically like-minded partners who offer unwavering support.[4] These networks are far reaching and often extend beyond immediate family and friends to Internet forums, other like-minded private organizations, and

Table 3.1 WRJ membership.

Pseudonym	Age	Occupation	Education	Politics	Membership (years)
Blake	22	Retail sales	College degree	Independent	2
Malcolm	44	Consultant/ counselor	Graduate degree	Democrat	5
Cassandra	31	Marketing	Graduate degree	Independent	3
Sean	62	Gardener (PT)	Some college	None	6
Bret	51	Writer	College degree	Democrat	7
Mark	33	Corporate sales	Some graduate school	Independent	7
Michael	36	Banker	College degree	Independent	4.5
Patrick	28	Writer	College degree	Democrat	2
Horace	41	Car salesman	College degree	Independent	4
James	36	Construction manager	Graduate degree	Independent	4
Simon	27	Engineer	Graduate degree	Independent	6
Philip	53	Grocery store owner	Some college	Democrat	5
Samuel	26	Music store employee	College degree	Independent	2
Duncan	30	Corporate sales	Graduate degree	Independent	2.5
Tristan	30	Waiter	Some college	Independent	5
Andre	24	Graduate student	Some graduate school	Independent	1
Colin	26	Student	Some college	Republican	1
Wayne	44	Retail manager	College degree	Democrat	5
Jerry	38	Music teacher	Some graduate school	None	7
Sherrill	35	Consultant	Graduate degree	None	8
Frederick	55	Federal employee	PhD	Independent	6

campus groups that exist in the shadow of liberal arts colleges and universities. As WRJ member James told me:

> I think I always understood myself as an antiracist. I was involved in a kind of multicultural group in high school that challenged the school's history curriculum for their exclusive focus on Europe. . . . Then in college with a few other groups I was involved with, I was a part of the black student union there too. After college, I really didn't have that network anymore. . . . I found a few websites in the late 1990s, and there were even more now. . . . After hearing of WRJ in a chat room, I sought them out. . . . Here I am.

Table 3.2 WRJ descriptive statistics.

Mean years active in organization (median, SD)	4.38 (5, 2.08)
Mean age in years (median, SD)	36.76 (35, 10.88)
Age range in years	22–62
Gender (male, female)	(19, 2) (90.4%, 9.6%)
Religion	
Catholic	2 (9.5%)
Protestant	12 (57.1%)
Atheist	1 (4.8%)
Agnostic	2 (9.5%)
"Spiritual"/other	4 (19%)
Where primarily raised (geographic location)	
Midwest	2 (9.5%)
North	3 (14.3%)
South	16 (76.2%)
West	0
Political orientation	
Democrat	5 (23.8%)
Independent	12 (57.1%)
Republican	1 (4.8%)
No affiliation	3 (14.3%)
Relationship status	
Single	13 (61.9%)
Married (mean length in years)	7 (9) (33.3%)
Divorced	1 (4.8%)
Mean number of children (median)	1.14 (0)
Highest level of education attained	
Some college	4 (19%)
College degree or equivalent	7 (33.3%)
Some graduate classes	3 (14.3%)
Advanced degree (MA, Ph., JD, etc)	7 (33.3%)
Occupational status	
Working class	1 (4.8%)
Lower middle class	3 (14.3%)
Middle class	8 (38.1%)
Upper middle class	6 (28.6%)
Upper class	3 (14.3%)
Yearly income	
<25,000	1 (4.8%)
25,000–49,999	9 (42.9%)
50,000–74,999	9 (42.9%)
75,000–99,999	0
100,000>	2 (9.5%)
Housing	
Own home	10 (47.6%)
Rent	11 (52.4%)

James's dedication to antiracism, like that of many WRJ members, is inter-twined with an energetic personality and vicious critique of other aspects of inequality in mainstream society. Many members take a holistic approach to social issues while concentrating on racism as the linchpin to human oppres-sion. Some joined WRJ after speaking with friends who were already mem-bers, but most cemented their membership in WRJ after becoming friends with other members. Others reported learning of WRJ via their quarterly newsletter, a flyer, or some other form of mass media.

The Average Meeting

Unlike the previous chapter, in which I presented "a day in the life" of NEA, I cannot fairly reproduce such an equivalent presentation for WRJ. WRJ mem-bers neither met on a daily basis like NEA, nor did they keep The Center open from morning to night. Rather, activities such as classes, workshops, lectures, and support groups took place in the late afternoons and early evenings. Hence, it is more appropriate to reconstruct the structure of a typical meet-ing rather than a day. Rather than condense every workshop and encounter that took place in my fieldwork, I have aggregated various experiences into a fictional WRJ meeting.

During the day members worked at their respective places of employment while The Center remained dark and silent. On a day with a meeting, one or two WRJ members arrived in the mid- to late afternoon. Most members had keys that allowed for virtually anyone to use the resources: several Internet-ready computers and printers, a fax machine, two telephone lines, and a small lending library. Generally, the first member in would begin to research infor-mation for an article in their quarterly newsletter, make phone calls to area coordinators, craft the lesson plans for an antiracist workshop, or write notes for an upcoming public forum. As more members arrived (generally during the afternoon there were no more than two or three members in the office), the work slowed as they sat around chatting about work, family, and the oc-casional racial issue.

As evening approached, more WRJ members trickled in. It was a frequent occurrence for members to bring guests (almost always white). By 6:00 or 7:00 pm, generally the scheduled time for an event to begin, there sat twelve to fifteen people (nearly all WRJ members). Most sat at a large conference table or in chairs situated in the corners of the room to facilitate more private conversations. Although events were always scheduled for a specific time, not once in my year of attending meetings did one begin on time. When I made this observation to one member during an interview, I was gently rebuffed: "Matthew!" said Horace in a slightly annoyed tone, "You can't tell people what to do. The meeting will start soon enough, don't force it."

When meetings did begin, generally thirty to sixty minutes later than planned, the guests were always introduced first. Guests of members were generally inquisitive as to why (and how) a bunch of white people would sit around and talk about racism and race relations. They always eyed the room suspiciously and spoke with a cautious hesitation. However, when I was introduced as a sociologist studying the group, their tone seemed to relax, as if my professional credential gave WRJ a kind of legitimacy. At the end of meetings, guests seemed relieved that WRJ was neither a religious faction nor a radical antigovernment group hoarding a weapons cache. However, many guests did express confusion over WRJ's stance that "whiteness itself perpetuates racism" and that whites should "oppose their own whiteness."

In addition to these guests, WRJ members from other chapters frequently attended. Whether these people were just visiting their friends or attending training seminars offered by the headquarters, their visitations afford a glimpse into the reach of WRJ's organizational logic. Different guest members attended twenty-one out of the thirty-three meetings at which I was present (64 percent). From these WRJ members' outings, I made three general observations: First, most members expressed high satisfaction with the training offered by WRJ headquarters. Echoing the comments of others, one guest from a New York state chapter told me:

> I was not expecting to receive the amount of in-depth training that I did. . . . especially along the lines of counseling techniques . . . [and] literature that I can use back at [her WRJ chapter]. . . . I'll admit to you that I had some reservations about how organized WRJ was at the top, . . . but these guys are great. I'm looking forward to the conference when I get to see them all again. . . . I made some great friendships and established some colleagues and networks that I will definitely be drawing upon. . . . It's good to know there are other committed antiracists like me working hard. . . . I needed the emotional lift.

However, many guest members acknowledged their frustrations in translating WRJ's focus on the psychological aspects of racism and white identity into pragmatic action. After agreeing to speak with me, one guest member asked me to step outside with him. We walked around the side of Malcolm's house and stood on the sidewalk under the glow of a suburban street light:

> Guest: I learned a lot. I wish others [from his chapter] were here with me. . . . I am a bit afraid that when I get back to [his chapter] that I will have difficulty convincing people that this is the way to go. . . . So many people [fellow WRJ members] want to directly oppose these racist structures.
>
> MWH: What racist structures in specific?
>
> Guest: You know, the police, different businesses, even capitalism on a whole, but how do we actually do that? [said with a tone of exasperation] I'm not sure how to oppose the racism in the police. . . . Even if I go through the steps [long pause] I know [long pause] some members are going to say, "It's just not enough." Do I just try to convince them? Do I alter the program? That doesn't seem quite right. . . . I feel stuck. . . . It's very satisfying being a WRJ member, but sometimes there's the action part that's missing.
>
> MWH: From what I know, you guys seem to do a lot of "action." Your rallies, public talks, your conference that is coming up . . .
>
> Guest: [interrupting] Yeah, but that's not what I mean. It's like there's not enough. . . . I don't know. [long pause] Change. There's not enough change, I don't see the change. How do I actually know that we're making a difference? Even mentally? I hear Malcolm about becoming "less white," less of an oppressor. I feel like I've changed a lot of my habits and my consciousness has been raised, but, I mean, alright [laughing awkwardly and nervously], this is [long pause] I don't feel less white. Is that bad? I mean, really, am I not getting it? . . . Sometimes I feel stupid.

Both guests and other WRJ members made statements akin to the aforementioned, evidencing a tension that WRJ struggles to resolve. Such a dynamic shows that not all WRJ members are static antiracists, buying wholeheartedly and unconsciously into the theory of WRJ activism.

Third, and related to the former, many WRJ guests hesitantly told me of an intense pressure to be perceived as an entirely committed member of WRJ. Indeed, the leaders make it clear that being a member of WRJ is a lifelong and thorough commitment. While both leaders and members spoke of such a dynamic with pride and the occasional egotistical posture that they are not "half-steppers when it comes to race," some admitted to me with sadness and/or frustration that they were neglecting their work, friends, and family to engage in what they felt was the proper amount of activism. "There are only so many hours in the day," remarked Simon. He continued, "I do a lot of work for [WRJ], I'm not asking for praise, it's just I feel incredibly guilty when I'm not doing everything I can. . . . I feel like I'm such an example to everyone too, maybe they don't feel that way, but I sure do."

After the introduction of guests, meetings began with the sharing of good news from either members' personal lives or from events covered in mass media. Such sharing generally showed the antiracist movement in a positive and victorious light. As Mark explained, "We intentionally afford time at the beginning of all meetings to start things off on a positive foot. . . . It's a chance to recognize the antiracist endeavors happening all the time, . . . that we might not give credence to unless we stop to intentionally think about it." This stage of the meeting did not generally end until every member said at least one good thing about antiracist work.

After the positive foundation was laid, members turned toward the illumination of problems in their own lives. In this stage, members told of how friends and family resisted or argued with their antiracist position, or they talked about a racist action they observed that week. Whereas the delineation of positive occurrences ran the gamut from the personal to the macro, the illumination of recent tribulations was almost always personal. Some members even simply repeated what happened to them weeks ago, sharing the story again because they felt that the hurt from racism needed to be laid bare and addressed. During one meeting, Tristan said:

> I want to just bring up what happened to me last week. You know, with my father? [Heads nodded around the room.] I just can't stop thinking about it, so I know it's doing a doozy to my mental and emotional state. When he said what he did [his father made a racist remark about Mexican immigrants taking "white people's jobs"] . . . it just blew me away. I mean, why or, um, how could he, just, say something so ignorant? . . . It makes me worry that a part of him is in me.

In speaking of personal troubles, members were allowed to speak as long as they wanted; some would take five minutes, while others would take thirty. On more than a few occasions, meetings never went past this stage, lasting almost three hours as members spoke of racist actions they were a part of, bore witness to, or resisted.

Sometimes the discourse shifted to the effect of social or personal problems on members' racial identity. It was in this stage that they demonstrated the most heterogeneous attitudes. Some remarked they felt constantly belittled and mistreated because of their antiracist stance and not taken seriously because they are white. Others expressed rather taboo subjects that were always accompanied by disclaimers that they just needed to get something off their chest or that they were "not really sure what they really felt" about something. One member named Wayne admitted that he often felt fearful of black men when they came into his store: "I'm just putting this out there because, well, it's honest, and I need some feedback from you guys. . . . I feel horrible for saying it, but, when black guys come into [his store], I get tense, . . . I recognize that I'm afraid." Rather than attacking him or explaining why such a fear is fundamentally unfounded, fellow members connected his feelings to a discussion about whiteness in general. In response, Horace said, "That's what being white is, that's what it does . . . makes us think prejudiced thoughts." So other members also agreed and chimed in with implorations about becoming "less white" as a way to stop such thoughts from occurring.

Simultaneously, other members often expressed that although it was necessary to acknowledge the hurt that whites inflicted throughout the world, that the constant "blaming" of whiteness was difficult for them. Ellen K. Scott describes this phenomenon as a central feature of white antiracist organizing in which:

> Individuals occupy one of two subject positions: victim or perpetrator. This discourse of agency in racial politics paralyzes action. Activists tend to vie for membership in the victim category and attach a great deal of shame to belonging to the perpetrator category.[5]

Even among actors who come together to explicitly confront the "shame" of whiteness, this confrontation proves a difficult task. WRJ members often felt their guilt accumulating and the need to release it. While WRJ's methods were a cause of much of this "stress," members often remarked how thankful they were for a supportive community in which they could confront their whiteness.

Discussions about the subjectivity of "being white" often led into a discussion of what one could actually do with his or her whiteness. That is, once it was agreed that "becoming less white" was the proper method and goal for antiracist action, it became necessary for the discussion to move toward the delineation of pragmatic goals. Members were often asked to refer to journals they were asked to keep as WRJ members. These journals were to record their own personal antiracist thoughts, struggles, methods, and goals. Here members pulled open three-ring binders, composition notebooks, or even leather-bound volumes with gold-leafed pages and discussed their own goals, methods for achieving them, and whether they were working.

Eventually the discussion of goals returned to how working toward antiracist goals made a member feel, a discussion on the "proper" role of whites in working toward a certain goal, or how the organization could improve so as to better facilitate the "reeducation" or "abolition" of whites. Sherrill stated:

> I don't want to derail this, and actually I think it's necessary for what we are talking about, but can we back up a second? . . . Seems to me that we are forgetting to talk about how this all relates to our every experiences and struggles; you know, I mean, I need to hear from more of you on how you are actually living this antiracist identity. I've been doing it for quite some time, and I feel like I am just starting to understand what this means for me, but I'm still so far away from the ideal, so especially the new members, relatively speaking, how does this grab you, or, uh, you know, make you feel, you know?

Another member, wishing to remain entirely anonymous, told me that this dynamic echoed the overarching character of WRJ:

> I just don't see how we can get out there and say we have a solution to things when we are still so confused about our own racism, about out own racial identity . . . more time needs to be spent counseling one another, learning and driving out the miseducation of racism in our own minds. . . . Out of this maybe we can put forth some personal, social, psychological resources, ideological resources that will be support systems, for other whites in our predicament. . . . For those that have woken up and seen the racism that is so normal; such a part of the world that lies right beneath the surface of everything.

Debating Whiteness

While the previous section details the structure of discussion, the overall configuration of meetings was stitched together by the thread of whiteness as an identity in crisis. For all members of WRJ, there is a consensus that white identity is a "social construction"; a belief that race is not an essential or biological identity but is rather an concept based in specific historical conditions and is subject to change based on particular legal, political, and social dynamics. Moving from this position, there is a tendency to view whiteness as little more than social privilege that masks the unfair allocation of material and symbolic resources by those socially marked as "white." For instance, as WRJ holds a number of classes on race and U.S. history, new members and guests are taught how Irish immigrants of the nineteenth century were not initially accepted as white. Through violence against blacks and Indians, support of slavery, and various attempts to de-ethnicize themselves (via changing traditional Irish names and distancing themselves from cultural traditions that would mark them as distinctively Irish), they slowly became understood as "white." Once "whitened," they were able to reap social (lack of discrimination allowing social mobility), economic (ability to gain employment and foster business deals), and political (voter enfranchisement and the holding of office) benefits. To many, such an arrangement means that whiteness itself must be abolished as a concept. Bret stated in a meeting:

> It's not been easy; it's been a struggle a lot of the time. But I finally accepted, or became comfortable if you will, with the fact that I no longer wished to be white. So many other people [referring to nonwhites] are resisting inequality, I feel like I am an authentic part of that struggle now . . . It took me a few years to work through this, you may do it quicker than I did, or it may take you a lot longer, with greater struggle, but either way, you know, you have to keep digging into yourself, expelling the bad ways of viewing the world, healing yourself, becoming more human, less white.

Others remarked that they did not understand why whiteness needs to be "abolished" to be antiracist. In an interview that Frederick would conduct only away from The Center, he said:

> I'm not sure if there is something wrong with my whiteness. I mean, I don't feel white.
>
> MWH: How do you know, I mean, what does whiteness feel like?
>
> Frederick: I guess, privileged, I mean, I do feel privileged and know that I am—I'm conscious of it and not just going through life blindly like a lot of whites do with their privilege, thinking that all that power is normal. That's part of the problem . . . but it's because I am conscious of these attitudes that most whites have that I know I don't hold anymore. . . . I guess I can say this because I used to be like that, so I know where I've come from. And yeah, I mean, that's it, I still *am white* [said with emphasis], I can't just stop being

white and, presto, like magic, I'm more human. I guess I am more human in that I recognize my privilege, but I'm still white. If you ask one hundred people what race I am, one hundred are going to say "white."

The differences exhibited between Bret's and Frederick's takes on whiteness are telling. They inform us as to the daily navigation of living a white antiracist life among WRJ members. There are many agreements among members, but there are also important points of departure.

Constructing a Color-Conscious White Identity

As with NEA members, members of WRJ understand whiteness as an identity in a state of crisis and uncertainty. Their activism is a response to widespread racism that is reproduced through white people's actions and understandings of their identity as normalized and superior. To WRJ, unless and until large numbers of whites begin to oppose racism and disavow their own privilege, the dream of a multicultural nation will not be realized. In this light, WRJ's understanding of whiteness is constructed on a tripartite foundation: (1) Whites are inherently carriers of unfair privilege; (2) whites are themselves victimized by racism through the internalization of unjust, stereotypical, and prejudicial attitudes; and (3) whites hold conscious and unconscious beliefs in their own normality and superiority.

As a remedy, WRJ members believe they must do their best to purge themselves of these hurtful feelings by examining and laying bare their feelings on race. After doing so, they can begin a process of unlearning racism by which they refuse to claim privilege in various situations. After this, they can more effectively "teach by example" and reach other "unconscious" whites, slowly spreading their message of antiracism. A key difference between NEA and WRJ is that NEA is outwardly oriented, while WRJ struggles with its inward fixation. Most of WRJ's workshops, meetings, and forums are not about political activism (although that goal is in mind). They focus on learning hidden aspects of history, cocounseling one another in their racialized feelings and thoughts and attempting to better understand how to live an antiracist life. Rather than using a logic of "color blindness" in which racial inequality and racism are explained away as the result of a lack of hard work, cultural deficiencies, or minimizing its occurrence, WRJ members are explicitly color conscious. Because of this consciousness, they believe that white recognition of inequality and racism will bring about a sea change in white attitudes and responses.

4 White Panic

*Blacks, black men in particular, I think the studies show, are
particularly violent . . . They engage in utterly reprehensible
behavior given today's moral standards . . . [They are]
overrunning our cities . . . It's genetically hardwired . . . Biology
has culture on a leash.*

—Laurence, National Equality for All

*Years and years of oppression, I think for one, have kind of
emasculated black men . . . I mean, I know how I would react
if I were in that situation, I'd lash out at the system that
oppresses me. Can you blame them for their violence? . . . It's all
learned, I mean, it's all cultural.*

—Michael, Whites for Racial Justice

Nonwhite Dysfunctions as a Normative Construct

In the midst of a so-called postracial era, there remains a widespread narrative that black and Hispanic people possess an array of dysfunctional traits:
from rampant drug use and unemployment to broken family structures and
violent crime. Evoking this discourse remains an effective endeavor for those
who want to say something about race—and command attention. Rhetoric
of "bad values" and "pathological behavior" reigns as a powerful tool for
whites to discuss people of color. That these discourses are particularly diffuse and firmly planted in the minds of most Americans is partially due to
their widespread proliferation in everyday life: in mainstream media, within
corner stores, and at family dinner tables. For example, after the housing market crash of 2006–2007, many believed that African Americans and undocumented Latinos and Latinas held millions of bad mortgages and effectively
caused the housing bubble to burst. The problem was—as with blaming Jews
for the cause and spread of the fourteenth-century Black Death—that it was
not true.[1]

This technique for framing the meanings of black and brown people, what
has been called the "black pathology biz," remains a productive strategy for
reproducing white supremacist ideology without making explicitly "racist"
statements.[2] The images of Willie Horton, gun-toting rappers, welfare queens,
and drug addicts have changed very little over time. They have become commonsense truths to many people.[3] And these "truths" are so diffuse and multifaceted that they show up across the political spectrum.

Conservatives often cite a deficient culture of essentially "bad," "broken," or even "un-American" values as the cause of African American and Latino or Latina habitually wrong choices. For example, right-wing media pundit Rush Limbaugh stated that "the black frame of mind is terrible" and that National Football League games look "like a game between the Bloods and the Crips without any weapons. There, I said it."[4] And in an increasingly loud voice from the New Right, we are told that black and brown "pathological" behavior has biological causes. In 2005, former Secretary of Education (1985–1988) and Director of the Office of National Drug Control Policy (1989–1993) William Bennett stated, "If you wanted to reduce crime, you could—if that were your sole purpose, you could abort every black baby in this country, and your crime rate would go down."[5] Recycling the logic from twentieth-century U.S. and German eugenicists—combined with the technological advances of the mapped human genome—most people of color are thought genetically predisposed to crime, violence, and hypersexuality. For example, James Watson (the codiscover of the DNA double helix) remarked in 2007 that he was "inherently gloomy about the prospect of Africa" because "all our social policies are based on the fact that their intelligence is the same as ours [white Europeans]—whereas all the testing says not really." And while he hoped that everyone could be equal, he continued, "People who have to deal with black employees find this not true."[6] In the worldview of Watson and others who share it, people of color have too much agency, are unable to delay gratification, and do not possess the biological capacity to compete with other races.

But politics makes strange bedfellows. On the other side of the political spectrum, a growing number of self-proclaimed "liberals" and "progressives" blame prejudicial behaviors for the emasculation of black and Latino men. As a result, so the story goes, this emasculation has created an overall "culture of poverty" in which the racial underclass remains trapped in a system of oppression. Take for instance the sociologist and Democratic senator Daniel Patrick Moynihan's controversial 1965 report: "The Negro Family: A Case for National Action."[7] In this opus, Moynihan remarks that discrimination and racism—from slavery through Jim Crow—had undermined the stability of black families, an uncontroversial statement in itself. But Moynihan went on to write, "At this point the present tangle of pathology is capable of perpetuating itself without assistance from the white world. . . . The cycle can be broken only if these distortions are set right." Fast forward to Massey and Denton's critically received *American Apartheid*, in which they wrote that structural segregation produces an "oppositional culture that devalues work, schooling and marriage."[8] Akin to conservative arguments, this worldview maintains that black and brown people are broken people, nearly beyond repair.[9]

This chapter demonstrates how both NEA and WRJ rely on the "black pathology biz" to construct an ideal white identity via two distinct symbolic boundaries. First, an ideal whiteness is set apart from a set of fictional black and brown behaviors thought endemic to those racial groups. Second, the white ideal is removed from those whites who fail to acknowledge and orient themselves in opposition to the aforementioned dysfunctional behaviors. Despite NEA and WRJ's shared use of these boundaries, they represent seemingly opposite ends of the spectrum on race. Still, NEA advances both biological and cultural arguments about the natural inferiority, common immorality, and hyperviolent character of black and brown people for the purposes of rationalizing their defense of a white nationalist political platform. WRJ makes arguments about the emasculation of black and Latino men and the overall dysfunction of nonwhite communities because of the historical effects of targeted racism. In either case, such rhetoric obscures white deficiencies and problems, reproduces a racist worldview in which racial groups are one-dimensional masses whose essential differences separate and arrange them in a social hierarchy, and leaves whiteness unchallenged as a hegemonic ideal that all should rationally emulate. The claim that pathological people of color are a threat to the social order makes either NEA or WRJ (depending on your leanings) appear functionally necessary and as a force for good. In some ways, these different positions are like two sides of the same coin.

NEA and the Threat of "Otherness"

The continued discrimination against people of color is often justified in the white imagination because of deeply rooted stereotypes and racist ideologies. Historically, African Americans were understood as property or as little more than animals without souls, or at least without souls worth saving. This imagery was not one-dimensional but took on specific gender- and sexual-specific forms. Patricia Hill Collins found:

> Because Black men did hard manual labor, justifying the harsh conditions forced upon them required objectifying their bodies as big, strong, and stupid . . . White elites reduced Black men to their bodies, and identified their muscles and their penises as their most important sites.[10]

The phobia of black male sexuality remained a pervasive tool for restraining interracial contact and for the surveillance of white women's actions alongside black men, even as white men engaged in sexual violence over black women. As Abby Ferber writes, "This narrative, which defines Black males as hypersexual, animalistic, and savage, is central to White American identity."[11]

Years later, many of my interactions with NEA members testify to the continued centrality of this discourse in the construction of a white nationalist identity. Most of the NEA members reside in nearly all-white neighborhoods, refuse to let their children have interracial friendships, and believe that there is a genetic explanation to racial inequality. Franklin explained:

> Biological differences explain much of today's racial conflict. . . . Genetics makes clear that there is a connection between race and intelligence where the more melanin you have the less intelligent you are, you know, the less mental capacity you possess. . . . DNA and genetics are proving what we knew all along really. Blacks, Hispanics, darker-skinned people are more aggressive and dangerous. . . . It's not racist, it's a fact.

Many of NEA's publications and newsletters focus on comparative studies between white and black crime. In these reports, it is argued that black crime is more frequent and has a greater detriment on society than crime committed by whites. NEA members often cite these reports when giving talks or defending their views in everyday conversation. For example, Harry, a lawyer with six years' experience in NEA, told me:

> Look, I see these guys all the time in the court system. . . . I used to do a lot of work out of New York City. And all the time, blacks, Dominicans, Puerto Ricans, Mexicans, you name it, they *filled* [said with emphasis] the booking stations, precinct jails, court rooms . . . It wasn't like cops were going looking for these guys. All they had to do was stop them on the street. . . . People today call that "racial profiling," but really, it's nothing but common sense. Say you're a cop in Manhattan or another of the boroughs, whatever. You're more likely to find contraband like guns or drugs on blacks and Latinos than you are on whites. If the object is to get rid of crime, then just stop them and lock them up or separate them from whites.

I questioned Harry on his argument, specifically the assumption that blacks commit more crime than whites and whether racial profiling would serve an efficacious strategy in finding such contraband. Harry responded matter-of-factly: "It's plain and simple. They commit more crime, and it's violent crimes and drug use and things like that." I rebutted that police racial profiling does, in fact, not seem to catch more illegal activities than other indicators,[12] that violent crime among blacks has been on a four-decade-long decline,[13] and that serious prowhite biases in sentencing, particularly in drug cases, seem to racialize the discussion of illicit drug use.[14] Still, Harry rebuked me:

> No, black people, Mexicans, et cetera are poor and have low education because they are black. . . . The violence that is hardwired in them prevents them from getting advanced educations . . . Sure, you have exceptions, but overall, I mean, no, you're just trying to explain away the reality of the situation that black people are more violent than whites. . . . White people just don't carry on like that. Our culture reflects our biology.
>
> MWH: So, white people, like you and your fellow members, are just biologically superior?
>
> Harry: Not just biologically, culturally. Maybe it's not all that much, but it's enough to keep us out of jail. We just know how to act right.

In another instance, NEA members discussed various aspects of an article in the NEA newsletter. After providing statistics on the propensity of blacks to commit violent crime, they agreed that more "layperson" examples should be used for those who might not be "numbers friendly." Adam, a consultant, stated:

> I mean, there's plenty of examples, really. . . . Mike Tyson and all his rapes of those women, he was a monster. . . . Then of course there's O.J. [Simpson] and all of his foolishness . . . from killing Nicole to that crazy chase in L.A. . . . Oh yeah, Kobe Bryant, that basketball player, he raped that girl in Colorado. Black athletes are a goldmine for that shit . . . I just need to go back and look through the paper over the past month or so, and I'm sure I'll find a few more to give it some local context . . .

Such white nationalist discourse relies on both cultural and biological justifications for racial inequality. According to former KKK member David Duke, "Science has been uncovering these differences dramatically over the last few decades. They exist in physiological areas, cultural areas, and in actual physical areas. We have these great differences between the races, and knowledge of these differences has been suppressed."[15]

An NEA article on the subject of genetic difference states: "Even when the other minorities have equal or lower education and class, blacks still murder, assault, rape, and engage in other acts of wanton violence at a pace that far outmatches whites." To NEA members, racial and gender differences are simply inherent and immutable, and it is rather fruitless to attempt to change them. Those that attempt to do so are engaging in little more than a pipe dream. As Mason told me:

> I used to be just like you, I did. . . . I wanted to believe that with enough social engineering that we could make the country a harmonious place, that we could have a real equality. It's an attractive and seductive proposition, I know. It still kind of pulls at my heart. . . . Look throughout history, the communists and Marxists tried to make it happen and failed. . . . I finally got to the point where I realized it was a child's dream, I mean no offence, but really, I can show you biological evidence that refutes any claim for racial equality. . . . I'm not going to put myself or my future family at risk by trying to make something work that just can't . . . Black men are violent . . . especially in regard to sexual violence . . . You can't fight your genes, you know?

Besides an overall construction of black men as violent and dangerous, NEA members demonize black women for licentiousness and promiscuity—qualities thought atypical in white women. Adam told me, "I mean, you may not want to hear it, but black women are, on average, just more sexually loose and promiscuous. . . . There's a reason why prostitutes are, by and large, black and Hispanic women." In *White Lies*, Jessie Daniels articulates how white nationalists often construct the black woman as a "'Jezebel,' or the sexually aggressive and promiscuous woman. This image originated in the context of slavery as a way to justify the widespread sexual assaults on Black slave women by white men."[16] Moreover, in her study of gendered ideology among white nationalists, Abby Ferber found that:

> the differences between white and non-white females is emphasized as a defining feature of the white race and signaling its superiority. The belief that white women represent the ideal of female beauty is widespread and considered common sense knowledge in this discourse. For example, *Instauration* asserts that "25,000 years of tough natural selection on the edge of glaciers" produced "these beauteous products of a very special kind of evolution . . . these magnificent-looking [Aryan] women" . . . And the *National Vanguard*

argues, "the White woman stands at the apex of beauty . . . But what about the Black woman? Alas, she is truly a pitiable creature. Whites have never found her attractive, and Blacks began to scorn her after they caught a glimpse of a White woman."[17]

In this same vein, NEA member Albert was adamant about the dysfunctions of black women. I held a kind of standing interview with Albert, in which he would often ask for a break or stop the interview until he could retrieve evidence that supported his point of view. In one such instance, Albert broke from an interview in The Office to spend a few hours behind a computer. Abruptly returning to where I sat, he walked up and blurted out:

> I found what I was looking for . . . Black women just have tons of babies . . . They don't know how to say no and constantly are evading their duties in the black family. . . . You just can't blame the men, you know. They aren't taking care of the children, letting them do what they want, . . . they act like children themselves . . . kids having kids [laughing]. . . . White women, and white people are the opposite of this. . . . *Looking at these images and hearing these stories, I know who I am* [my emphasis].

The claims that black men are hypermasculine to the point of being "beast-like" and that black women are sexual jezebels constitute a long-standing racist discourse that is still evoked, although with less overt fervor, more political correctness, and under the guise of "scientific" status.[18] As Albert stated, this historically entrenched but newly modernized script provides a guide for the construction of white racial identity.

While the emphasis on interracial boundaries provides a template for white racial identity formation, the marking of white intraracial distinctions were just as important. In her landmark study of the social construction of white femininity, Ruth Frankenberg observed that some whites think there two types of whiteness: "those who are truly or only white, and those who are white but also something more—or is it something less?"[19] While no one can fully embody all the dimensions of the ideal or hegemonic form of whiteness, those who socially claim a dominant status can more easily define the standards and the intraracial distinctions between them and the whites that are "something less." Hence, NEA members made frequent efforts to claim a hegemonic status and avoid a subordinate and marginalized status. Members failed in their intraracial boundary work when they were unable or unwilling to adequately demarcate the difference between them and the negative traits thought characteristic of people of color. One NEA member I call Will told me:

> We had to kick a member out a few years ago. . . . We started sending a couple of folks to these interracial discussion groups that some city committee was sponsoring. It was to facilitate learning across and trust across the color line. . . . [laughing] I mean, I wouldn't say we were going there to "spy." That would be too harsh a word. But we didn't want good white people duped by that nonsense. . . . She became friends with a few black women in the group. . . . Next thing I know, she's doing drugs with them. Like heroin or something. . . . It was clear to us that she had no clue as to her heritage, who she was really. I mean, it's very sad. When white people lose their way like that. They can't be a part of NEA. . . . She strayed too far from our ideals. . . . She stopped believing in our ideology. . . . She stopped aiming for our ideals.

As further indication of intrawhite boundaries, Josh, a first-year NEA member and an artist, told me:

> I don't want to say I don't get a lot of respect here, but, okay, I guess I just don't get a lot. . . . I don't really buy that black folks are all that bad. I just don't think we can successfully get along, so the nationalist approach just seems pragmatic. Does that make sense? I mean, I have a couple black friends that are black nationalists . . . They wouldn't identify like that, but they don't believe that black and whites can get along either, so until that day, we're friends. . . . They're intelligent people, I think one has a master's or doctorate or something like that. She's raised smart kids. Her husband is a nice guy too. There's nothing wrong with them, so what's the big deal? . . . I can't really say that around The Office, you know? [laughing] I mean, that's not kosher to say, I mean, unless we're talking to a TV camera, that blacks are intelligent. . . . I think they are, so there's a limit to how far I can go here.

It should be clear that the dominant meanings of white racial identity are not formed in relation to a paramount racial "other" but also in relation to forms of whiteness deemed other. The simultaneous presence of inter- and intraracial boundaries demonstrates that NEA actors cannot simply claim a white status but must perform the right type of whiteness as intersubjectively understood by others.

WRJ and the "Culture of Poverty," Redux

WRJ often held public forums to gain support for their activities, attract new members, and, in general, educate the public about the "disease of racism," as many members frequently called it. During one such forum, Cassandra remarked:

> I think it's important to really hit people with this information in their hearts, you know? . . . We can make all kinds of logical appeals and throw numbers at people, and I guess that will reach some people, but anyone can spin numbers in any direction so that, eventually, those same people could be brought right back to believing that racism is not all that bad . . . by, um, you know, showing how there is some progress in certain areas . . . I see these [informational] tables as a way of really showing people the human cost of racism, how it affects people's lives and really handicaps them.

As Cassandra made clear, WRJ used their public outreach programs to inform people that racism not only has larger social implications but also contains an emotional and mental consequence.

Several of WRJ's evening educational sessions concentrated on the effect of racism in areas they felt most would not readily think of, such as gender and sexuality. As Malcolm told a group of first-time attendees of a class about racism:

> Racism had hidden costs . . . We as whites are often taught not to see it and to acknowledge it only when it is most blatant and in your face . . . Well, what happens when racism has an effect you are not expecting? . . . Maybe one that is so subtle to you that you don't see it? What if racism also works on gender relations? On people's very notions of gender identity? . . . What might seem normal in that area might be the effect of racism.

During this educational session, Malcolm lectured on an array of topics: from the legacy of slavery, Jim Crow, and the black codes, to the modern prison-industrial system that engages in hyperincarceration of people of color at an unprecedented rate. He returned to a key point throughout the night: Racism has ravaged the social organization of "the black community" and has effectively reversed the "natural order" of black gender relations so that most black men today deal with the consequences of "emasculation." Malcolm continued:

Black men today are an effect of years of oppression, . . . of having to see their women and children taken from them, of not being allowed to be the man of their household, of constantly being told to call white boys a fraction of their age "sir," while they were in turn called "boy" . . . The legacy of such degradations has not allowed black men to become men. [long pause] Some of you might think that black men are dangerous and destructive, violent criminals and what not. Many are. But how would you respond? Would you steal and do what you had to do to survive? . . . Would you do it if pressed by your family to support them? . . . How would you respond to a society that says you are little more than a boy? I think you might do some childish things . . . Whites haven't had these pressures, we don't have to resort to such behavior. But we are the cause of much of blacks' problems, and we have to start fixing it here.

Black Male Emasculation and Black Macho Women

Malcolm's words reflect the dominant WRJ picture of black men as less than the "average man." Much of WRJ's framing of black masculinity is accomplished via appeals to what some scholars call the "emasculation thesis." This position advocates that the processes of racism, colonialism, and imperialism weaken, or even "feminize," black men. First gaining critical purchase through *The Negro Family in the United States*, E. Franklin Frazier argued that the history of slavery, oppression, and disenfranchisement had borne out a cultural pathos by which the "natural" order of the black family was replaced by a tendency toward matriarchy.[20] This thesis was later injected into public discourse via the Moynihan Report, which claimed that the black family was caught in a "tangle of pathology." The report reiterated claims from various scholars and gave steam to the notion that men of color, especially African American men, were caught in an inescapable cycle of bad values.[21] Moynihan wrote:

> At the center of the tangle of pathology is the weakness of the family structure. Once or twice removed, it will be found to be the principal source of most of the aberrant, inadequate, or antisocial behavior that did not establish, but now serves to perpetuate the cycle of poverty and deprivation. It was by destroying the Negro family under slavery that white America broke the will of the Negro people. Although that will has reasserted itself in our time, it is a resurgence doomed to frustration unless the viability of the Negro family is restored.[22]

During the civil rights era, many liberal dissenters argued that black masculinity was an embodiment of anger in reaction to the denial of manhood. That denial then led to riots, black social unrest, and aimless, dangerous, and self-destructive behaviors that Grier and Cobbs called *Black Rage*.[23]

This position gathered even more support after the publication of Frantz Fanon's *Black Skin, White Masks*, in which he wrote, "At the risk of arousing the resentment of my colored brothers, I will say that the black man is not a man."[24] While it is unclear how to exactly define what *emasculation* means in everyday life, Fanon argued that it was reinforced via economic exploitation and a process of ideological internalization that created an inferiority complex of self-hatred. The depiction of "feminized" black men continued with the publication of Robert Staples's *Black Masculinity*, which advanced the thesis that slavery, monopoly capitalism, and even feminism were undermining black male strength.[25] While other scholars carried this notion forward, William Julius Wilson's *The Truly Disadvantaged* propelled the notion of black male dysfunction by alluding to the "ghetto specific cultural characteristics" of blacks.[26] Just one year later, the 1988 election campaign of George H. W. Bush activated this discourse by playing on the shared "culture of fear" that equated black men with dangerous and violent criminality.[27] The Bush campaign highlighted how democratic nominee Michael Dukakis's prison furlough program enabled convicted murderer William Horton, an African American male, to commit rape and robbery over a weekend leave. This trope continued into the 1990s with the publication of Majors and Billson's *Cool Pose*, in which they argued that black men dealt with joblessness, educational failure, and violent behavior via a coping strategy called the "cool pose" that takes on a life of its own (that is, it becomes "pathological") and sustains dangerous and self-destructive patterns.[28]

WRJ often advanced the argument that black women, because of black male emasculation, were forced into an unnaturally masculine identity and made to unfairly play the role of the black man—as providers and heads of household. To WRJ, such matriarchy is unnatural and unfair to black women, unfairly burdening them with the responsibilities that only a man should, and can, handle. As Bret told me, "I feel sorry for black women . . . their men act like children, and they are forced to hold it all together." So, also, Horace said, "Black women are so overburdened today. . . . All those kids, no constant man in their lives . . . They're the ultimate victim."

A view of both macho black women and emasculated black men provides the conceptual basis for much of today's academic research and layperson conjecture about black gender relations. Just one year after the publication of the Moynihan Report, Jessie Bernard (widely cited as one of the founders of sociological studies of the family) advanced the notion that slavery gave black women unnatural superiority over black men in her text *Marriage and Family among Negroes.*[29] While a great deal of scholarship has since attempted to refute that claim, the idea of black family role reversal is firmly embedded in mainstream logic and pop psychology. What is most insidious about the claim of sexual and gender role reversal is that it acquiesces to patriarchal and white normative notions of domesticity, sexuality, and gender politics. As the cultural critic bell hooks writes, the emasculation thesis is "a reaction against the fact that they [black men] have not been allowed full participation in the power game" with white men.[30] In the end, the thesis results in a picture of black masculinity that is inextricably tied to the social and sexual control that men think they should have over women. Accordingly, WRJ often spoke of black woman as incomplete, as in need of man to fill a void in her life. Sherrill told me:

> It just kind of bothers me how loose and overly sexualized black women are portrayed . . . and I think they buy into it as well, or at least it promotes what is already going on as far as the decay of their families and communities. Women in need obviously need men in their lives, and there is a shortage . . . and racism is so bad that black women are not going to start looking to white men, or Latino men, or Asian men to fill the void.

As the comments of WRJ (as well as the comments of NEA before it) reveal, gendered ideology is a key part of to racial pathology worldviews. Gender and race help to mutually construct one another. The controversy surrounding nonwhite pathologies reveal our racial and gendered assumptions about sexual morality, marriage, and family roles and amplify long-standing racial and sexual myths and stereotypes. Even when black men are scolded for dereliction of duty regarding fatherhood or breadwinning, even more blame is heaped on women of color, who are expected to be "guardians of morality and cultural values."[31]

WRJ members frequently spoke of the unhealthy reversal of black gender relations that emasculated black men while unfairly saddling women with stewardship over the family. For example, as I sat at the kitchen table of WRJ member Sean and his wife, while three of his four children milled about the house, Sean stated:

> We don't have a lot of the issues that black, or Native, or Latino families possess. That's white privilege. We don't have to worry about, well, she [referring to his wife] doesn't have to worry about taking care of the children *and* [said with emphasis] working. She can work, or stay at home, or put the kids in day-care, or whatever we decide is best. She, and I too, are not discriminated against when we leave the house. So we have a rather healthy family. . . . Blacks can't, unfortunately, say the same. . . . I'm fortunate to be white. That's privilege. I can be a man, and my wife sees me as that. The attraction, the relationship, the way she sees me, *and hopefully looks up to me and respects me* [said as he turned and looked adorningly at his wife] is constant. . . . If I were under the constant barrage of racism, how could she respect me? . . . I don't have a mind that makes habitually bad decisions like so many men of color. I mean, it's not their fault, you know?

Later in the conversation Sean told me:

> Look, sure, there are many white families that have problems too. It could be because they are poor, or gay, or what-have-you. . . . This will sound a bit callous, I know, but really, there's no excuse for white families. They have a huge advantage. Their development has not been stunted, or retarded, like that of black families in a white supremacist environment. *They have no excuse!* [said with a raised voice]. . . . If you're white and not making it, while not all whites have the same advantages, I know, still, there's really something wrong with that individual.

Sean's words illuminate the collusion of inter- and intraracial boundaries and narratives in the making of white racial identity. First, Sean is clear in his demarcation of white and black characteristics. White families, and white men in particular, do not acquire the dysfunctions that men of color possess. To Sean, white men don't have minds that make "habitually bad decisions." Rather, whites differ fundamentally from people of color because they do not reproduce the social and moral dysfunctions that result from racist discrimination. Second, if whites are not successful, the cause is not a group characteristic or group effect but is because "there's really something wrong with that individual." Here the boundary shifts from the distinction between white and nonwhite groups to distinguishing among white individuals. This shift illuminates how morality and dysfunctions become racialized in particular ways—as the domain of either people of color or atypical whites who are well below par. With the usage of these symbolic boundaries and their linkage in shared and recognizable narratives, we bear witness to the construction of hegemonic whiteness. Sean relies on the discourse that the ideal white person neither has (group-level) pathologies like people of color nor has (individual-level) dysfunctions like some whites.

These distinctions were carried out in an array of WRJ activities. During my fieldwork, I found that WRJ members defined and defended themselves against both people of color and other "lesser" whites through how they maintained their lawns, gardens, and the outside appearances of their homes. Whereas black and Latino properties were discussed as dilapidated or as lacking in necessary attention, WRJ members took care to cultivate their properties. So too, WRJ members saw poorer whites with overtly racist tendencies, often framed as "rednecks" or "white trash," as either unable or unwilling to take care of their property and homes.[32] In both cases, the ideal white identity was expressed not just through overt discourse but also through specific actions of property maintenance.

Displays of patriotism and nationalism were another way that these symbolic boundaries and narratives materialized in everyday life. Members of WRJ largely conceived of patriotism as a kind of uncritical and anti-intellectual flag waving. They interpreted patriotic people of color and other whites, respectively, as either duped victims of nationalistic false consciousness or as weak-minded individuals who require a source of meaningful national identity. When one WRJ member mentioned that he put up a flag for the Fourth of July, another stated: "What? Why? Come on . . . why don't you just burn a cross on the your lawn instead?" Meaningful patterns of boundary work are embedded in the environment, not just the atomized words, of WRJ members. Such recognition suggests that white idealizations are shaped by the definitions of group membership as they are reproduced in mundane everyday activities.

Hegemonic Whiteness: Defining Pathology

While a tenet of NEA logic is that blacks, especially black men, are both culturally and genetically hardwired to act in dysfunctional and immoral ways, WRJ argues that the pathologies of people of color are the result of

racist maltreatment and discrimination. Regardless of intention or pathway, a crucial similarity remains. In both worldviews, the existence of immoral, flawed, and unfit group-level characteristics among people of color is
a taken-for-granted and "commonsense truth" that is evokes a kind of white
moral panic.[32] As a result, a white supremacist vision of people of color is juxtaposed against whites as the antithesis of such behavior. The following two
quotations, from Philip of Whites for Racial Justice and Franklin of National
Equality for All, together illuminate the similarity. Philip stated:

> Discrimination against blacks, reinforced by prejudicial media messages and
> unfair policies, creates a reality for blacks that is so ugly and violent that some
> whites are scared of their own creation. I think this then goes on to reinforce
> those stereotypes . . . but, of course, this is the way that whites designed the
> system . . . I think that sociologists like you are too involved in trying to refute
> every bad thing that blacks do . . . strange because I've read Marx too, and you
> have to be more structural . . . I think we try to show to others how harsh rac-
> ism is, you know, the material realities of things. The fact is that many fears by
> whites are realistic because of how we have treated blacks. If people are treated
> terribly, they will become terrible. Now, we may not like to admit that, but
> look at drugs and crime. Those are black things. If I get scared when a bunch
> of black boys walk down my street, should I be scared, and if I am, am I racist?
> I'm not sure, but I do think that it's logical to assume that black boys are more
> dangerous than white boys. . . . I think that if you aren't scared more of the
> black boys, then you don't really understand the realities of racism; racism has
> fucked up black people.

And as Franklin explained:

> Sure, there is racism against blacks; it's against whites, too. But you don't see
> whites running around shooting each other and getting high all the time. If
> prejudice really had that much of a social effect, you would see it on both sides.
> Blacks can't help it . . . they are not as intelligent or moral, and it's unfair of us
> to expect them to be. Racial conflict is going to happen, prejudice is going to
> happen, . . . that's natural. But that this happens everywhere and whites suc-
> ceed and blacks fail, well, that's a social experiment right that there for you
> [laughing], the conclusions are right there. Whites are clearly superior, and
> we deserve our own space. Maybe, with time, if blacks had their own space
> and environment, that would somehow stabilize, but probably not much, it

is biological. In the meantime they are screwed up, and it's not "racist" [said by denoting "air quotes" with his fingers] of me to acknowledge that, yeah, to number one, acknowledge it and, number two, act on it. That's not racist to say that black people are criminals.

We do not commonly expect a white antiracist with a quasi-Marxist understanding of black boys as a lumpen proletariat group of violent thugs under the thumb of a racist white bourgeoisie to resemble the logic of a conservative white nationalist who reasons that black criminality and immorality are the result of biological and cultural dispositions. The underlying logic, regardless of a formal white antiracist or white nationalist political position, is quite similar.

People are complex beings. At any moment, one could reasonably identify any given action as immoral, illogical, or wasteful. Hence, we must realize that *dysfunction* and *pathology* are raced, gendered, and classed terms that are deployed toward or against certain peoples' interests. The operation of these terms often results in the deification of certain white formations contra the demonization of nonwhites as a whole. NEA and WRJ do not focus on black "social problems" because they are extant reality but because such focus allows for the redrawing of symbolic boundaries and the retelling of stories that, in turn, bring a settled, orderly, and pleasing meaning to whiteness. The discourse of NEA and WRJ actors is not just words and ideas that float about disconnected from who they are. Words are neither pure descriptions of the world nor simply reflections of one's mental logic. Discourse is constitutive of the very people that speak it.

Consider the following. Whereas strange, abnormal, or deviant behavior is a characteristic of various human societies across space and time, it takes specialized patterns of meaning making to turn these actions into "crime," "immorality," or "pathology." It takes even more specialized and repeated discourse to link those concepts to certain groups of people. Hence, words create the world as they represent it. The fact that crime, drugs, and violence are highly politicized and raced concepts seems natural to many Americans. Many cannot imagine a world in which the face of immoral pathology à la crime, drugs, and violence is not that of a darker hue. So, what would happen if we took this worldview and flipped it on its head? In *Yo' Mama's Dysfunktional*, Robin D. G. Kelley does just that. He writes:

This tangle of deviant behavior . . . is characterized by a "rejection or denial of physical attributes" leading to "hazardous sessions in tanning parlors" and frequent trips to weight-loss salons; rootlessness; antisocial behavior; and "an inability to make practical decisions" evidenced by their tendency to own several homes, frequent private social and dining clubs, and by their vast amount of unnecessary and socially useless possessions. . . . the culture of the rich is engulfed in a web of crime, sexism, and poor health. Drug use and white collar crime are rampant, according to every available index . . . In sum this group is engaged in a permanent cycle of divorce, forced child separations through boarding schools, and rampant materialism that leads to the dreaded Monte Carlo syndrome. Before they can be helped they must close tax loopholes, end subsidies, and stop buying influence.[34]

That such wording may seem alien is the point. While many whites engage in behaviors considered self-destructive or even morally and mentally "sick," these problems are not racialized. Rather, those whites who commit them are seen as a kind of lesser white, or even as an exception to whiteness. NEA and WRJ shore up the meanings of an ideal white identity vis-à-vis (1) the pathologies of people of color and (2) whites who do not view people of color as pathological or those individual whites who embody dysfunctions of their own. In a hegemonic white regimen in which the "black pathology biz" achieves commonsense status, unjust racial arrangements are internalized and endlessly reinforced in not only the identities that overtly rationalize such relations (white nationalists) but also within the identities of those who have been delegated to fight against these relations (white antiracists).[35]

5 The Ironic Value of Dishonor

I'll grant you that at one time things were very hard for blacks, but now, well, things are very different. Whites are being crucified for just being white! . . . I'm a white nationalist because we're under attack. Period. There's nothing left to say.
—Tim, National Equality for All

Our purpose is to help defend others from racism, to unlearn the racism in our own minds so that we don't oppress others . . . we end up on the receiving end of a lot of racism, a lot of the time I think we get it worse than blacks.
—Philip, Whites for Racial Justice

IN MARCH OF 2011 CNN RAN A STORY ENTITLED "Are Whites Racially Oppressed?" The article began:

> They marched on Washington to reclaim civil rights. They complained of voter intimidation at the polls. They called for ethnic studies programs to promote racial pride. They are, some say, the new face of racial oppression in this nation—and their faces are white. . . . A growing number of white Americans are acting like a racially oppressed majority. They are adopting the language and protest tactics of an embattled minority group . . .[1]

The article was not about members of organizations like NEA or WRJ. Rather, the story outlined that 44 percent of Americans believe discrimination against whites is equal to bigotry aimed at blacks and other racial minorities.[2] Other polls demonstrate similar interpretations among whites: Of whites, 71 percent were satisfied with the way society treats blacks;[3] 43 percent of whites said that racial discrimination toward blacks is not serious;[4] and 55 percent of whites believe that racism is not widespread, while 42 percent believe racism against whites to be widespread.[5] Simply put, more and more whites regard themselves as oppressed. To nearly half of all whites in the United States today, social and economic changes are interpreted as threats to white normality, privilege, and culture—a culture that many whites understand as inherently superior and moral. Despite the apocalyptic tone of the CNN article, this phenomenon is far from new. Such worldviews and discourse were evident when whites discussed slave revolts during the eighteenth century, in the whites' backlash against a handful of newly elected black congressmen during Reconstruction, through visceral reactions to the New Deal, in white resistance to the civil rights movement, and in the increasingly loud claims of white disenfranchisement that rode the wave of Barack Obama's election to the White House.[6] In fact, framing such white reactions as repetitious history is likely to generate a backlash in and of itself—most whites resist viewing themselves as a racial group, unless they interpret themselves as a group under attack.[7] If talk turns to whites receiving unearned privileges, then the concept of a collective falls conveniently to the wayside.

Although the last chapter highlighted the shunning of pathology as one dimension of the hegemonic ideal, this chapter demonstrates an odd reversal. Members of both NEA and WRJ often feel that they, as whites, are the victims of racial discrimination, inattention, and stereotyping. To emphasize the differences between these two groups even as they reproduce similar constructions of whiteness, WRJ engages in "demotion discourse"—they believe that the stigma of their white antiracist activism is equitable with the racism experienced by people of color. In contrast, NEA evokes "sympathy narratives"—they invite pity for their social position as whites victimized by a social order that can turn decidedly antiwhite. Despite their differences, both groups' construction of a stigmatized whiteness is taken for granted and remains a particularly "commonsense" understanding of white racial identity. The possession of racial stigma (that is, suffering because they are white) becomes an ironic value and honor to which both NEA and WRJ members aspire. By claiming persecution because of their whiteness, they collectively pursue an ideal image of a white martyr who suffers greatly yet makes the choice to "keep up the good fight." Stigma becomes a badge of honor: an emblem of their individual character, a mark of their commitment to a social cause, and a sign of what white people must endure to make unpopular political (either nationalist or antiracist) choices.

The Logic of White Stigma

As we sat in The Office of National Equality for All, Nick peered over a local newspaper that had captured his gaze for the past half-hour. Tapping his pen on the table to gain my attention, he asked, "Have you read this?" "I don't know. What story?" I replied. Nick placed the paper on the table and spoke:

> Second page. About us. We're "white supremacists" that have, wait. What was it? [long pause] Here. We have "undue influence." This guy, I don't recognize

him [the columnist], but, uh, says we have "undue influence in Riverside's political sector." Here's the kicker: "White supremacist organizations have experienced increased growth in recent years as disaffected whites look for an answer to their class-based economic woes." I don't even know what that really means, but wait, here it really is: "NEA threatens the hard-won victories of racial reconciliation and progress born out in the mixed neighborhoods and schools of Riverside. They seek, with myths of racial inferiority, to dismiss these victories as little more than social interference of our natural impulse to separate. They represent the worst of race relations . . ." blah blah blah. He goes on, but the point is, here we go again. We're the big bad racists.[8]

Across the room, Lisa interjected. "I read it. Here it comes again. You're ready for the phones to start ringing, right?" Nick: "Yeah, ready, I guess. We should call in others to man the phones and get a press release ready. Want to write a letter to the editor?"

Such a scene played out several times in The Office of NEA. When stories about NEA appeared in local or regional papers, such coverage dominated members' conversation and guided their agenda for days after. Like many organizations that deal with the politically sensitive topic of race, NEA was image conscious. However, while NEA members certainly disliked many of the outcomes associated with negative coverage in the media, the process by which members navigated such exposure went far beyond aversion or a back-and-forth war of opinions waged over media airwaves and in the pages of newsprint. The constant demonization of their political project was co-opted and used as a bargaining chip in social interactions. Their repeated trials in the court of public opinion became prima facie evidence of their status as victimized cultural warriors, fighting for the rights of white Americans to be free. Public disparagement conditioned the strength of their convictions.

An array of sociologists find that white nationalists, and even whites writ large, evoke the claim that they are the victims of the racial order. For example, in *White Lies* Jessie Daniels wrote that the:

> image of the triumphant white warrior is constructed in opposition to the view of white men as victims of racial Others, especially Black men. . . . [and] the potential physical and sexual attacks to white men imagine themselves falling victim [reinforces] . . . the image of white men as victims and Black men as predators.[9]

Karyn D. McKinney found that "for young whites, the new 'white man's burden' is whiteness itself."[10] And Forman and Lewis find that mainstream whites frequently reduce, "claims of Black disadvantage or White account-ability." These narratives, they continue, "represent one part of a larger set of understandings which explain White dominance as deserved and, therefore, in need of protection rather than challenge."[11]

Perhaps paradoxically, the white antiracists of Whites for Racial Justice frame their identity in comparable ways, even if they arrive at that destination by a different path. On a cold October day in 2006, I sat with Michael near a window in The Center. A thirty-six-year-old banker by profession, Michael had accrued nearly five years in WRJ. Michael leaned back in his chair as he took in a deep breath. We had been speaking for nearly two hours about his activism in WRJ, and he was tiring of the dialogue. As he exhaled, he seemed to let down his guard to begin a measured sentence. "To tell you the truth, this whole 'white antiracist thing' is more than a little difficult. . . . White people, we're, we're conditioned to see the world in racist ways, as though we're the natural owners and administrators of the planet. That weighs on me constantly, you know?" Turning from me, he settled his vision through the window and continued with an uncomfortable laugh:

> I sometimes wonder if what we're doing is pointless, because, you know, we're just conditioned to feel superior. But, then again, what's the alternative? Give up? It's a struggle to figure it all out. But if that's the worst of my worries, then so be it. . . . But then, you know, it's like not only are we constantly fighting our own racism, but we're fighting the stigma of being "antiracist whites." People either don't know what we do or think we're communists or crazy ideologues or something strange that's not mainstream. I'm tired of paying that price. . . . I'm sick and tired of being looked at as the weirdo when all I'm doing is fight-ing the good fight.

White antiracist politics are problematic endeavors. Despite the emergence of new and explicitly marked forms of white racial identity projects, whiteness and antiracism are often considered antithetical to one another.[12] Hence, the antiracists of WRJ interpret their whiteness as inherently racist and ruefully privileged while concomitantly in need of recuperation and repair—a mean-ing making process that poses an identity paradox for those involved.

I found members of both NEA and WRJ to construct and perform their racial selves as victimized and culturally stigmatized largely because of their whiteness. Both groups struggled to present their whiteness as a "normal" identity worthy of appreciation rather than disdain, while they also wrestled with how to call attention to their "stigmatized" status to legitimate and rationalize their activism and their worldviews. NEA and WRJ members understood whiteness as unfairly stigmatized in three key areas of practice: (1) publicity and political correctness, (2) socioeconomic mobility, and (3) the effects of miseducation.

Publicity and the Meanings of Political Correctness

The members of NEA spoke often about the stigma they earn as "white nationalists," and they openly lamented the barrage of insults and "misinterpretations" heaped on them. As I bore witness to NEA's attempt to publicize white nationalism as a pragmatic and rationale endeavor, they expressed considerable frustration with their detractors and opposition. On one such occasion I accompanied NEA to a rally to protest undocumented immigrants in the United States. NEA was a participating organization in the rally because they (along with other anti-immigrant, nativist, and white nationalist organizations) felt that immigration enforcement was too lax, that "illegal aliens take jobs from whites" (as one NEA member told me), and that "illegal immigrants put an unfair burden on the tax base of lawful citizens" because of their "rampant crime."

While we were at the rally, a series of confrontations took place between NEA members and an immigrant-rights group. After NEA members were called various names from "racist" to "Nazi," I turned on my audio recorder to capture the words of NEA member Steven as he shouted at several immigrant-rights activists:

> Would you say that to the NAACP? Would you? No, because you people don't think about how we are just looking out for ourselves and our nation like black people do everyday. It's not a matter of race that we're here, it's a matter of law and order! . . . We want this nation to be a white nation, . . . We want it to be a moral and orderly nation . . . We're just sticking up for our rights as whites. [Looking at some of the white immigrant-rights activists] If you were smarter you'd know we're working for your rights!

Such rhetoric repeated when I visited NEA members at their homes. In trying to convince me of their embattled status, family members would tell me that their activism is just like that of any black or Latino civil rights group—except that they are stigmatized for it.

Unsurprisingly, members often told me they felt hemmed in by a "doctrine of political correctness." As Franklin told me, "It is increasingly difficult, in most sectors at least, to get across our message as realistically legitimate when we must constantly fight off cries of 'racism.'" Harry stated, "It's blatantly unfair. . . . How can you people say blacks can have 'black pride' but whites can't have 'white pride'? It's a double standard. . . . In this 'politically correct' world gone mad, we fight an uphill battle. . . . We fight for what others are given." A great deal of everyday discussion revolved around white victimization at the behest of an overly politically correct world. My field notes from different days in The Office record such an atmosphere:

Afternoon. Slow. Not much work being done/few members hanging out and catching up. . . . Derek, John, Nick speak of PC culture of Riverside. Discussion of local official, white man, made gaffe about race—seen as unfair toward whites. Asked about comment. John said was about crime, and blacks in certain neighborhoods commit more crime. Official "jumped on" for being "a racist," and if a black guy that would not happen. Nick: "Shows you that whites can't speak the truth about race."

Another entry from my field notes demonstrates this understanding of whites as victims:

Lisa/Joey describing frustrations: feel unable to speak their mind. Don't want to be called racist. Told me they feel afraid when in public, want to say exactly what they want. Joey: relates feeling to first amendment rights, how one should "be able to speak freely because it's a constitutional right." Lisa: people should be restricted in some things they say, but that honesty about race is more important—shouldn't be restricted unless words would cause a riot. . . . Joey: U.S. controlled by "guardians of political correctness" that don't want to confront the "reality of race" b/c discomfort and b/c it will disturb ideas about "multiculturalism and interracial harmony." . . . Joey: PC hurts whites: "more than anyone, whites are hurt the most."

One of NEA's public documents states, "[NEA] is committed to confronting and abolishing the politically correct smut that is rampant across our once fine nation. . . . [political correctness] is little more than an attack on white rights . . . it [political correctness] is against being white . . . you can be on the right side of it [political correctness] if you are black or Latino or Indian . . ."

NEA's frequent distribution of flyers and pamphlets, coupled with their hosting of, and participation in, lectures, forums, and panel discussions at colleges, community centers, libraries, and museums illustrates both the textual and performative sites in which white nationalist identity was formed contra, and buttressed by, the stigma of a politically incorrect agenda. In an array of activities, white victimization was visibly rooted in everyday life. Across the spectrum of these varied social contexts, one event emerged as a highly interactive site in which the dominant meanings of political correctness were debated and a stigmatized white racial identity was solidified—NEA's attempt to host a white nationalist conference in 2007.

NEA attempted and failed to host several "white nationalist conferences" in the years before my research. In attempting to plan their own, they often looked to other such white nationalist conferences as examples. Such meetings take place across the nation at least once or twice a year. They are often hosted by a local white nationalist organization and generally draw a small array of nationalists, sympathizers, and overt "hate groups" like the KKK and neo-Nazis. NEA members told me that their conferences never reached fruition because "outside politically correct forces" generally opposed and stopped them. As Paul told me:

> Yeah, they never took off because of outside politically correct forces in the community or because of negative publicity. . . . Really, this is all about First Amendment rights. We have a right to say want we want, to assemble as we want, to publicize our events in the press, you know, this is basic First Amendment stuff. . . . If the liberals want to keep up their drumbeat about how they are the side for protecting civil rights, then they're gonna have to wake up and change their, you know, ways that they do things. . . . Some groups [white nationalists] get their meetings off the ground, some don't. It all depends on how much they're, uh, how much resistance they face.

By couching their conference plans (and subsequent resistance) within constitutional rhetoric, members felt that not only were their wishes and wants at stake but also their civil rights as white people.

Armed with the myth of white oppression and the goal of a white race standing victorious, NEA members prepared for the conference by hosting a number of parties and fundraisers that known financial backers, sympathetic friends, and fellow nationalists from other organizations attended. These soirées were billed as functional necessities and precursors to putting on a conference. In form they appeared as tributes to Victorian bourgeois Western culture. Complete with catered hors d'œuvres, a violinist, and a ready supply of cigars that the men—and only the men—took up to retire to the "sitting room" in Laurence's home, these evenings were elaborate rituals that enhanced white racial solidarity. No official speeches were ever on the agenda, but key NEA members occasionally commandeered a room to voice their confidence in the white nationalist agenda and the necessity for a conference that would "bring like-minded people together . . . away from the overlords of groupthink," as Adam once proclaimed. According to Eric, such nights were important for his, and NEA's, identity:

> I always look forward to those nights. It's almost like I felt like when I was younger and going on my first date. It's weird, I know, so don't judge me. . . . I actually get, what's it called? "Butterflies"? Yeah, that's it. . . . Once the night is going, I feel great . . . and a couple years back I met a [U.S.] representative. I mean, where else am I going to have that kind of chance? My dad was a butcher. [laughing] And his son is having a drink with a congressman [said with a roll of his neck]. I feel like, well, again, don't judge me, but I feel so close to everyone. We're all laughing and having a good time, and we, we can forget our troubles for at least a little bit. . . . It's how white people should be. It's what white culture is all about. . . . It's a good time.

As witnessed, Eric's racial and personal self is bolstered by the amity generated from these celebratory interactions.

As plans for the conference began to solidify into action, the mechanisms for behavior shifted to a more strategic display of raced and gendered performances. The male-dominated NEA quickly discovered that their ability to execute a publicly advertised conference would not be easily won. Once mainstream media caught wind of their plans, a printing company refused to produce their programs, a bevy of hotels regularly declined to rent out their meeting rooms, and even catering companies did not contract with them. In response, NEA engaged in a strategic display of front-stage femininity in which female members stood as the temporary public face of an organization needing a softer and gentler edge. In the back stage, the women bore the burden of nurturing the bruised and disappointed NEA male egos not accustomed to being told "no" by a nonwhite service class or being questioned by aggressive reporters. In the former, the women members of NEA became the "receptionists" for NEA. They fielded phone calls and spoke directly with reporters in light, even flirtatious, tones. Normally dressed in business suits and flats, with her hair pulled into a bun, Lisa would demonstratively order Josh to fetch her coffee. But in the moment of NEA conference crisis, she wore skirts or dresses, high heels, and long, curled hair that bounced on her shoulders as she laughed with innkeepers and traded eye shadow color suggestions with female reporters.[13] In the latter, female NEA members consoled men as the defeats mounted and the likelihood of pulling off a conference dimmed. As I spent one late-night evening in The Office, John illustrated how these all white rituals of conference became a site of collective racial and gender identity:

> I just can't handle the public like they [women] can. They have a way that's naturally softer and just better with calming folks down. . . . Like I told you a while back, I was having trouble with that one reporter that kept calling every day, digging for dirt. I couldn't get rid of him. [. . . laughing] But, I mean, once she talked to him just once, that was it! He didn't call anymore! . . . Men are just too rough, we just can't do what they do. . . . White women are a valuable possession, I mean, they keep us all together and calm us down. They keep us balanced and calm, and happy. . . . It's been rough the last month, but I don't what I'd do if they weren't here to keep us balanced. . . . I want to yell and scream sometimes, but they just put a gentle touch on things.

As with much of the white nationalist movement, the gendered division of labor is entrenched in a patriarchal worldview.[14] Women are understood as the helpmates and servants of white men's important work "for the race" and as the natural administrators of "emotion work"—the labor that involves managing one's own and others' affect to remain consistent with organizational and contextual display rules.[15] Like the smoke-filled, male-dominated sitting room of Laurence's house, The Center temporarily became a site in which a narrow and myopic type of gender performance was allowed and rationalized toward a particular end. The collective agreement that women can naturally handle emotionally turbulent times as they simultaneously attempt to soften the hard walls of political correctness put up by a resistant service industry and media meant that NEA held themselves accountable to one another within the specific interactive contexts. For example, when Steven attempted to call a reporter, a supposedly demure, supportive, and quiet female member wrenched the phone out of his hand, thumped him on the head, and slammed the phone on the table as she yelled: "What the hell do you think you're doing?

Can you handle the press? You can't even get a publicity statement out." Yet, not to be found derelict in her "emotion work" she was, just ten minutes later, speaking supportively to Steven and rubbing his shoulders after he received notification that another hotel would not host the conference.

Given all the problems with conference planning and implementation— not to mention its eventual failure—it would seem that such an endeavor was an improvident strategy for making and strengthening alliances, recruiting members, and publicizing NEA practices and ideology. So why do NEA members continue with their conference-based publicity plans when other white nationalist organizations successfully host conferences and in view of the fact that NEA seems doomed to disappoint in this area?

I argue that eventual failure of conference preparations is not only the ef- fect of incompetent and overreaching planners or just the result of a public who did not want white nationalists in their community. Rather, conference planning was just as symbolic, ritualistic, and performative as it was utilitar- ian. The planning and implementation can be read as a social drama in which NEA members constructed an unfairly stigmatized, yet ultimately valorized, white identity with which others could express sympathy and solidarity. This is not to say that such a process was intentional or conscious. Members would gladly have hosted a conference if they could have and, regardless of the out- come, would still claim they overcame unfair interference. No matter the functional result, the process became a site in which NEA members aligned themselves against the specter of political correctness, convinced themselves of the necessity of their work, and assisted one another in their collective per- formance as unfairly stigmatized whites who met their specific gender expec- tations. Due to the logistical cooperation required and the emotional capital expended, conference planning necessitated a high frequency of communica- tion between members that created solidarity and trust. As David told me, "I don't think I really knew everyone before all this. . . . Now they're like my brothers and sisters. They were there for me." In these tight-knit and frequent interactions, NEA members became their own audience for exhibiting and embracing stigma as an "authentic" white nationalist trait. These interactions serve as an important in-group ritual for strengthening a bright boundary between themselves and "politically correct" people of color and their allies, as well as highlighting in-group distinctions and dominance—the ideal white nationalist identity is attacked, suffers, embraces its stigma, and then emerges to keep up the good fight.

Immediately after the conference plans were abandoned, NEA members spoke regularly of the "antiwhite, politically correct culture" that they believed unfairly stopped them from hosting their meetings with white nationalists, white supremacist churches, and militia groups across the country. As Daniel told me in an interview:

> This politically correct nation has become so hostile toward any expression of white pride or even any subtle attempts at whites claiming their rights that it is a distinctly racist society toward whites. While there is surely prejudice toward all people, that is nothing new. That's what happens when races mix: There's trouble. But now, things have changed so that it's just not accepted for whites to stick up for themselves. . . . *It's like we are the new black people of a couple hundred years ago* [my emphasis]. Except that now blacks and Mexicans are the ones that get to say whatever they want.

Given the magnitude and frequency of NEA's claims, one might expect the antiracist members of WRJ to exhibit an oppositional worldview. With that assumption in mind, it is important to illuminate how political differences fail to negate a strikingly similar orientation toward white victimization.

A thirty-year-old corporate salesperson, Duncan had spent two and a half years in WRJ when I met him. One day, as Duncan was piecing together an article for the WRJ newsletter, he told me, "I have to be careful how I phrase things." I replied, "I mean, sure. But don't we all when we put anything out there for the public to view?" Duncan retorted:

> Yeah, but it's different. I mean, well, all right, it's like I have to really be careful how I present WRJ. We're a special type of white group, some might think we're Nazis or something because we're all white, so it's hard. . . . On top of all that, I mean, we're not allowed to organize the way blacks do. They've got it easy. They can come together, and people understand that as good, I mean, some can be too militant, and then they get grief for all that, but in general they are respected. We try to the do the exact same thing, the exact same thing! And we're damn near criminalized for standing up against racism.
>
> MWH: So do you think that is why you guys get grief? For standing up against racism?
>
> Duncan: Yeah, yeah, I do. Right? But, I mean, there's more to it, right? We're not the mainstream kind of whiteness, we're an unpopular kind of white

group. So, our whiteness works against us. We have to fight against our whiteness, so that, I mean, I guess you could say we're held hostage by it.

MWH: Hostage?

Duncan: Well, yeah, I mean, even [long pause] I mean, yeah, like held down and oppressed by it.

Duncan felt his white identity somehow disallowed him from being an antiracist with the same ease of antiracist people of color. Duncan and I continued to talk through the afternoon as he began to share more about his feelings of white marginalization. He continued:

Being in WRJ is a commitment that I love. I get a lot out of it, but you know . . . at the same time it gets old real quick. Whenever I bring up how I feel [about racial issues] it seems that I'm attacked. I mean [long sigh] it just doesn't just seem that way, *I am attacked* [said with emphasis]. Being white with these beliefs puts me on center stage, right in the line of fire. People of color think I'm crazy and wonder what my ulterior motives are, and other white people, well, they think I'm crazy too and that I'm a communist or something or other. . . . It's like being white with these beliefs, like I said, makes you a target *just like black people* [my emphasis].

Duncan's supposition that white identity is "in the line of fire" and is a "target just like black people" is parallel to NEA's ideas that whites are being "corrupted" and that whites are "the new black people." Another WRJ member I call Sean, a sixty-two-year-old gardener, stated:

Being white in today's climate means not being able to speak one's mind openly. I believe that not all things should be said; some things should be kept quiet because it hurts the public good, but today's politically correct climate is engineered in such a way that I can't say what I feel about racism, even though I am critiquing it! If black people want to critique racism then that seems all fine and well, but watch out if I do! [said with a sarcastic tone] That's why I'm a part of WRJ—I can express my opinions freely. . . . In the end I guess you can attribute all this to the effects of racism, we all end up being oppressed equally. It does seem unfair [long pause] that people of color can stand for antiracism and people think that's normal, but when I do, or we do, it's seen as deviant behavior.

Sean and Duncan echo one another. Together they represent a view of whites as fundamentally repressed in how they are allowed to publicly engage in racial discourse. They both understand whiteness *as equally* victimized as blacks, which contradicts much of WRJ's overt statements concerning how society is a racialized hierarchy in which whites benefit unjustly in every arena of life. Much of WRJ's official literature proclaims that members abide by a fundamental principle that, as the beneficiaries of unequal power, they feel morally obliged to share power by equalizing society. However, Sean refutes this principle one step further when he indicates that whites are *more* repressed than blacks. The idea that whites have to "pay" for their comments with the stigma of "deviance" while blacks get to "stand up for antiracism" with little to no repercussion because it is "normal" is an odd reversal of WRJ's overt antiracist politics. This arrangement is disturbingly predicated on a reversal of racial power dynamics that reinstalls whites, not people of color, as victims of the racial order and thus deserving of assistance. As Colin told me:

> I would be lying if I didn't tell you I feel like my choices, my decisions, . . . my identity is under attack by our politically correct society. . . . It's like being white and being in [WRJ] is too much for some people to understand. I feel like it's such a stigma . . . It's just not normal for whites to stand up and take this stand . . . I'm proud of it . . . At the same time . . . I feel so constrained by how we talk about race, like my identity is always under investigation . . . I'm not allowed to express how I feel, . . . There's no space in our society for a white antiracist.

So, also, a music teacher named Jerry stated:

> People of color can crack [racial] jokes, but if I do then it's racist. That's not fair. I mean, I'm different than the other whites who are saying those things because they're racist, I'm not! Look at me, I'm a member of [WRJ]. That would be crazy . . . Why can't I say those things, I mean something totally different? . . . I guess I relate to blacks in a way as they are oppressed too.

Like the members of NEA, WRJ antiracists understand the performance of their racial identity as similarly constrained by politically correct discourse.

The following example illustrates how this feeling is rooted in practical activity. At ages twenty-four and twenty-six, respectively, Andre and Colin were some of the youngest members of WRJ. Joining at approximately the same time, and having been members for only a year, they were still tenderfoots in formal antiracist activity and were often quick to talk with me about their discomfort with WRJ expectations. Unsurprisingly, they became good friends and relied on one another frequently—both inside and outside of The Center. They worked together in recruiting members for WRJ, and, as both were students at a local university, they often studied together and engaged in leisure time sports watching or movie going. Both standing over six feet tall, Colin and Andre were young, handsome, and single, straight men from working-class backgrounds. Together they regularly went out together to experience the Fairview nightlife. As a moderate-sized town, Fairview had a downtown area with a number of nightclubs that sprang to neon life on late-night weekends. In this context, Colin and Andre became each other's "wingman."

At one Friday night in The Center, they asked me to come with them. Agreeing, I met up with them later that evening at a bar and club I call the "Z Lounge." A favorite spot of Colin's and Andre's, the place was a known meeting ground for eligible twenty- and thirty-something singles who desired a great DJ, nice company, and top-shelf drinks at lower-shelf prices.

Entering the club, I was greeted to a bassline that shook my body, the noxious intermixture of a hundred different perfumes and colognes, and the explosion of multicolored lights as they reflected off mirrors, disco balls, and ice-laden drinks on the bar and tabletops. Almost immediately, Colin and Andre were exchanging half-hug/handshakes with male friends and embracing women whom they knew. Soon we stood together at the bar. Colin suddenly made a point of telling me the following: "Okay. Hopefully, we'll be able to meet some girls tonight. Just play it cool. Don't be a 'researcher,' you know. Just be Matthew. We're all students, so just, you know, play that card." Nodding in the affirmative, Colin turned and started chatting with Andre. After a while, they nudged me to accompany them to a table where four white women sat. Taking the lead, Andre introduced us, Colin told a joke that coaxed out our laughter, and soon they accepted Andre's invitation to procure a small, private table in back of the club where it was not as loud and drink orders would be served rather than ordered from the bar. After a while, one of the women asked how we all knew one another given that we went to different schools. Sheepishly, Colin squeaked out that they were members of an "organization" and that "we had known one another for a few months."[16] Such vague answers did not often satisfy, and finally all the cards were put on the table. During one such evening, Colin stated:

Well, honestly, we're members of Whites for Racial Justice, maybe you've heard of it? [The women all shook their heads negatively]. Well, anyway, we work to educate people about how to fight racism, especially white people, and we've been members for about a year, and Matthew here, he's a sociologist, and he's studying what we do, so that's cool. So, yeah, we're all here just having a good time.

After such declarations, responses would vary. Some were clearly turned off, some did not seem to care, but the most common response was a quizzical look and questions. On this night, one of the women stated: "Antiracist whites? So like, why, so isn't that stuff, like racism, just black people's problem?" Andre replied: "Well, no, we don't think so. White people receive a lot of unearned privileges, and we benefit a lot from other people's suffering; so it's important for everyone to work for justice." In response, the woman stated, "I guess. Just seems a little radical. I mean, do you guys like march and protest with signs and stuff? . . . I mean, I think racism would just go away if people stopped talking about it." At this point, the atmosphere grew tense, and the other women at the table were clearly devising a plan to excuse themselves. Andre's mention of "unearned privileges" straightened the back of everyone at the table, and it was clear that such politically charged talk didn't fit with the sights, sounds, and scene of Z-Lounge. As expected, the women came up with a polite reason to leave, thanked everyone for their time, and soon made their way to the dance floor where they formed a tight circle and laughed as they danced. Colin and Andre sat at the table, stirring their drinks. "Does that happen a lot?" I asked in an attempt to break the awkward silence. "Yeah," they replied in unison.

Given that I accompanied Colin and Andre on several other outings over the next few months, I can confirm that these interactions did happen with great regularity. In another such dialogue, a young woman flatly told Colin: "Antiracists? I don't get it. Racism is over. . . . You guys are the racists." After a while, it seemed that Colin and Andre went to the Z-Lounge not only to see old friends or engage in flirtatious behavior but to activate a political and moral holier-than-thou attitude toward "normal" white people. After one night, they remarked flippantly, "Wow, can you believe what some of those girls were saying? I mean, they have no idea who they are or about *any* [said with emphasis] type of inequality in the country. It's sad. I guess I used to be like that. . . . I'm so glad I woke up."

As these interactions, judgments, and identity-management continued, I was shocked by one particular evening with Colin and Andre. Traveling to a

more upscale and quiet bar, I found Colin and Andre in the midst of a conversation with a two women. As the dialogue progressed, I noticed that Colin
and Andre deftly avoided mention of their work in WRJ, claiming they knew
one another through school and that I was just a "graduate student" they
happened to meet a "few months back." Leaving the bar together, I turned to
Andre and said, "So, what was up with not mentioning the activism?" "I knew
you were going to bring that up," Colin stated. He continued:

> I just get tired of dealing with all the antiracist stigma sometimes. It's too
> much. I just wanted to be a student. . . . Andre and I talked about it earlier, and
> we decided not to bring it up, just to see how it goes. I feel horrible, but it's too
> much sometimes. Wasn't it kinda cool though? I mean, we hit it off with them
> [the two women from the bar] really well. . . . I just wanted a break. I wanted to
> just be white rather then some "crazy white person," you know?

This was the only instance of deception I saw from Colin and Andre. Moreover, a few days later in The Center, Colin approached me. Sitting me down
he said:

> I feel horrible. I can't believe I lied like that. I'm such a hypocrite. . . . I mean,
> I used my white privilege like some kind of social lubricant for the conversa-
> tion. I know you say that, and I just want to say, I'm not that kind of person. I
> don't do those things. I wasn't being true to what I believe and what really, uh,
> makes, me, uh, tick. I can't be with someone who's not on the same page with
> me anyway, you know in regard to, uh, race and equality. . . . I just wanted you
> to know. That's not me. I'm sorry.

The guilt that Colin expressed was a result of pursuing the hegemonic
white ideal. While there was an emotional trade-off in which stigma was exchanged for acceptance, Colin was unable to use that capital in a meaningful
way. The temporary moment of flirtatious acceptance was not connected to
his white antiracist identity. Through Andre and Colin's ongoing social ritual,
they held one another accountable to an overt and proud performance of a
white antiracist self. Such support was an important aspect of social cohesion
and order, as rejection for reasons of being too serious or radical to potential
female partners began to mount. Over time, the rejections built a sense of
stigma into the white self that became both a white badge of courage and a
marker of antiracist authenticity—the two became intertwined so that, eventually, the ideal white antiracist was one who was regularly attacked for his

or her beliefs, was stigmatized on their behalf, and did not allow that stigma to impede his or her activism. Hence, the patterned repetition of this practice increased the likelihood that these members would comply with the ideals of hegemonic whiteness and come to see those ideals as indelibly normal, proper, and natural.

Many members of WRJ recounted an array of consequences that resulted from knowledge of their activism. Some mentioned that they had been demoted or fired from jobs, some remarked that others refused to date them, and one member said that he had not spoken to his brother in years because of his membership in WRJ. For these activists, the meanings of a public antiracist lifestyle were grounded in an interlocking set of judgments, negative consequences, and losses in their everyday lives. As the thirty-five-year-old consultant named Sherrill told me, "It's simply not fair . . . Being white is so hard these days. . . . You can't say what you want about race, otherwise you're a racist. . . . I guess that's a big reason why I come to [WRJ], otherwise I would feel so alone." In comparison, a white nationalist counselor I call Tim told me in a group interview:

> The PC domination of our world began when whites couldn't say how they felt, I mean really, it's a step closer to fascism . . . [NEA] gives me, or, I mean, . . . it's a vehicle for expressing the truth without being called "racist." . . . It's great to be around others that see it for what it is . . .
>
> MWH: Is that important to you, to be around others that see it the same way as you?
>
> Tim: Yeah, I don't feel that sense of loneliness like I get in other places.

While there are key differences, namely that NEA believes that mainstream society is now antiwhite, while WRJ believes that whites are, by and large, privileged in relation to various social structures, both understandings of white identity reveal an important correspondence. Both groups are similar in their construction of their white activist selves as unfairly stigmatized and even racially oppressed.

The Allusions of Advantage and Assistance

Another realm in which both groups understood whiteness as a social stigma was in the realm of socioeconomic mobility. Members of both groups thought that white identity served as an unfair detriment in economic competition and for social status. However, there were pronounced differences between both groups. Members of NEA were unanimously opposed to policies like affirmative action, reparations for slavery, and any system that used "racial quotas." Across the board, such programs and policies were labeled "reverse racism" against white people. They spoke of the need for a "white civil rights movement" in which white people should "march, protest, or boycott" until they had equal protection under the law and in practice. They often spoke of antiwhite biases as so pronounced that defeat was almost a foregone conclusion. In one interview, a twenty-year-old NEA member and student named Josh asked me, "Why should I even think about applying to a top Ivy League school? The spots are already reserved for minorities." Of all the whiteness-as-stigma discourse, this aspect was most pronounced in the everyday language of The Office. Moreover, such talk of reserve racism against whites was a primary theme in their publications, radio announcements, Internet discussions, and speaking points at public forums. Will, a six-year member of NEA, told me:

> These policies [referring to affirmative action and racial quotas] demonstrate beyond question how whites have been left out in the cold . . . If you're white, it is fundamentally, across the board, harder to get a job than if you are black. That's against our civil rights. If you support those programs you're a racist against whites, European immigrants, uh, you know?

On the other side of the political spectrum, WRJ members make a 180-degree turn from the white nationalist stance of NEA. As WRJ member Horace told me, "Whites have so many advantages wherever they look. . . . Have you seen that 'white privilege checklist'?[17] I mean, aside from the fact that I'm more likely to get a job or less likely to go to prison, even the Band-Aids I want to buy are the color of my skin. That's a kind of advantage that has to be equalized." Together, WRJ members are avid supporters of affirmative action and even reparations for slavery. Members often described how their white privilege was offset by affirmative action and how it helped to create a "level playing field." Their activism was guided by the idea that such programs, even if imperfect in either theory or practice, were steps in the right direction—toward a just society in which all individuals would have equal opportunities and chances to be who they wanted to be.

While such clear-cut political divisions make for fine talking points, abstract discussions of policy, and delineations of where one stands relevant to "hot button" topics, political lines blur in members' everyday lived experiences. The prism of practical activities refracts these distinctions and broadcasts a new spectrum in which white antiracists and white nationalists can exist on the same wavelength. Members' understandings of who is entitled to assistance and who achieved upward socioeconomic mobility on their own are influenced by the stories of their trusted friends and families. As my time in the field with both groups lengthened and intensified, I met more friends and family members who were not only curious about my interest in WRJ or NEA but wanted to share their opinions on the group as well. During these interactions I learned that friends held an array of stories about white disadvantage that they frequently told to their NEA or WRJ acquaintances. Most times, these stories were retellings about someone they knew who was unfairly denied a job offer or school acceptance "only because they were white." For example, one such story was recounted to me as I spoke with a work associate of the NEA member I call Nick. His friend, a white female in her late twenties who wished to remain anonymous, stated:

> I tell Nick all the time, I mean, I'm not a nationalist or whatever. I just consider myself conscious of my race and what's going on in the world. . . . So, yeah, take affirmative action. I know a couple people that didn't get into the school they applied to, and they knew some black girls who did, and those black girls had much lower grades than them, you know? So, how is that fair? I mean, I get the idea of trying to make things equal and all, and sure, blacks had a rough time with slavery and all that, but I mean, how is denying hard-working white students into school any different?

The odd and improper conflation of slavery and school attendance notwithstanding, Nick's friend evinces a common critique of affirmative action: that less- or unqualified nonwhites are frequently admitted to schools at the expense of white people. Nick then picked up where his friend left off: "Yeah, I know a few white people that have had the same thing happen. . . . Being white is a detriment with school applications. . . . We can't get a break compared to blacks or Latinos."

The friends of WRJ members told similar stories. After WRJ meetings, Tristan (a thirty-year-old waiter and five-year member) would often wait to be picked up by his girlfriend Sarah. Together, they shared a young child and planned to get married. After one meeting in which the group discussed affirmative action, Sarah arrived to pick up Tristan and their child, whom he had brought to the meeting. As Tristan and I continued our discussion from the meeting, Sarah and Tristan together buckled their child into the car seat. Suddenly looking up, Sarah stated: "My girlfriend in high school didn't get into her top college, but this black girl with low grades did. I mean, I get that we need affirmative action, but that's not fair. What if she [referring to their daughter] doesn't get into school because she's white?" As the conversation continued, Tristan stated:

> Yeah, affirmative action is unfair, but I mean we do need it for nonwhites that can't get jobs because of discrimination. It's the lesser of the two evils if you will. It's wrong, but functionally necessary . . . I mean, at the same time I wonder, because I know a few [white] people that didn't get a job they should have gotten because it was given to a minority, and, I mean, they're white and poor. They've got privilege in other areas, like not being followed around in stores, and they can get bank loans much easier than a Latino, I am sure, but they are struggling with paying the bills, . . . and they are good white people you know, like us, they are conscious of racial things . . . They shouldn't be harmed by affirmative action. Like with our daughter, . . . maybe certain whites shouldn't have to abide by affirmative action, like some should be exempt somehow. It doesn't seem right that the good ones have to suffer right along with the ones that use their privilege everywhere they go.

Tristan's logic is telling, as his parceling out of good and bad whites functions as a method for navigating this complex issue. By demarcating the good and bad, Tristan can support affirmative action in abstract while claiming exemption from it. In this same vein, another WRJ member named Philip stated: "I support affirmative action, . . . but it's flawed. It hurts the good and bad whites alike. I don't feel I should have to give up a job the same as some redneck racist should have to. . . . It's imperfect, but the best we can do."

As shown, members' friends and family bring these issues "close to home." In so doing, the political dialectic of either supporting or opposing social welfare programs like affirmative action was lessened in the face of "real-life" stories that supposedly besmirched the effectiveness and rationale of those policies. The stories of white people, disenfranchised and oppressed by the behemoth of affirmative action, mounted and carried substantial emotional currency. The specter of this program as prima facie evidence of an antiwhite society haunted the white racial meaning making of these actors. Even for the white antiracists, whiteness was translated as a mark of stigma and a sign that they, their friends, and their family members would have a tough time of gaining employment or attending the college of their choice—all because they are white.[18]

As Erik (NEA) told me, "Blacks are lazier than whites. That's proven. Affirmative action is nothing more than an undeserved handout that's morally bankrupt. It penalizes whites with work ethics. . . . This program doesn't work because it doesn't take into account that the races are fundamentally different." Comparatively, Bret (WRJ) said:

> Slavery, Jim Crow, modern racism today, you know, those legacies have handicapped the average black person. They don't have the value system or skill set that most whites do. The competition is unfair. . . . If we're going to make a just society, we have to give them a helping hand through job preferences. If we [whites] have to pay a bit of the burden for them to catch up, then so be it. We made that bed.

Bolstered by the trusted narratives of friends and family, National Equality for All and Whites for Racial Justice framed the meanings of social advantages and assistance in terms of racial group attributes, rather than the different barriers that different groups face. Neither the NEA critics nor WRJ defenders of affirmative action seem to focus on the different conditions and contexts in which people navigate the social hierarchy. Rather, both focused on the assumed characteristics and behaviors of white versus nonwhite people. For example, while NEA members seem to think affirmative action rewards unqualified people of color at the expense of deserving whites, WRJ members see affirmative action as providing handouts for dysfunctional and damaged people of color who can't compete without help. In either case, affirmative action is framed as a kind of win-lose scenario in which preferential treatment rewards some and punishes others. Neither group came to interpret affirmative action as a program designed to level and equalize social conditions but as a policy that addresses the essentially different traits, attributes, and values of different racial groups.

The debate over social welfare policies and their implementation is disparate and varied—from claims that affirmative action is "reverse racism" or that it is "morally bankrupt," to the notion that the policy is "wrong, but functionally necessary" or that it is "imperfect, but the best we can do." The cornerstone of this multifaceted structure of interpretation is the assumption that different racial groups possess fundamentally fixed and distinctive abilities that together occupy a racial seesaw in which nonwhite gains then translate into white stigma and a fall in their social mobility. Here we see both (1) the logic of racial essentialism in which a racial group is understood as relatively homogenous in relation to key features such as values, worldviews, and behaviors that then forms an unholy alliance with (2) the assumption of a zero-sum game in which one group's gains must mean another's loss. This synthesis propels both groups' understanding of whiteness as under attack and unfairly burdened by an inability to climb the socioeconomic ladder.

The Mis-Education of the Caucasian

In 1933 famed historian Carter G. Woodson published the now celebrated *The Mis-Education of the Negro*.[19] The central thesis was that the U.S. educational system taught that blacks were little more than primitive and incapable subordinates to white civilization. As a result, Woodson argued that blacks had been brainwashed into accepting a false understanding of their history and a distorted images of themselves in the present.

The members of NEA and WRJ also worried about the depiction of racial identity in history books, popular culture, and everyday discourse. They spent a great deal of time researching, writing, and teaching about race in the Western world. By and large, NEA members feel that the essential morality, technological achievements, and quality of philosophy from certain European sources are together undervalued, if not obscured, by an overall focus on "inferior" sources of knowledge: from philosophical relativism to multicultural history. Comparatively, WRJ members argue that history is incorrectly told with a wrongheaded focus on conservative "dead white men" to the exclusion of women and people of color. While they differ in significant ways, both believe there are few accurate sources of information about race and they specifically worry about the information white people receive about themselves. Members of both groups believe that mainstream information about race is detrimental to the proper development of a white racial consciousness. As NEA member Harry told me,

> I've had a lot of schooling. I have three different degrees. . . . I don't think that I learned much of anything about how great whites have been. I did learn about a lot of white thinkers. But, when I did, they weren't called *white* [his emphasis]. But when anytime a black or a Chinese or a Hispanic person or whatever did anything, it became a celebration of how great that was for blacks or the

Chinese. Do you understand? I don't know what that did to my own development, but I did feel for a time like I had no place to look for role models. Like
there were no real *white* [his emphasis] leaders and examples even available,
and I know that's not true. . . . It makes me angry that the same could be happening to younger white kids today. . . . Education is like propaganda.

In a similar vein, WRJ member Andre sat down to talk to me after teaching
an evening course on the history of black political leadership. Among many
of the things he said that night, his first words stood out: "Education today
is little more than propaganda for a white supremacist nation. It breeds un-
thinking hordes, masses of people, especially whites, who think that the world
belongs to them. Whites might be the most hurt by this mess."

That Harry and Andre both possess critical views of education is, in and of
itself, of little value or consequence. However, it is unexpected that both understand white people as the greatest victims of the educational system. As I
spoke to more WRJ members about white miseducation, I found that Andre's
views were widely shared. I wondered how WRJ members could reconcile a
view of whites as the paramount victims of the educational system, given that
such a stance would seem to contradict or even undermine the white antiracist position that whites are the unfair beneficiaries of educational opportunities and attainment. When I questioned WRJ members as to this seeming
contradiction, they reconciled the ambiguity by distinguishing between the
"mental" and "physical" effects of racism. I reproduce the following back-and-
forth discussion to illustrate their logic:

Andre: We know that whites benefit from the schooling system; clearly this
is irrefutable, there's so much evidence that it's unreal. And they get that
advantage over nonwhites through tracking and gaining a picture of themselves as upright and moral and as natural leaders and what not, getting into
better schools, getting better attention, even nutrition in school . . . That's
how blacks get screwed over because whites get better resources. At the same
time, all that really hurts us, you know? It's like we benefit materially but get
hurt mentally.

Cassandra: That's the point: That we as whites get really screwed up in the
head with all kinds of superiority complexes and entitlement issues. So we
benefit materially the most, but I think get hurt mentally, or in our consciousness, most.

MWH: Okay. So you're saying that whites, mentally, suffer more mental racism than nonwhites?

Mark: Well, kind of, I mean, you know, it's complicated. Racism is complicated, it's a really complex issue. . . . I mean, how do you even measure racism and its effects? It's like an invisible force that's always there. Like the air we breathe. . . . While we have internalized feelings of white superiority, blacks have feelings of inferiority. . . . I don't think that you can say that one group benefits more or less from racism.

MWH: . . . I hear a lot from all of you about how nonwhites are on the receiving end of racism and how whites benefit at their expense. So, how do you measure that?

Andre: I mean, it's just apparent, right? Whites have all the jobs, make more money; you look at demographics, housing patterns, employment, the schools, et cetera. Whites are at the top of all that.

MWH: Right. So, whites benefit from racism more than blacks?

Andre and Mark: Yeah [in unison].

MWH: So how are whites hurt more than blacks?

Mark: It's mental, and that's hard to measure; I mean, just look at how screwed up and racist most whites are. It's obvious.

Cassandra: Again, I think it's a real complicated issue, and, in some ways, these questions are a distraction from what we should be concentrating on, . . . that's trying to end racism.

These antiracists understand whiteness as an identity that is mentally malformed because of "superiority complexes" and "entitlement issues," while blacks suffer more from material deprivations like school segregation, vocational rather than collegiate tracking, harsher grading, lower graduation rates, and the like. Yet, at many times throughout my research, such a distinction would fall to the wayside as WRJ members spoke of the negative cognitive consequences of the educational system on people of color. To many observers, such discourse would certainly seem contradictory and inconsistent. How can we explain these shifting words and logics? Why do these antiracists appear to claim a "more oppressed" status than people of color? The answer emerges in the recognition that symbolic boundaries and narratives constantly shifted and aligned in relation to expectations of particular interactions. White antiracist activism is constantly called on to legitimate itself against a sea of detractors, unbelievers, and those who are simply puzzled by their existence and agenda. These members rationalize "white antiracism" by placing extra emphasis on how racism corrupts the white psyche as much, if not more, than that of their nonwhite counterparts. Yet, they run the risk of betraying a key ideological tenet of WRJ—that whites are the unfair beneficiaries of educational advantages. They are burdened with speaking of whiteness—and themselves—as simultaneously oppressed and advantaged more than people of color.

In my exchange with these antiracists, my particularly line of questioning directly confronted this contradiction and put WRJ members in between the proverbial rock and a hard place. By calling on the handy distinction between mental and material consequences, they could simultaneously speak—albeit it awkwardly—of white oppression and advantage. Such compartmentalization allowed for members to transform the stigma of "superiority complexes" and "entitlement issues" into both a rationale for their activism and as a sign of their antiracist "authenticity." In coding their lives as genuinely victimized by a white supremacist educational system, they could valorize a stigmatized and oppressed identity as an ideal form of whiteness.

Given that a key dimension of an ideal hegemonic white identity is bound to the display of a properly victimized and stigmatized whiteness alongside a genuine respect for the depth of nonwhite oppression, members would often unite these logics in creative ways. For example, Frederick remarked:

> I look at it like this: We [whites] have some screwed-up views of race, resources, power, et cetera. So, in some ways, yeah, we are more victimized by racism than people of color because we in turn reproduce it . . . and that form is worse than any other form of racism . . . because we hold the keys to ending racism . . . If white people don't stand up and take a stand against it, it will go on forever, so when we are affected by it, it makes it worse for everyone. It's like what Malcolm [X] said about whites working with whites, that we have to fix things in their community first before there can be racial unity. . . . Curing racism in white people's consciousness is the linchpin of the whole system . . . it's key to ending the vicious cycle.

NEA members also understood white identity as negatively affected by wrongheaded educational disciplines and techniques. NEA members stand on one side of the "culture war" debate over curriculum revision and what

counts as the canon of accepted knowledge.[20] NEA members are severe critics of the curriculum reform movement of the 1980s and 1990s that aimed
to insert the perspectives of women, people of color, and LGBT (lesbian, gay,
bisexual, and transgender) into the humanities and social science literatures.
As a result of such changes, two-year NEA member George told me, "White
people's last line of defense was knowledge and education. Since *multiculturalism* [said with a sneer], we have nothing."

The panic over the decline of white civilization vis-à-vis the introduction
of Zora Neale Hurston and Chinua Achebe into college reading lists could
certainly be interpreted as silly and absurd if it were not for the fact that such
beliefs propel serious actions in the name of whiteness's defense. NEA members were adamant that multicultural education had poisoned the average
white mind against white nationalism but in favor of nonwhite ethnic and
racial pride and nationalist movements. Members became very defensive, if
not hostile, toward those who did not share this view. For instance, after NEA
member George framed black and white nationalism as equivalent political
programs deserving of the same consideration and legitimacy, I remarked
that I did not understand them as corresponding ideologies or practices.
George responded: "That is exactly what I'm talking about. They've got you
brainwashed and . . . " Interrupting, I said, "Wait. Who has me brainwashed?"
George continued:

> The government, media, schools, the liberal university, they have all bought
> into this lie. *It's a lie!* [said while screaming]. See, blacks and race traitors,
> nonthinking people like you. Sorry if this is harsh, but it's the way I feel.
> They're the ones running the country now. Honestly. I mean, really. I'd be
> dishonest to myself if I didn't say your comments made me sick. . . . Here we
> are, you've been with us for months, and you see what we do. Did you see any
> of us do anything remotely "racist"? No, you didn't. . . . It's why I do what I
> do, but I tell you, it gets really old sometimes especially with people like you.
>
> MWH: What? People like who? Who do you think I am?
>
> George: It just makes me sad in a way, you're wasting that space in the uni-
> versity when some smarter white person could be in there, not engaging in
> your liberal activism. . . . It's exactly because of folks like you, and the black
> nationalists, and the other multiculturalists and postmodernists, and who-
> ever else that is taking our space and our rights. . . . *We're the victims here,
> not you* [my emphasis].

George and I never truly recovered from this exchange. While we spoke several times over the next few months, and he allowed me to continue interviewing him, his responses were often curt and peppered with a thinly veiled animosity. However, his angry outburst is telling. The white nationalists of NEA honestly feel as though they are the victims of the racial order. Although their claim lacks a great deal of evidence, they are responding to a climate in which overt white nationalist views are not to be expressed in polite company, and this is something with which they struggle to adjust. They translate having to think about what they say and how they say it as "oppression."

NEA and Sympathy Narratives

Whiteness represents a range of dramaturgical performances that actors manifest in specific interactions. The meanings of racial identity and expected behaviors of different racial groups often appear natural because people adhere to a set of mythologies learned in formal institutional rules and everyday interactions. Over time, racialized myths are accepted as extant reality. Because white nationalists understand race as innate—a biological fact with essential characteristics and traits—they interpret any social situation in which whiteness is inferior, in either practice or meaning, as the product of unfair and politically correct publicity, socioeconomic engineering, and ideologically biased educational agendas. Accordingly, sociologist Mitch Berbrier wrote, "I recognize . . . a priori that white supremacists and separatists perceive themselves as stigmatized persons; their arguments presented . . . are part of a larger strategy of impression management and the management of a stigmatized identity."[21]

For NEA members, the meanings of white racial identity are bound to an ongoing reproductive process: First, whiteness is interpreted as a naturally superior yet unfairly stigmatized identity. Second, because of the intermixture of superiority and stigma, white nationalist activism is understood as rational and ethical. Third, because such activism is coded as both logical and principled endeavors, any critique of white nationalism or white people is interpreted as unfair and unfounded—which in turn leads back to an understanding of whiteness as essentially superior yet unduly victimized. And because such a process takes place not in a vacuum but in everyday interactions, NEA members manage their "superior yet spoiled" white racial identity by inviting and rationalizing sympathy from both fellow members and outsiders. By pointing to political correctness, socioeconomic immobility, and miseducation as both reasons why whites are unfairly victimized and why white nationalism is necessary, they generate a platform for sympathy and approving identification that legitimates each of the prior three interpretations.

The tripartite understanding of white racial identity as essentially superior, socially stigmatized, and (hence) deserving of sympathy is together a powerful reconstruction of the meanings of whiteness in today's day and age. In everyday practice, these interpretations work to reinforce one another and rationalize a host of white nationalist mythologies. White stigma becomes both the goal to be overturned and the meaningful fuel toward that goal. The dishonor of stigma becomes a valuable part of their identities. As much as the white nationalists might want to honestly overcome their stigma, their cutting-edge critique of society would be significantly dulled without this self-understanding; if whiteness is not unfairly under attack, then why should anyone—like NEA—arise to defend it?

NEA members attempt to construct a white nationalist image that carefully balances between a passive person who suffers and an active person who acts against such suffering; between the overt protection of white self-interests and the playing of the sympathy card.[22] NEA constructs an identity from both categories—a suffering white racial activist who emerges as the savior of white people and white civilization. They create an idealized white racial identity they are bound to pursue: the heroic white actor who, through dedication to logic and morality, and in full awareness that he or she too will be stigmatized, dares to tread on the politically charged ground of defending a unfairly victimized whiteness.

WRJ and Demotion Discourse

Akin to those in NEA, members of WRJ interpret their whiteness as stigmatized due to political correctness, a lack of socioeconomic mobility, and the effects of miseducation. They believe that their antiracist activism is misunderstood and unfairly attacked because they are white. They understand social welfare programs designed to benefit people of color as necessary but believe such programs unfairly penalize good, moral, and antiracist whites. And, finally, they believe that the educational system is unfairly biased, which in turn creates a malformed and racist white mind enslaved to superiority complexes and entitlement issues—something to which people of color are immune. Such understandings are not abstract political talking points but are reproduced through the constraints of their lives as they attempt to perform a white antiracist identity. First, they understand white racial identity as unfairly advantaged by de facto racial privileges across an array of social structures. It is this recognition that motivates much of their antiracist work. Second, because of those privileges that support a racially unequal world, they believe that white people are conditioned to hold racist worldviews that rationalize that inequality. Third—and as a result of the first two understandings—white antiracist activism is legitimated as a necessary, but socially stigmatized, endeavor. That is, members judge that white privilege and racism must be combated but also believe that such activism stigmatizes and oppresses them akin to people of color. Fourth, to reconcile a paradoxical view of whiteness as simultaneously privileged and oppressed, WRJ members intentionally recognize, and try to shun, white advantage.

As outlined, the antiracists of WRJ do not seek a great deal of sympathy from outsiders as NEA members do. Rather, they seem to readily embrace their stigma both as whites conditioned to hold racist thoughts and as whites who choose a strange and radical antiracist politic. However, they balance the costs of their conditioned "racist mindsets" and their attempts to be "antiracists" by relying on a false equivalency. They explicitly make meaning of their white antiracist identity as oppressed to the same degree as, if not more than, people of color. Such "demotion discourse"—in which WRJ members eagerly construct a vision of themselves as racially subjugated and stigmatized—provides members with a powerful feeling of solidarity with people of color and works as evidence of their antiracist devotion and authenticity. The constant self-marginalization and denigration enables the transformation of stigma into a valuable and ethical commodity. These antiracists know that they cannot overturn white privilege and racial inequality overnight or even in their lifetime. They see few opportunities for creating parity between the races. One option they do see, and one they hold as meaningful and moral, is to confront their own racism and refuse to use their racial privilege, at least as much as they are able. Instead of making the world equitable, they try to demote their whiteness to the level of the racial underclass.

Such meaning making is not without consequence. And some of the implications betray their own antiracist mission. Quite ironically, WRJ imagines a decidedly antiwhite world to manage their white antiracist identities. That worldview is not distillable to a choice they made. Rather, many of the WRJ members legitimately feel they are racially oppressed, even as they spin that white supremacist understanding into a white antiracist position. As

WRJ member Tristan told me, "I do feel like I learn something from being victimized by affirmative action . . . I relate better to people of color." WRJ's construction of whiteness remains bound to the reactionary logic of white supremacy members claim to reject. Much as NEA members see their activism as the same as any ethnic pride or civil rights movement, WRJ unintentionally undermines the claim that nonwhites face patterned and substantial disadvantages across an array of social structures.

WRJ members continually emphasized or downplayed particular aspects of their whiteness. At one moment people of color were understood as oppressed by white racism, while at the next the experiences of whites and nonwhites were framed as relatively equal. As tempting as it might be, one should not read these shifts as hypocrisy or confusion on the part of these activists. The particular ideal of their identities morphed and shifted depending on the particular demands of the context. However, these changes did not occur simply because of arbitrary social currents—what Goffman called a "rampant situationalism."[23] Rather, the ongoing process of white racial identity formation is simultaneously constrained and enabled by a "loose coupling" to the dominant and ideal meanings of whiteness.[24] WRJ members, like those in NEA, emphasized a stigmatized whiteness because it was one dimension of the white ideal—an aspect of identity thought commonsensical, natural, and taken for granted by an array of whites far outside the context of their activism.

Hegemonic Whiteness: Ideal Victimhood

I began this chapter with a CNN story about whites' growing belief that they are racially oppressed. To conclude, I draw attention to another media spectacle. Just weeks after the CNN story in March 2011, a white UCLA undergraduate student named Alexandra Wallace uploaded a video to YouTube.com entitled "Asians in the Library." Speaking directly to the camera, she stated:

> The problem is these hordes of Asian people that UCLA accepts into our school every single year . . . In America we do not talk on our cell phones in the library . . . I'll be like deep into my studying, into my political science theories and arguments and all that stuff. Getting it all down, like typing away furiously, blah blah blah. And then all of a sudden when I'm about to like reach an epiphany. Over here from somewhere: "Ohhhhh! Ching chong, ling long, ting tong! Ohhhhh!" Are you freaking kidding me?[25]

After her video went viral and was covered by ABC, NBC, and *The New York Times*, some called for Ms. Wallace's expulsion from UCLA. In the end, the university did not discipline her. She published an apology letter in *The Daily Bruin* and then, citing that she had been "ostracized from an entire community," withdrew from UCLA.

When Ms. Wallace turned to the Internet to find solidarity in her beliefs—that she was victimized by the improper manners of Asian hordes in "our" space—her expectations were not universally confirmed. As a result, those who disagreed were often framed as victimizing her still further. And when she decided to withdraw from UCLA under the auspices of ostracism, her victim status was solidified. At each step, the claim to victimhood excuses and/or marginalizes racist language, while positioning the wielder of that discourse as yet another example of a white person not allowed to speak openly about race. As one white nationalist blogger noted of Alexandra Wallace:

> She's not as experienced in fighting against forced diversity as those of us who are White racialist activists. . . . She has experienced the enforcement side of diversity first hand. Will the apology merely be a temporary tactical maneuver, or will it be a permanent and unnatural accommodation to forced diversity and multiculturalism? . . . most people support Wallace, even if she isn't exceptionally polished, recognizing that she's a young White woman speaking out on a level comprehensible and approachable to her peers. Additional support for Wallace has been posted on the Vanguard News Network Forum. This gal is also getting a hell of a lot of support on The Blaze, a news website run by Glenn Beck.[26]

The CNN story and Wallace debacle both illustrate that the white-as-victim narrative is widely shared and carries resonance in diverse registers. The story of white victimization is, in our post–civil rights era, a dominant feature of our national conversation on race—what anthropologist John Hartigan Jr. calls the "sprawling, unwieldy, often maddening means we have developed in the United States for discussing and evaluating what counts as 'racial.'"[27] The aforementioned pages reveal a glimpse of these "maddening means." Despite the conflicting political orientation of NEA and WRJ, they are both informed by, and held accountable to, a broad public discourse that validates white racial victimhood. In competing to play the victim, one vies not just for social sympathy, but for a (white) badge of courage that marks the battle wounds of systematically unfair treatment and discrimination. For

NEA, the white racial victimhood motif grows out of growing white displeasure with legal and policy initiatives (for example, affirmative action) that seek to remedy years of racial discrimination toward nonwhites. To these white nationalists, such programs have overstepped their bounds; they don't redress past discrimination, they enact it in the present. For the antiracists of WRJ, a white supremacist world has scrambled their moral compass and damaged their psyche. They fight an uphill battle against their own internalization of supremacist logic and in teaching others how to live an antiracist life. And importantly, members of both groups regularly express aggravation toward the politically correct expectations of what you can (and can't) say about race. Their overt discussions about race—whether nationalist or antiracist— prove too weighty a subject for most. As a consequence, they feel social pressure to limit, curtail, and significantly edit their racialized speech. Regardless of politics, when it comes to race, whites are increasingly competing to play the victim.

Such talk of white victimhood and stigmatization persists in the face of mountains of evidence of white privilege and even after the most obvious acts of white racism. We should examine these robust and widespread claims to victimhood as holding serious potential for social change. Whether through NEA's sympathy narratives or WRJ's demotion discourse, the constant evocation of white oppression and stigmatization reflects a sobering possibility—they can lead to the reversal of hard-won victories for people of color and further mystify the realities of a white supremacist nation. For example, many white Americans now interpret social welfare programs and policies birthed from the New Deal and the civil rights era as "unearned handouts" for people of color. Ironically, many of these programs actually give whites enormous and unearned benefits.[28] Whites today fare better and reap social benefits at rates that far outpace their nonwhite counterparts: from income and wealth accumulation, employment rates and competition, and health and disease to police profiling, sentencing, incarceration, and recidivism, educational achievements and outcomes, and home ownership.[29]

Despite the realities of a world that afford whites an array of social advantages, whites are making meaning of their racial identity as unfairly victimized—whether in mainstream news outlets, YouTube videos, or in white nationalist and white antiracist organizations. White victimhood is a historically entrenched and intersubjectively shared worldview. Rather than recognizing how white racial preferences continue to skew the playing field, many whites believe that their race affects their lives only in negative manners. Increasing numbers of whites interpret white victim discourse as rational and legitimate gripes that should be addressed through voting, social activism, and even violence. We must not miss the paradoxical recovery of white domination inherent in the project of white stigmatization. Given that claims to white victimhood are intertwined with racial inequality and stratification, the evocation of white victimhood can yield material results in the form of status, credentials, and valor in a variety of disparate settings: from everyday whites to those practicing either an antiracist or a nationalist lifestyle.

While NEA and WRJ evince disparate political projects, they are together bound to a similar understanding of whiteness—both groups make meaning of white racial identity as unfairly victimized and stigmatized. While it might seem counterintuitive at first blush, the construction of whiteness as victimized and stigmatized is a dimension of the white racial ideal. How is victimhood an ideal dimension of white racial identity? Either an NEA or a WRJ member who claims to be victimized by his or her race asserts a moral position by which his or her unjust suffering or demoted social position becomes a sign of dedication, authenticity, and virtue—not just as a member—but as a conscious white person. Those members thought the most dedicated to the nationalist or antiracist cause were also considered the most subjected to antiwhite bias, discrimination, and prejudice. Members received everyday implicit instructions—whether in trying to organize a white nationalist conference or in trying to convince fellow club goers of their rationality and legitimacy—that a "real" nationalist or antiracist does not have an easy life. Accordingly, the same members that reported lesser amounts of stigma also told me they felt substantially inferior to other members. For example, Nick stated of his fellow NEA member Laurence: "I mean, look at him. That guy gives his all to NEA, and he pays a hefty price. . . . I heard someone say one of his brothers or sisters doesn't talk to him anymore [because of his membership in NEA]. . . . I can't imagine that level of sacrifice. He's on another level. . . . I'm nowhere in his league."

Both NEA and WRJ pursue an ideal white identity that is stigmatized, and thus honored, committed, and valuable. By emphasizing two symbolic boundaries, they together reproduce the stigma dimension of the ideal white racial identity. First, both memberships reproduce an interracial boundary.

They claim a racial double standard in which white actions are unfairly stigmatized while similar nonwhite actions are praised. White subjugation and marginalization are interpreted as signs of a bona fide, committed, and principled nationalist or antiracist member, which in turn solidifies the second, and intraracial, boundary: Those whites who do not perform an identity adequately oppressed and stigmatized are coded as somehow lacking in relation to those members who righteously suffer on behalf of their noble cause.[30]

6 Saviors and Segregation

*This is a white nation, and I make no apologies for it. . . .
The problem I have is that we are being overrun by them
[nonwhites]. . . . We are committing national suicide if we let
this continue. . . . It's not wrong to want to preserve morality,
civility, and what not . . . You have to regulate where these
people [nonwhites] can go, or the country will go into an even
steeper decline than it already has. . . . If anything, I'm a
preservationist.*

—Paul, National Equality for All

*This nation was founded on white supremacist principles,
and it has fundamentally altered the psychology of whites and
nonwhites alike. We [whites] are often born with this sense
of superiority, and they [nonwhites] are the reverse, right?
They see themselves as inferior a lot of the time . . . This leads
to a lot of problems, of course; look at the all black areas all
over the country and how they are bogged down in violence
and corruption. We [whites] are best equipped to fix this. . . .
Sometimes I look at how black folks act in white places, and it
makes me so mad, 'cause I know what those other whites are
thinking, you know? There should be a law about where people
can and can't go. . . . for their own good, you know?*

—Duncan, Whites for Racial Justice

Race and Place

While many of the official laws that enshrined racial segregation are today a
thing of the past, the logics, meanings, and habits that accompanied them are
far from gone. We possess implicit and vigorous understandings of where certain racial and ethnic groups belong. For example, the words *urban* and *ghetto*
have become such common pseudonyms for black or Latino areas that they
are used in both common parlance and in the explicit language of marketing. Furthermore, what one wears, how one talks, or how one carries oneself
in particular places is often viewed through a racial lens. Consider the recent
debate over "sagging pants" (a style of wearing one's pants partially below the
waist that is symbolically linked to young black and Latino men). Attention to
this phenomenon functions as a racialized social panic in some municipalities. The town of Delcambre, Louisiana, made sagging pants a crime punishable by six months in jail and a $500 fine.[1] The city of Opa-Locka, Florida,

banned sagging pants in city parks and public buildings.[2] The city of Dallas, Texas, funded a series of public service announcements denouncing saggy pants, attempting to link the practice with the supposed stigma of homosexuality.[3] In 2008, the interim police chief in Flint, Michigan, ordered the arrest of men wearing sagging pants under the offense of "disorderly conduct."[4] And in May 2011 the Florida House and Senate passed the so-called droopy drawers bill (SB 228), criminalizing the public showing of underwear.[5]

White supremacist logic cements the linkage of race and place as "natural" and "common sensed." In defending the Washington, D.C., police practice of racially profiling black people in the predominately (and symbolically) white area of Georgetown, a 2006 *Washington Post* story recounted one's opinion that "black people were an unusual sight in Georgetown" and that to be "suspicious at the sight of a couple of young black men hanging out . . . is not racial profiling, it is common sense."[6]

The aforementioned examples lay bare the informal, but robust, coupling of racial identity with specific words, bodily performances, and places. Certain racial groups and areas are conveniently framed as fitting and belonging whereas other racial groups entering into the same areas can become racial persona non grata, an out-of-place social menace. It is important to note that this race-place relationship is a coconstitutive process. That is, the meanings of racial identity and the meanings of the places those identities inhabit simultaneously inform one another. For example, as whites engaged in flight from inner cities to the outlying suburbs during the 1950s and 1960s, those distant spaces formerly understood as inconvenient housing located far from resources and sites of employment were reinterpreted as places for safe and tranquil family dwelling, where homogenous white ethnic enclaves could be reproduced. For those whites who stayed behind, the purity of their racial identity was marred by their supposed "inability" to "escape" the city—a place quickly being recoded as crime infested, dirty, and the home of dysfunctional and dangerous people of color. Accordingly, Kai Erikson writes:

> The paths along which most white people made their way out to the suburbs were formed by the opening of new roadways and railings. The paths along which . . . [people of color] made the same journey, however, were formed . . . by the policies of lending institutions, the effects of restrictive covenants, the behaviors of realtors, and all the other workings of racial segregation . . . race makes place, and, in doing so, place makes race.[7]

Erikson makes clear that the racializing of bodies by their spatial context, and the racializing of spaces by those bodies, is a circular rather than a linear relationship.

While identities and spaces are linked, not all spaces and their appropriate racial identities are equal or interchangeable. Dissimilar racial identities are differently constrained. Shannon Sullivan remarks:

> The fact that white people sometimes feel uncomfortable and even fearful when in predominantly black spaces, such as black neighborhoods, does not necessarily indicate that white existence is constrained in a similar way that black existence is. Unlike black people, white people are seen by a white racist society as having the right or authority to enter freely any public space they wish. That they cannot do so comfortably in, for example, prominently black neighborhoods tends to be seen as a violation of the "natural" order of things, as an "unjust" limitation.[8]

Sullivan makes clear that we share in a racist logic and order that rationalizes black bodies in the white spaces of Georgetown as "suspicious" and out of place but then frames whites' feeling of discomfort in black spaces as prejudiced and unnatural. An unequal arrangement privileges the movement of white bodies across and between differently racialized spaces, while nonwhite movements are literally and figuratively policed, surveilled, and disciplined by whites who are understood as the natural owners and administrators of that space. Such an arrangement well demonstrates the claim that "space is fundamental in any exercise of power."[9]

In the following pages I demonstrate how NEA and WRJ members are conditioned by the symbolic violence of similar place-race linkages. This is not a totalizing effect; the members of NEA and WRJ approach racial segregation of public and private spaces in drastically different manners. NEA members explicitly desire an all-white nation or, at the least, a return to the officially segregated institutions and interactions of a pre-*Brown vs. Board* (1954) era in which people of color's movements in white spaces were legally constrained. Conversely, WRJ finds the project of legal segregation repulsive. They desire no such return to the "separate but equal" era of Jim Crow but explicitly advocate the free movement of people regardless of race.

However, many of these formal political distinctions melted away in the heat and pressure of everyday decisions. In situations in which these actors were compelled to save face, where they wished to portray themselves as knowledgeable and committed activists, and when they demonstrated a care and concern for specific close friends and abstract strangers, unusual interpretations were made and different racial meanings were drawn on and implemented. At moments of uncertainty or conflict, the logic of racial segregation and control was used to ground members' pursuit of an idealized white identity—a kind of paternalistic savior of people of color.

Instances of varied paternalistic logics were frequently observed.[10] In specific, I witnessed three kinds of paternalistic strategies. First, "messianic messages" rationalize the segregation of racial areas. This technique includes two subcategories: (1) labeling people of color with "inferiority complexes" or "slave mentalities" and (2) anthropomorphizing spaces and resources at the expense of the people who live in and use those spaces and resources. The second strategy is what I call "intersectional paternalism," whereby both NEA and WRJ members' understandings of race and gender collide to produce different interpretations of both white and nonwhite women. This technique also holds two subcategories: (1) protecting the purity of white women and (2) saving nonwhite women from men of color. The third technique manifested in a unique example—members' use of the "Red Campaign" to help alleviate HIV/AIDS in Africa. While Table 6.1 catalogs the frequency and variation of the paternalistic strategies that members exhibited, the following pages contextualize these meaning-making endeavors in the everyday lives and social imperatives in which they emerged.

Constructing a White Nation: Messianic Messages

Adam, a formal white nationalist for six years, once gave a public lecture at a community college on restricting U.S. immigration to "Anglo-Europeans." During the speech he opined that a strong national border was a key principle of contemporary white nationalist thought. After the speech he was questioned as to what he meant by "white nationalism," to which he answered:

> We as whites, as now what we might call European Americans, have both a common genetic link and cultural history; we are a better fit for the control of this nation . . . We are already in possession of the more superior areas as far as land use and aesthetic beauty and are best suited as the caretakers of the nation . . . We hold more economic and political power and should not try to upset this natural occurrence through social engineering . . . This country was founded as a white nationalist nation, and it should remain as such . . . Those that *offend and upset* [my emphasis] our country with cultural values not in

Table 6.1 Paternalism techniques.

| | Messianic Messages | | Intersectional Paternalism | | | |
	Inferiority complex/ slave mentality	Anthropomorphize spaces and resources	Protect cult of true womanhood	Save brown women from brown men	Inspi(RED) Paternalism	Subtotals
Derek (NEA)	14	3	3	6	4	30
Erik (NEA)	0	8	2	4	4	18
John (NEA)	1	5	4	6	5	21
Nick (NEA)	4	5	8	7	3	27
Laurence (NEA)	8	7	9	5	4	33
Paul (NEA)	5	8	2	3	4	22
Lisa (NEA)	6	7	9	16	6	44
Josh (NEA)	2	3	3	7	0	15
Joey (NEA)	2	3	7	9	2	23
Chris (NEA)	0	0	11	13	3	27
George (NEA)	7	6	0	1	0	14
Tim (NEA)	2	4	14	4	7	31
Will (NEA)	4	3	15	8	8	38
Steven (NEA)	0	3	1	2	1	7
Mason (NEA)	6	6	3	8	5	28
Albert (NEA)	2	0	2	0	4	8
Charles (NEA)	5	5	13	9	7	39
David (NEA)	13	0	15	15	4	47
Franklin (NEA)	3	5	4	6	6	24
Joseph (NEA)	2	4	17	14	3	40
Harry (NEA)	4	0	2	1	2	9
Adam (NEA)	7	5	6	14	5	37
Robert (NEA	0	4	12	15	7	38
Subtotals	97	94	162	173	94	620
Blake (WRJ)	13	0	2	5	7	27
Malcolm (WRJ)	12	7	3	3	4	29
Cassandra (WRJ)	15	7	6	3	11	42
Sean (WRJ)	6	0	0	2	1	9
Bret (WRJ)	9	3	7	10	8	37
Mark (NEA)	6	15	14	12	0	47
Michael (WRJ)	8	14	5	7	14	48
Patrick (WRJ)	16	16	6	9	4	51
Horace (WRJ)	5	3	5	15	8	36
James (WRJ)	16	4	7	3	3	33
Simon (WRJ)	12	16	12	8	4	52
Philip (WRJ)	13	5	9	11	0	38
Samuel (WRJ)	6	0	5	3	1	15
Duncan (WRJ)	8	8	6	7	8	37
Tristan (WRJ)	12	11	4	1	2	30
Andre (WRJ)	3	0	9	15	7	34
Colin (WRJ)	6	1	6	11	4	28
Wayne (WRJ)	0	0	2	2	2	6
Jerry (WRJ)	3	0	6	9	9	27
Sherrill (WRJ)	12	7	11	10	5	45
Frederick (WRJ)	11	2	4	8	6	31
Subtotals	192	119	129	154	108	702
Column Totals	289	213	291	327	202	1,322

line with that of a civilized nation-state should not be allowed within our bor-
ders. . . . This is for the betterment of all involved actually . . . We [whites]
should handle the problems that arise.

In subsequent interviews with other members of NEA, I asked pointed questions about white segregation. I inquired as to their reasoning for making either all or a part of the United States an entirely white nation-state. With little
hesitation, members explained that it is both "unnatural" and "unhealthy"
for races to blend with one another. They believe that the cultural and social
intermixture of the races would do particular damage to whites because of
nonwhites' intellectual inferiority and biological predisposition to violence
and crime. Joseph, a forty-one-year-old lawyer who joined NEA about a year
before I began my research, told me, "Blacks, Latinos, even Asians, for that
matter, have to be watched and looked after. You can't trust them to govern. . . .
unless you're talking about complete separation, then I'm sure they would be
fine, or, well, I don't know. Maybe they would wipe themselves out."

For the members of WRJ, such assumptions were decidedly racist. Tristan,
a five-year member, told me:

There are people out there that are trying to go back to the Jim Crow era. They
feel threatened by a changing world and want to conserve what they can or
simply create a nation that never was. I mean, this nation has always been a
white supremacist nation, but there has always been resistance, you know?
The oppression is never total or complete. There's always resistance.

Furthermore, Mark told his fellow WRJ members:

It's kind of normal now that whites are expected to be in charge of this country, to tell people where to go and what to do. It's a lot of pressure in many
ways, that, I guess, assumes whites are superior . . . It's based on a lot of assumptions about how we [whites] are supposedly more naturally intelligent
and what not, and all that racist *Bell Curve* shit.

While Tristan and Mark expressed severe distaste for an overt and direct white
nationalist doctrine of telling people "where to go and what to do" based on
essential cultural and biological distinctions between the races, they—along
with many other members of WRJ—came to rely on these logics in an array
of different social circumstances and interactions. I observed that the logic
of white control of nonwhite movements in white spaces was often rational-

ized by moral intentions and social expectations. As a result, WRJ and NEA members alike constructed an ideal white racial identity in which patronizing attitudes and paternalistic behaviors came to indicate who was a competent, knowledgeable, and even caring white person.

The members of WRJ attempted to live their activism. Their friends and family all knew of their work, and these members were usually proud to talk about their activism with colleagues, family, and even strangers standing in line with them at the grocery store. Careful not to come off as "radicals," members walked the line between committed and fanatical. WRJ members seemed especially enthused when they spoke about race with their nonwhite friends, as they felt empowered to share "inside information."

One summer evening, I accompanied WRJ members Mark, Sherrill, and Michael to a party at friend's house—an African American man in his thirties whom I call Lamont. Michael and Lamont, both employed as loan officers, met years ago when they worked at the same bank. Lamont moved on to a different banking institution but remained close friends with Michael. They make time to see one other every few weeks and continue to develop their friendship. As I walked into the party, I immediately noticed an interracial mixture of about twenty people. The party was laid back and enjoyable. After a few hours, the guests gradually excused themselves until only Lamont, Michael, and myself remained. We sat at the kitchen table, picking over the remaining food. Lamont and Michael had known each other for just over four years—about the same time that Michael joined WRJ. "Oh yeah!" Lamont said, as he laughed and leaned back in his chair. "I remember when Mike joined. He was excited, to say the least." They exchanged a knowing glance, and Lamont continued. "I'm not really into all that race stuff, like Mike. . . . Trust me, though, I know about it. My father marched with [Martin Luther] King. Other than what being a black man entails. . . . Mike loves to study race relations. *He's the great white hope!* [said with sarcasm and humor]" At Lamont's last remark, they both laughed. It was clear they were close friends. Michael was a serious and fairly prideful person. I had not previously witnessed anyone joke with him as Lamont was able to do.

They continued to reminisce about "old times" until the conversation turned back to some of the guests at that evening's party. "So, who was that one guy? The guy with the purple shirt. New co-worker of yours?" Michael asked. "Yeah. New loan officer at the bank. Nice guy. We started golfing on the weekends," Lamont replied. Resettling himself in his chair, Michael straightened himself and said, "What do you know about him?" To this, Lamont sighed, put a smirk on his face, and turned to face me. "This is what Mike does. He thinks he has to vet every new white friend I get," said Lamont. Turning to Michael he continued, "You don't know everything about every white person. Some people are just okay folks." "Alright, alright!" Michael said as he raised his hands in surrender. "But remember," he enjoined, "most white people are conditioned to be racist. So, just, you know, be careful."

Shortly after this exchange, yawns were apparent, and we all began to comment on how late it was. Soon Michael and I were standing at Lamont's door, thanking him for a wonderful evening. As I walked back to the car with Michael I asked, "What made you ask him about the guy in the purple shirt?" Michael responded:

> Let's just say, Lamont is a little naïve when it comes to race. He thinks he knows a lot. But, I feel bad saying this, but [long pause] he didn't know half of the stuff happening at the bank. . . . I've never told him much of the racist things people said about him. He was, I think, the second black employee we've had since I've been there. That bank is just a racist place. I hate working there, sometimes it's just, well [long pause], Lamont, he, just, he shouldn't have been there. . . . I actually encouraged him to leave and take a position somewhere else, at a blacker bank where he'd be more comfortable. . . . I worry that he would become friends with these racists and not even know it. . . . He's like a kid when it comes to race.

Michael cared about Lamont. But it was striking to witness such affection and concern laced with secrecy and criticism. "Why don't you just tell him?" I asked. Michael responded, "Oh, he wouldn't be able to handle it. He'd probably freak out that so many of his judgments about white people have been wrong. . . . Instead I just try to watch over him. . . . I'll shoulder that problem."

Michael's willingness to "shoulder that problem," coupled with Lamont's "great white hope" joke, were together reminiscent of the logic of the "white man's burden"—a view that white people have an obligation to oversee the development and livelihood of people of color who do not possess the capacity to determine their own destiny. Accordingly, I asked Michael, "Does that seem a bit paternalistic?" He responded, "Well, no, not if it's for his benefit. I mean, I'm the one that has to look out for him. It's not like he's privy to that hidden racism. . . . What am I supposed to do? Just stand by and do nothing?"

Michael frames the situation as dichotomous: Either stand by and do nothing, or save Lamont from the racism he cannot see.

Michael strongly disagreed with my categorization of his antiracist agenda as paternalistic. In fact, WRJ's formal activism critiqued the paternalism of whites as people with "Messiah complexes" who were little more than "racist whites who see no intelligence amidst darker-skinned people," as Mark once told me. Understandably, WRJ members resisted any such characterization of themselves as racially paternalistic—such whites were either the enemy or potentially reprogrammable allies and members. While such demarcation of different politically attuned whites stood as a powerful "other" against whom WRJ members officially positioned themselves, they systematically relied on the logic of racial paternalism to guide many of their interactions with people of color.

One WRJ member—whom I refrain from identifying even in pseudonym—was an extremely committed activist.[11] On top of the work with WRJ, this member occasionally hosted a "multicultural book club." Every two weeks a multiracial group—anywhere from six to ten people—descended on this member's home to discuss their chosen text. After describing their last meeting, I was invited to the next: "You'd probably get a lot out of it for your research. . . . I think it would be really interesting to have you there." After witnessing few interracial interactions with WRJ members, I happily accepted her invitation.

I became a regular at the meetings. I was not sure what to expect, but they were lively and engaged discussions. All the members seemed to carefully read each text, and when they met everyone was afforded an equal voice in relation to one another. In turn, the meetings held a focused yet laidback air, and I found myself looking forward to seeing the group. After a few meetings, I noticed that this member held a special bond with a participant I will call Maria, a thirty-something Latina. The child of immigrants from El Salvador, she was a single mother who worked a variety of office administration jobs. The two had met a couple of years earlier when Maria had a temporary position at an office where a WRJ member worked. Maria told me that they instantly hit it off and became close friends and that the WRJ member was now one of her daughter's favorite friends.

After several months of attending the book club, I took note of Maria's absence at several consecutive meetings. Finding this unusual, I asked the WRJ member about her disappearance. "Oh, she's mad at me," the member stated. "Why? What happened?" I replied. The response shocked me:

> I'm not sure if you knew, but Maria was planning on buying a house. . . . I agreed to be a cosigner for her loan. She deserves it, and they both [Maria and her daughter] are such kind souls. Well, she found a house in this all-white neighborhood. She told me it had a great school and everything, and I could tell she was really in love with it. But she just doesn't know about that neighborhood. . . . Everyone knows that only whites live there. She would have such a hard time if she moved there, because, well, I hate to say it, but the people there are known for being really racist. . . . I wouldn't want a cross burned on her lawn or anything. . . . So, I told her I wouldn't cosign the loan. I'm not going to support her living in that neighborhood. . . . We had a big fight about it. I haven't heard from her in a couple weeks.

To this WRJ member, Maria's choice to live in a white racist neighborhood was an ill-conceived plan that would endanger her and her daughter's well-being. When I asked the member if Maria knew the risks involved, the member responded, "Oh, she knows. She knew beforehand, and she certainly knows after I talked to her. . . . I'm not going to let her make that decision." "Well, I'm sorry you two had a fight about it. You seem like such good friends," I said. The member responded:

> Don't be sorry. I'm not. She's just showing her true colors, I guess. I went out on a limb to offer her money *and* [said with emphasis] she doesn't want to listen to what I say, so, I don't know, I guess, it's just, I just thought she was on my level, but, well, whatever.
>
> MWH: What do you mean, "on my level"?
>
> WRJ Member: I just mean, okay. So, maybe this is a bit paternalistic, or maternalistic, of me [laughing uncomfortably]. But I recognize that, you know, there's just not an equal footing between us. I mean, we don't have equality of experience. She just doesn't understand things like I do. . . . But what you need to understand is that there is a closeness between us. I care for her, and that puts heart into the relationship, you know? So it's not like I'm being controlling or anything, but, I mean, I care for her, and I thought she cared, I mean, even that she loved me. . . . It hurts to say, but she's just not that smart, and she doesn't listen. I know better, I mean, I study racism and work to fight it, and if I tell someone "Don't live there," then, don't live there.

MWH: So what has happened in that neighborhood that makes you really worried? Do you just want her to live in a Latino neighborhood?

WRJ member: Yes! That would be better for her. And that's what I told her. But she kept going on about better schools and safety. Yeah, "safety"! [said sarcastically] I mean, well, you asked about whether things happened, and no, nothing that I can recall specifically, but it would be bad for her. I mean, and, really, she doesn't have a husband. Those whites will just look at her as a typical "broken" Hispanic family and begin to assume all kinds of things. . . . She has to trust me. And, really, she doesn't know how much this has hurt *me* [said with emphasis]. I love her, and I'm just trying to save her. [long pause] It doesn't matter anymore. . . . I don't care what I promised I'd give her. She's not getting money for someplace I disapprove of. It's for her own good. . . . I think she's going to try to get someone I know to cosign for her now, and I'll do my best to stop that, too.

This member was clearly distraught over their disagreement. The intermixture of friendship, money, and racism sparked a disagreement over the legitimacy of one's knowledge and who has control and authority. The member was so upset that she felt compelled to intercede into future arrangements with third parties—all with the intent of stopping Maria from living in the white neighborhood of her choice. In revisiting the topic with this member weeks later, I was told rather matter of factly:

I just don't see what's wrong with her [Maria]. Why can't she just find a nice Hispanic neighborhood in which to live? . . . Maybe she just hates her own people and thinks she needs to live in a white neighborhood. That's probably it. . . . You know how racism can make people of color have this inferiority-type complex in which they try to be as white as they can? I think that's particularly prevalent with Latin women anyway.

The disagreement illustrates the operation of an implicit white paternalism embedded in the dominant expectations of interpersonal interactions. The member's promise to cosign the loan was—evidently unbeknown to Maria—conditional. The arrangement of white benevolence and nonwhite gratitude was thrown into disarray when Maria's autonomy was translated as a combination of unrequited love and care, lack of intelligence and wisdom, and disrespect. This framing laid the groundwork for the white savior coup de grâce: Maria's actions were interpreted as evidence of a racial psychosis of self-hate. The result of these interactions and interpretations reproduced the historical pattern of racial segregation; in the end, nonwhite movement and agency were controlled and curtailed while the white space of the neighborhood was policed and left intact.

There were many instances of such paternalism amidst the WRJ membership, even as they officially decried the logic of white supremacy inherent in such paternalism. In brief, Bret (a fifty-one-year-old writer) told me frankly that he discourages all his nonwhite friends from pursing doctoral-level educations because "It would just be too hard for them. . . . I don't want my friends' self-esteem and respect crushed under the ideology of white supremacy that they teach in today's universities." The threat of a white racist other served as a potent device for constructing an important intraracial boundary. In opposition to this white racist other, WRJ members emerged as the saviors of supposedly ignorant and/or overly trusting nonwhites who were the prey of unspecified, yet omnipresent, white racists. In conjunction, white antiracist meaning making of nonwhites depended on their obedience to their messianic messages. Deviation from their counsel was often coded as insolence, ignorance, or self-contempt stemming from either the nonwhites' character flaws or the traits associated with their racial group. Rarely was the rejection of white paternalism understood as a difference of opinion coming from an equal. As these examples show, WRJ's messianic messages expose a benign pattern of life and work in symbolically violent ways to reproduce the racial order of white stewards and nonwhite servants.

NEA members also exhibited patronizing interracial interactions. Despite their stereotype as activists with purposefully all-white networks, many of the members of NEA held interracial friendships. They found that interracial acquaintances were efficacious strategies for destabilizing the claim that they are "racists." As one member asked me, "How can we be racists if we have black friends?" Yet, as witnessed by the interactions of WRJ, the possession of nonwhite friendships does not preclude the operation of racism within those friendships.

Joseph, a lawyer by trade, joined NEA about a year before I began my research. A formal and rather strict individual, Joseph was not one to mince his words. Our discussions were characterized by a no-nonsense tone; he spoke openly but matter-of-factly about his childhood in inner-city Baltimore, his slow disillusionment with his Methodist faith, his divorce, and his desire to have children. Then forty-one years of age, he felt as if his window for having children was slowly closing. To supplement his desire for children, he told me of his regular volunteer work at an orphanage I label "Riverside Boys' Home" (RBH).[12] Joseph spoke at length about his concern for a young African American man I call Donald.

Donald, then in his senior year of high school, has been raised in RBH since he was a few months old. Joseph made his acquaintance over ten years ago when he volunteered as a summer league basketball coach. Telling me that he was immediately struck by Donald's "basketball IQ," he spoke at length about Donald's positive outlook on life, hard work ethnic, and commonsense approach to life, which was "an exception to most black people." With pride, Joseph told me of his mentorship of Donald and how he felt he had helped to raise a "fine young man."

Joseph then told me that Donald had become an academic standout in high school and that he was considering his options for college. I did not expect what he said next:

> So, Don and I have come to an agreement. You know, I told you before how much I care for him. . . . Sometimes I feel like he's my de facto son. But, anyway, I told him, that, I, I would, uh, pay for his college tuition if he went to Howard or another reputable black school. . . . Only if he went there.
>
> MWH: Why only a black school?
>
> Joseph: It's complicated. I think that, well, [long pause] simply put, we need more intelligent black voices and black thinkers. Don could really be one of them. He's a bright guy. . . . If we're going to separate, then black people have got to be able to run their own institutions and take care of their families. White nationalism is just not pragmatic right now because separation just can't happen. . . . I think it's like the U.S.–Mexican relationship. They [Mexicans] are in such disarray that they need the U.S., and they keep coming here. If they can become economically and politically stable, then we can actually be separate, not just by some invisible line in the desert, but in reality. We won't need them, and they won't need us. . . . Don could be one of those guys that helps black institutions get it together.
>
> MWH: It sounds like you're helping Donald because it helps your agenda.
>
> Joseph: Our interests are aligned, that's true. But I've come to really care for him. . . . If he can go to a school like Howard, that's great. But you know by now that I'm not going to have Don take the place of some white student at Columbia or Virginia. Black schools are for black people, and the same goes

for white people and white schools . . . But, really, I'd feel horrible if I didn't help him out, and so, yeah, I get something out of it, too, in that respect. I feel quite proud of myself as a, a kind of, well, like a champion for his cause.

As Joseph makes quite clear, his financial assistance, mentoring, and friendship with Donald are motivated by a future white and black separation (as well as the current protection of elite education for white students). Even a nearly two-decades long camaraderie across the color line does not mitigate the symbolically violent connection of race and space. Rather, the misrecognition that racial groups properly belong *only* in their respective spaces (for example, black students in black universities, or Latino families in Latino neighborhoods) serves to guide interracial interactions and the development of interracial "friendships."

This stout linkage between race and place also manifested in NEA members' tendency to anthropomorphize (attribute human form and value) places coded as black, Latino, or Asian at the expense of the people of color residing in these places. For example, NEA member Erik's apartment was decorated with photos and artistic renderings of African landscapes, the Brazilian rainforest, and cool blue Caribbean waters that lapped onto sandy white beaches. In talking to him, I felt that he seemed to deeply covet these areas. I once asked him if he had ever visited any of the places he so prominently displayed in his apartment, to which he responded curtly: "No! They're too dangerous and unstable. Such a shame with all they have to offer. . . . Kind of like areas in New York or Philly." Puzzled as to his connection between Northern urban centers and depictions of bucolic beauty, I asked what he meant. He told me:

We have to protect the resources in black areas. . . . infrastructure like buildings, roads, electric, sewer, all of that. I think that blacks, other nonwhite people like Latinos and Asians will return to their homelands in Africa, parts of South America, and Asia. . . . Areas in the U.S. South or the Caribbean have so much to offer in terms of farmland, natural beauty, specific crops that can grow only in those climates or minerals in the ground . . . It's necessary that we protect those areas for future white use and population.

So, also, NEA member Steven told me:

Places like the West Indies, Mexico, a lot of the waters off these areas are beautiful places that have to be preserved for future white generations to enjoy. . . . It's a shame what is happening to these places—they are really gorgeous, you know? I think, they, in a way, give life an inspiration to the people that live there. They are special places that have something to offer. . . . Look at the beauty of the plains, and then we give those areas to Indians? Come on! . . . We all too easily make this dividing line and paint all whites as these evil creatures and people of color as these unfairly oppressed, angelic martyrs. Well, sometimes blacks or whoever just can't take care of their land. They obviously need white people's help. . . . They have these slave mentalities anyway. I think they want us to take control anyhow. . . . If these places are going to retain their beauty and potency, then it's important to take control of them before it's too late.

Such paternalism was witnessed in both NEA and WRJ's patterned interactions with people of color and in their descriptions of those interactions. Members of both groups found themselves frustrated and annoyed with nonwhites when they behaved in unexpected and undesired ways. They interpreted those exchanges and observations in ways that redeemed their own actions as little more than neutral and logical, while they idealized a specific kind of heroic white racial identity. These interpretations were built out of a legacy of white supremacist worldviews in which people of color are either a significant threat (in the case of NEA) or an unfortunate victim (in the case of WRJ). In either case, nonwhites were understood as in possession of a "slave mentality" or struggle with "inferiority complexes," while whites were the proper saviors of both nonwhites and the places they reside.

Under either white nationalist or white antiracist practice, paternalistic techniques reproduce white supremacy. Some may think of paternalism as a form of overt control that is a historical artifact rather than a contemporary pattern of interaction. In so doing, we may misrecognize the violence of paternalism as little more than benign friendship.[13] The racial paternalism evidenced in the preceding passages was not an occasional phenomenon but consisted of patterned interactions that rationalized asymmetrical relations of power. When members of NEA spoke of their goal of building either an all-white nation or a segregated portion thereof, they concomitantly spoke of the need to take over and "help" blacks get their lives in order so that they can exist autonomously on their own—the end goal being very simply to leave whites alone. When WRJ members spoke of their target of a racially healed nation in which people of all colors can live harmoniously side by side, they spoke of having to do things for blacks and other people of color because they believed those people were fundamentally incapable of doing for themselves.

NEA and the "Cult of True Womanhood"

The paternalism evident in NEA's everyday interracial interactions intersected with their understandings of gender. Patronizing and controlling understandings of white women's place in white nationalism were dominant. These gendered and raced meanings derive from the eighteenth and nineteenth centuries when the United States witnessed an unprecedented growth of new professions in which white men became lawyers, office workers, factory managers, merchants, and doctors. In turn, a new kind of white middle-class family structure emerged whereby: (1) Surplus income became available, which enabled the "luxury" of women staying home with children; and (2) surplus income and flexibility slowly normalized the idea that white men should support the family through work outside the home. In turn, this belief gendered the public and private sphere—the outside world was a masculine place full of temptation and trouble that was no place for "weak and delicate" women. For this reason, (3) the new middle-class family came to epitomize the backbone of society. The home was sanctified as the site of (white) civilization's reproduction and protection.[14]

Alongside the ideal of the white male savior, a feminine ideal materialized. Often called the "cult of domesticity" or the "cult of true womanhood," this way of thought assumed that white women naturally possess the virtues of piety, purity, and submissiveness and a desire for domestic livelihood. This feminine ideal was found in women's magazines, advice books, religious journals, newspapers, and novels—it saturated popular culture by providing an overview of women's duties and expectations while cataloging the cardinal virtues of white womanhood for a new age. There was a fearful obligation and solemn responsibility to help to uphold the temple of this "cult"—the family. If anyone dared to tamper with or subvert this structure, then that person could easily be condemned as an enemy of God, nature, and nation. This structure was indelibly racialized as white. At the point when the cult of domesticity became the ideological norm for white women, many women of color were enslaved, subject to de facto surveillance and violence, or were becoming workers in lower-class jobs outside their own homes or within the homes of white women as their domestic handmaidens.[15]

Crucial pillars of all "true" (read: white, straight, and middle- or upper-class) women were their demure affect and their sexual virtue. Whereas women of color were often portrayed as mammies and jezebels, white women were implored to protect their virginity. In popular literature, a seduced woman often atoned for her sin via death, a demise often accompanied by poverty, depravity, or intemperance. In fact, it was thought that just the contemplation of losing their sexual purity could bring "hysteria" to young white women. Accordingly, white men were seen as the protectors of this cult, and white women were encouraged to be thankful for, and deferential toward, their male benefactors. Men and women often held one another accountable to gendered expectations.

Social relations carried gendered and racialized obligations that people were both aware of and worked to enforce. Men's control over women's bodies was both normalized and rationalized given the racial, sexual, and gendered expectations of how social interactions should, or should not, occur. Given this background, the "paradigm of American racism, available during slavery but crystallized in the period following Reconstruction and still influential today, [is one] in which White men's control of Black men is mediated by the always-about-to-be violated bodies of White women."[16]

This understanding did not magically disappear with the slow shift from industrial to service capitalism. Rather, the class-racial-gender-sexual symbolic order has retained much of its form through misrecognition as natural and everyday impression management techniques in which we communicate our identities to others and elicit predictable responses.[17] For white nationalists today, the paternalistic control of women symbolizes the protection of the white race and civil order in general.[18]

For the majority white male members of NEA, an ideal identity was one in which they disciplined white women to abide by the "cult of true womanhood." Many of NEA's public lectures included admonitions against interracial dating and marriage and advice to white fathers on how to successfully "protect" their daughters from nonwhite men. Some of NEA's literature states, "The lust and desire that the black male brain carries is so overpowering that it drives them insane, . . . they can be bent on having and possessing women, and white women are the greatest prize." However, such overt pronouncements were not common. The practices that bound white male members to the pursuit of their ideal savior identity were witnessed in their domestic interactions with their wives, girlfriends, and children.

Half of the twenty-four NEA members I interviewed had children ($n = 12$). Of these twelve children, eight were female. Of those eight female children, NEA members and their families consented to my meeting and speaking with five of them (ages five, eight, nine, fifteen, and nineteen). Four of the NEA daughters seemed very well acquainted with their fathers' activism, while one seemed largely aloof to what her father did—a practice that seemed intentional as I was instructed not to speak explicitly about the work of NEA while in this member's home.[19] Allowed access to these member's homes, I was often taken on tours of different rooms. In one daughter's room, I observed a copy of *Mein Kampf* (Hitler's 1925 autobiography and manifesto) on a shelf right next to a dictionary. Another girl's room contained an album by "Prussian Blue" (a controversial white nationalist folk teen duo) and the nineteen-year-old girl, while away at college, kept a room at home with a simple bed, dresser, and a desk on which was taped a piece of paper that read, "White rights are human rights." Rooms like these contained many other items that one might not readily recognize as "white nationalist." For instance, in one girl's room there hung a poster in which Rudyard Kipling's poem "The Stranger" was superimposed over the image of a large white man wrapping his arm around a white woman with long, flowing blond hair. White nationalists often reference Kipling's poem as it symbolizes an identity politic based on white biology and solidarity while expressing distaste for the "stranger within my gate." A portion of it reads:

> The men of my own stock,
> They may do ill or well,
> But they tell the lies I am wonted to,
> They are used to the lies I tell;
> And we do not need interpreters
> When we go to buy or sell.[20]

When I spoke with many of the NEA daughters about their "white nationalist" items, they often commented that they felt pride in "being white" and that they wished to have full and equal rights like "other races." When I asked one daughter about the aforementioned Kipling poster she said:

> I like to think of that couple as me and daddy. He protects me, and that's what men should do. . . . I'm starting to get older [she was fifteen at the time] and will get to start dating next year; so, I want a white man that will do that for

me. . . . Like the poem says, a white man will understand me and give me what I need. Like where it says, "This was my father's belief, and this is also mine." That's so true. I want a boyfriend, uh, I mean, you know a white boyfriend, right? Uh, that will watch out for me, and one day, I mean, not soon [laughing], I will have a strong husband. . . . I really thank my dad, and mom too, but really my dad, for this part of who I am . . . He's been there for me. . . . I'm not like those other girls that don't have fathers.

The discourse of white men (whether fathers, boyfriends, or husbands) as the essential protectors of white girls is a key component of the white nationalist worldview. Without those men in their lives, white women are seen as misguided and directionless. As another daughter told me, "My dad has always told me what is right and wrong. . . . He has always helped keep a lot of the black guys away." Such racialized and gendered paternalism rests on an ideology in which black men are preconditioned to violate white women. Such an ideology was widespread and not simply endemic to a father–daughter relationship.

One of the few female NEA members, Lisa, stated:

I think I have told you this before right? I have, I mean, again, a big part of the reason I help out here is because these guys are, well, number one, they are serious. They are not playing around, I mean, they really believe in what they are doing and want to protect the race. They don't just talk about it like a lot of other whites do; they are acting on it. And, uh, number two, they really do, I mean, this is on an emotional level for me, so they really make me feel safer. The more men in [NEA] we can get, I mean, I try to recruit people all the time, the more safe I am, other white women will be. We need strong white men to protect us . . . especially as society goes through further cultural decay. . . . I mean, there are drawbacks sometimes, like my ex-husband used to tell me what to do all the time, and that got old, but I mean, sometimes I wonder if I was just too hard on him, he was just trying to protect me. I didn't always listen. I was stubborn and did what I wanted. I should have obeyed him more. He always told me where I could and couldn't go. . . . I guess it was for my own good.

In a similar manner, many of the daughters expressed a mixture of frustration and thankfulness for white male paternalism. One daughter told me:

I just can't stand it when he [her father] is so controlling. . . . Sometimes I just have to take a deep breath and tell myself that he knows more than me and always will and that his intentions are good. . . . I mean, really, it's not his fault. It's the blacks and Mexicans that rape women like me that are the problem. It's really not his fault.

The placement of blame for the white male control of white women's movement in physical space is telling. When Lisa stated that such control of movement was for her "own good" coupled with the daughter's statement that "it's really not his fault" but the fault of "blacks and Mexicans that rape women like me," the surveilling control of white men was reconstructed as both normal and necessary. White women are seen as inherently incomplete without white male supervision. Even as they gain maturity and adulthood, such paternalistic white men will know "more than me and always will."

WRJ and "Saving Brown Women from Brown Men"

In "Can the Subaltern Speak?" Gayatri Spivak coined the phrase "white men saving brown women from brown men" to describe how British men rationalized colonial takeover through supposed acts of Indian female liberation—in specific, the nineteenth-century British abolition of Indian widow burning or "sati."[21] Since the apex of colonialism, the objectification of nonwhite women as things to be salvaged and saved from barbaric men of color has been a useful and seductive trope. Such framing reemerged in the wake of the World Trade Center and Pentagon attacks of 2001 when First Lady Laura Bush said in a radio address, "Because of our recent military gains in much of Afghanistan, women are no longer imprisoned in their homes. . . . The fight against terrorism is also a fight for the rights and dignity of women."[22] In response, anthropologist Lila Abu-Lughod writes:

> These words have haunting resonances for anyone who has studied colonial history. Many who have worked on British colonialism in South Asia have noted the use of the woman question in colonial policies where intervention into sati (the practice of widows immolating themselves on their husbands' funeral pyres), child marriage, and other practices was used to justify rule. . . . The historical record is full of similar cases, including in the Middle East. In Turn of the Century Egypt, what Leila Ahmed (1992) called "colonial feminism" was hard at work. This was a selective concern about the plight of Egyptian women that focused on the veil as a sign of oppression . . . [23]

I in no way wish to lessen or dismiss the very real intersecting oppressions with which women are faced. Rather, I suggest that women's oppression, movements for liberation, and colonial engagement have a complex interrelationship. This complexity is often reduced and distilled into a narrative in which colonial interventions are interpreted as humanitarian acts of "white men saving brown women from brown men." The habitual practices of white male supremacy are mystified through a focus on nonwhite women's victimization at the expense of nonwhite men's demonization. This general process is not limited to the special cases of nineteenth-century India or post–9/11 Afghanistan. Rather, systems of inequality are reproduced through generic patterns of impression and identity management whereby we coordinate our interactions with others (in terms of speech, gesture, clothing, and the like) so that others may recognize us as members of particular social groups and so elicit predictable responses from others.[24]

In this vein, WRJ members' patterned misrecognition of the objectification of nonwhite women and the demonization of nonwhite men enables the management of a seemingly moral, progressive, and valorized white savior identity. Saving women of color—interpreted as an imperative for antiracist and antisexist work—WRJ members labor to adhere to the expectations of a proper messianic white identity. Failure to embody these characteristics can be interpreted as a sign of a member's callous affect or his lack of commitment to the antiracist cause. Hence, WRJ members are well aware that race is not the only meaningful category of difference. Members often pepper their public discussions of race with at least some mention of class, age, sexuality, or gender. Members do realize that ignoring these social categories is detrimental to the goal of social justice, as they believe many of the causes and mechanisms of racism, classism, and sexism are intertwined.

At one particular business meeting, members discussed a letter they received from a nearby women's shelter called "Safe Haven."[25] The shelter, specializing in care and counseling for female survivors of domestic abuse, asked WRJ if members would give a series of talks on how white men can resist the combination of sexism and racism. With the permission of Safe Haven's administrators, I was invited to accompany WRJ members Malcolm, Mark, Patrick, and James to the shelter. Meeting at The Center, we all piled into Malcolm's car and headed to the shelter. On the way, members remarked that they were excited that their mission had reached the ears of the shelter directors, yet they admitted they were slightly apprehensive. "I've never been to one of these. What's it going to be like? Do they want us to just talk about oppression?" said Mark. Like Mark, the other three members had never been to a women's shelter, and they did not know what to expect. Other than reading a few of Safe Haven's pamphlets on domestic abuse and sexual assault, they were unacquainted with the larger topics and Safe Haven's particular operation.

On arrival we attended an hour-long meeting with Safe Haven's director and assistant in which they made clear their wish that WRJ conduct monthly seminars at the shelter on how racial and gender stereotypes and inequality develop and persist and how to personally work against them. Specifically, they asked WRJ members to relate their lectures and workshops to the impact racism and sexism have on family violence and on children and the development of their racial and gender identity and what people could do to work within the confines of state policies and laws related to race, gender, and violence. ". . . and I think it will really help to see white men discussing these issues," the director concluded. Everyone seemed both in agreement and somewhat relieved that their request could be managed. After setting up a tentative schedule for the following month, Mark asked if it would be okay if they could meet some of the women in the shelter. "I'd just like to get a feel for who we'll be speaking to," he said.

On the condition that I—as a non-WRJ member and researcher—could not interview the shelter's residents, they checked with some of the women and hesitantly agreed. "You can observe, but not interview. Introduce yourself, and that's all," the director's assistant told me. As I tailed Malcolm, Mark, Patrick, and James around the shelter, the WRJ members introduced themselves, told residents that they would soon return to give a series of talks, and attempted to get to know some of the women residents. Almost all the women in the shelter were black or Latina and seemed to hail from working- and lower-class backgrounds. Some of the women spoke to the WRJ members about themselves and their experiences openly, while others only mentioned they were there because of personal "setbacks" or "accidents." Two women in particular were quite explicit about their residency at Safe Haven. Telling the WRJ members that they were at a stage at which they were trying to work through their feelings of anger, depression, guilt, or sadness, they both told blunt stories about sexual violence, malicious beatings, and constant psychological abuse that, as one woman stated, "wore me down until I hated every ounce of who I was." After an hour of these introductions, the WRJ members thanked those with whom they spoke, briefly touched base with Safe Haven's director, and headed out the door. As we climbed back into Malcolm's car, Patrick began to cry. Wiping away his tears, he explained that he "cognitively" knew that women all over the world were abused and hurt every day but that hearing and "feeling" those stories was too much to bear. "I had an idea, but I had no idea," he said. The rest of the drive back to The Center took place in utter silence.

A few days later, I walked into The Center to find members engaged in an impassioned discussion about how best to help the women of Safe Haven. I sat down and turned on my recorder:

Mark: So if we can focus our work on the pragmatic issues like who, where, and how the abuse takes place—I mean, it's mostly men, right? . . .

Malcolm: I don't know about the others, but I, I mean, geez, there were a lot of black women, Latinas, you know Latin women, and uh, I didn't see any Asian women or anything else. But, I mean, there's clearly a connection here between race and abuse.

James: I don't follow you, I mean, well, like black and Latin women are more likely to be beaten.

Malcolm: Yeah, I mean, I don't know the stats on all that, I'm sure they [the shelter] has that, but no, you're right, I didn't expect so many either. . . .

Andre: I think it's a kind of trickle-down effect. So, if their men are being discriminated against, they are going to want to figure out how to exercise power somewhere. They're doing it [exercising power] in the home because they don't have any other choice, really.

[members seem confused by Andre's comment]

Patrick: No, no, that makes sense. It's just so sad. . . . but I mean, so, okay, so how do we phrase this at the talk? So, if I get up there and start talking about how "bad" black men are, I mean, I don't really believe that.

Andre: No, it's not that black men are bad. They're forced into a situation in which they have no other choice. I mean, what would you do? I mean, wait, I'm not saying any of us would beat our wives or girlfriends or whatever, you know, but I'm saying, can you imagine the frustration of not having any say in this world? That's really a class issue. We should talk about all three. . . . If you're poor 'cause you can't get a job because you're a black man, you're going to take that out at home on black women. . . .

Duncan: So, I get it yeah, but honestly, come on, guys, I mean [long pause] . . .
Okay, I wasn't there at the shelter, but this all sounds a little too abstract. I get
it, the theory and everything and the displaced frustrations, but what do I say
when someone asks me what to do about it? I don't have any answers. That's
just not it, I mean, no, that's not right.

Sherrill: So, this needs to be said. . . . From a woman's perspective, all I could
imagine is what someone is going to do to stop the man from hitting me.
If you're not telling me that, I mean, do you think I'm even going to hear anything you have to say if you're not telling me that?

Malcolm: She's right. She's right. I mean, we need to talk about identifying
the threats and neutralizing them. Nothing else is really germane at this
point. . . .

Duncan: . . . If we don't take control of the situation, who will?

This discussion illustrates how WRJ members were unsure as to the correct course of action. As the meeting broke up, both Sherrill and Bret spoke
with me. Sherrill stated, "I think it is really important for whatever we do, to
try to do it as equals. We can't do much unless we learn to see things their
way." Bret remarked, "Yeah, if we don't see it their way, and they see it from
our way, in a way that we both really get where we are coming from, I mean,
I'm not a woman, not black, and I've never been abused. I don't know what to
do. I have to learn." While Sherrill and Bret's dialogue emphasized the import
of exchange, dialog, and equanimity, another logic deeply imbued with paternalistic superiority was at play. Such paternalism emerged not out of a desire
to control or dominate but from the frustration and anger of dealing with the
close-up and graphically violent effects of sexism and racism. Members began
to interpret such violence and their roles in addressing it, so that they felt empowered to act. As Colin, a twenty-six-year-old student, told me:

We have to do something. I mean, these women, especially the women of
color, have been beat down so that they now just accept everything for what it
is instead of fighting for their rights. I think there are lots of possibilities that
they just don't use. They don't know any better, so we have to change their attitudes toward things.

This kind of self-perception began to transform the meanings of WRJ
members. Slowly, they saw themselves as omniscient beings capable of provid-

ing advice on a host of issues regardless of the situation. This logic reframed the women, themselves proactive enough to seek out Safe Haven, as unable or unwilling to make the right decisions because of their "ignorance" and their "attitude." After the third workshop with Safe Haven, Mark told me:

> I think Safe Haven is great, but I don't [long pause] . . . I hesitate to say this, but you just asked what I think, right? That's all? . . . Well, I mean, it just seemed like, when I was there, like well, like, all they were doing is enjoying relaxing and talking with each other. I mean, there are plenty of things they could be doing, like going out and getting a job so that they could remove themselves from the situation, but they are just there sitting and talking . . . I think that is more important to them. . . . Maybe if we stay there long enough we can be a role model.

Moreover, James told me:

> I can't imagine what violence does to the psyche. I mean, they are some *screwed up women* [said with emphasis]. Seriously, Matthew, I mean, they are crippled and like, I mean, they are like children. *And they have children* [said with emphasis], some of them, at least. They need good men in their lives. I don't know how they are going to make it without a man. . . . I'm so thankful they [Safe Haven] contacted us.

As indicated, a dominant self-concept as role model and savior existed alongside a rendering of women as overly passive and mentally adolescent, thereby burdening men, especially the men of WRJ, with administering and fixing their identities and lives.

As we will see from the following discussion, the members of WRJ were frustrated with their inability to stop domestic violence. Such a feeling of frustration is telling. Violence has been a long-standing characteristic of human society across cultures for thousands of years and is (I say with great despair) not likely solved in the near future. That the members of WRJ were irritated that they could not immediately solve domestic abuse in Fairview and surrounding cities speaks to the sense of entitlement and influence they felt. Such frustration was most tangibly directed not only at the passivity of women but also at the inherent danger of black and Latino men—the imagined perpetrators of violence. Accordingly, the rationale of policing and controlling the movements and actions of men of color as essentially violent and criminal beings had so impregnated the cultural logic across the political spectrum that the previously explicit logic of NEA now found a home in the implicit rationales of WRJ. As Colin told me:

> If we want to get to the root of the problem, we will have to obviously solve racism. As that is not happening tomorrow, we have to be pragmatic in some way and physically do something about the men that are hurting these women in, uh, the meantime.
>
> MWH: What do you mean, "do something"? Like what?
>
> Colin: I don't know yet, I mean. Black men are mad and angry. They've lost respect in the home. . . . But they have to be taught a lesson. . . . We've got to start being more active if we want this to stop, and that means challenging black men. Now you can call that culturally imperialist or racist or what have you, but that to me is just tough love. Sometimes you have to do that. Just like with a child, if you love them, you have to be tough. If we stop violence against black women, then that is a great thing. . . . That's why I've dated women of color. I don't beat women, and I figure if I can be political in my personal, even my romantic life, then that is a step forward.

Colin always laid bare his thoughts. I came to respect his sense of forthrightness, and I often marveled at his unadulterated honesty. His words reveal quite a bit about WRJ's activism in relation to women (especially women of color) in abusive environments.

For WRJ members, saving these women from sexual and sexist violence meant navigating a tricky space between reactionary and progressive politics. For example, Patrick stated:

> I don't know what helps except, well, if there were some type of harsher penalties that worked as a deterrent, then that, of course, might help. But that, I mean, that's less than ideal obviously. I'm not comfortable with encouraging, let's say, more police on the street when black men are obviously unfairly racially profiled. No way. But there's just no easy answer here.

Such a rendering created a catch-22 for WRJ members. Neither approach was satisfactory. While they wished to surveil men of color for their imaged hyperviolent and sexist behavior, they had no effective model for enacting such surveillance. They also did not want to put such surveillance in the hands of police who were coded as a racist and violence-prone force in and of themselves.

To solidify the meaning of their own identities as moral and sacrificing saviors for the well-being of nonwhite women, they instructed women to stay clear of places and spaces thought to be dominated by men of color. As Duncan explained to a group of nine women (six black, two Latina, and one white) during a workshop at Safe Haven:

> Racism and sexism are powerful forces. . . . Contemporary capitalist economics only worsens the oppression of men of color because they can't get jobs and can't get a sense of pride. Think about it. You didn't see the Crips and the Bloods out in California until black and brown unemployment rose. Violence breeds violence, and racism only generates a desire to oppress others more. . . . I think that if racism toward men of color lessens, then they will, will, uh, be less violent toward women. . . . Until that day, be smart. Stay out of black and lower-class neighborhoods. Don't go to black men's houses at night. They say most sexual abuse occurs from people you know, so even if you think he's a friend, you have to ask yourself: "How might racism make him want to hurt me?"

Similarly, when Bret was asked to speak to a high school classroom full of black women, he stated:

> I'll tell you like I would tell my own daughter, regardless of her race, but especially since you're black, you know, it makes sense, and you have to realize that it's just dangerous to be in areas that are dominated by black men. . . . Don't be alone, so use the, the, it's called the "buddy system," right? Yeah, so don't be alone. Have white friends with you, like, uh, chaperones . . . But I'll tell you, you may laugh, but when you date, consider white men. Don't think that you have to subscribe to outmoded ways of doing things when like, you're considering who you like, so, you know, statistically, I think, because white men, we don't suffer racism because of our privilege, so we're less likely to be sexist in an interracial relationship. . . . But, really, consider white men as partners. . . . and let me just tell you. I think most white men have a thing for black women, they just won't tell you.

Duncan and Bret's arguments to stay away from black male areas, to use white "chaperones," and to reduce chances of violence by dating white men collectively attempted to rationalize the surveillance and segregation of black men and black women. More disturbingly, the statement that "white men have a thing for black women" reproduced the very sexual objectification of black women that WRJ members said they were trying to contest.[26] With this logic in play, the white antiracist identity is easily constructed against the dangerous and sexist men of color. They—the "good" whites who are doing only what they feel they can—must rescue women of color from the "bad" and inherently misogynistic men of color, who stand as an embodied threat to democratic and egalitarian principles. This racial and gendered paternalism was clearly articulated in debates in WRJ meetings on how to assist Safe Haven and continued to motivate their work with the shelter.

In the end, colonial paternalism was reproduced through demands to conform to a proper messianic white antiracist identity. This identity was idealized and was one of the dimensions of hegemonic whiteness to which I have referred throughout. To live up to this aspect of the ideal was to be seen as a worthy and committed member. This meant signifying that one possessed the qualities of compassion, intelligence, rationality, tenacity, moral courage, and the ability to solve others' problems. Someone who joined WRJ slowly learned the implicit scripts and unspoken rules associated with this dimension until they became practical knowledge and embodied disposition. Displaying these characteristics was not a matter of conscious or awkwardly forced performances but could reflect the member's ability or desire to adhere to socially shared expectations that carried substantial rewards and penalties. Failure to embody these characteristics could be interpreted as a sign of a member's callous affect or his or her lack of commitment to the antiracist cause.

Empowe(RED) Paternalism

During the 2006–2007 timeframe in which I conducted this research, the "Red Campaign" gained a great deal of momentum. Designed by U2 singer Bono and Bobby Shriver, the chairman of DATA (Debt, AIDS, Trade, Africa), the campaign was designed to raise awareness and money to help curb the spread of HIV/AIDS in Africa.

The Red Campaign teamed up with some of the world's more conspicuous brand-name products to make what they called "(Product)Red" branded commodities like red iPods, laptops, and cell phones. Perhaps the most iconic product became the Gap brand T-shirt—a solid red shirt emblazoned with a word such as *endeavo(red)*, *inspi(red)*, *admi(red)*, or *empowe(red)*.[27] The Gap T-shirts were a success in both Riverside and Fairview, as many scrambled to buy a T-shirt so as to broadcast their support of a noble cause and as a sign of their global awareness.

Weeks after the Red Campaign began, I walked into WRJ's headquarters to find members discussing it. They were debating whether WRJ should officially support the campaign among the organization's national membership. Two of the Red Campaign shirts lay on a table in the center of the room. I sat down with the members and listened to their conversation, already in progress:

> Patrick: It seems prudent that we support it; I mean, if we don't, what kind of example is that [said in mocking sarcasm]: "Oh, so you guys are antiracists, but you don't care about the inequality in Africa?" Yeah, great.
>
> Andre: I'm not saying that, it's just, I don't know, . . . okay, look, it's a little commercialized, right? I mean, I want to help, and I think it's good, but okay. I don't know how these products are made and just don't want to support capitalism. How do we know that these products are not made in ways that actually take money out of Africa?
>
> Sherrill: That's a good point. Really.
>
> Colin: Yeah, but at the same time, I think, we need to consider that we should do something. They can't help themselves. There's not much there to help.
>
> Malcolm: I'm just not sure, is it better than nothing?

WRJ members were not convinced of the efficacy of the project. Far from cultural dupes or consumerist robots, these activists took seriously the complicated relationships among capitalism, profiteering, health and disease, and antiracism. A tension arose between a worry that they would be perceived as inauthentic or sophomoric activists if they did not support the campaign on the one hand, while on the other they worried that the Red Campaign would largely assist the sponsoring companies rather than Africans with HIV/AIDS. Toward the end of the conversation, they reached a tentative conclusion:

> Andre: I'm not entirely sold on supporting this. . . . It is getting lots of attention, and people are buying into it.
>
> Horace: Think of it this way: If we support it, we're going to attract a lot of people to our cause anyway. Besides, it's better than nothing. We have to buy things anyway, might as well be something that gives money back. . . . It will mainstream our message.
>
> Colin: There is so much devastation there, we have to take charge of this, and if there is one way to do it, then I am for it. That's plain and simple to me.

Sherrill: It seems in the end, you know, after all is said and done, that we are either doing something or nothing. This is something . . . We have to take care of them [Africans]; who else is going to do it? That seems like something that is at the center of our mission, right? . . . Think about the colonialism and oppression of Africa. They don't know the right thing to do, *they're past the point of clear thinking* [my emphasis]. This campaign is not perfect, but it's the best thing they have. We have to help save them.

Patrick: She's right. Come on, the campaign is designed so that the money has to be used correctly. Besides, it's a great way to really expand our mission and attract people interested in Africa.

Malcolm: What do we all think, sound good to go with this? [Most of the room nodded their heads in affirmation.]

As evidenced, the logic of paternalism helped to resolve the conflict. By describing an amorphous group of "Africans" as "past the point of clear thinking" and concluding that WRJ's role was to "help save them," an essentially hierarchical racial relationship was imagined and reproduced in the antiracist headquarters.

In trying to be good and moral white antiracists, who clearly felt their mission scrutinized by others, the WRJ members felt a real pressure to take control and solve the problems that Africans were seemingly unable to do for themselves. Such paternalism was mixed with a sense of entitlement and chauvinism. After the discussion, Malcolm told me in a frustrated and exasperated tone: ". . . and really, at the end of all this, if people, especially black people, aren't supportive of what we're doing, then they're stupid anyway. We don't need their support." James, who had been entirely quiet during the meeting, replied: "Yeah, I rarely know how to help. This makes me feel better." The group interaction and navigation of the topic illustrate how the specter of racist and white supremacist logic haunted the best of intentions when dominant group members perceived themselves as implicitly superior to the subordinated group.[28]

Weeks after WRJ decided to officially support the Red Campaign, I walked into The Office of NEA and found John, a forty-two-year-old consultant and six-year member of NEA, wearing a Gap "Red" T-shirt, emblazoned with the word *admi(red)*. My face must have shown my surprise, for John looked at me quizzically as he blurted out a defensively toned, "What?!" "I just wasn't expecting you to support HIV/AIDS research in Africa," I said. John responded:

It's great! [Laughing] Who can really say that white nationalism is selfish, right? I mean, if Africa doesn't pull their shit together, how are we going to rationalize our aims? . . . [laughing] Well, I like the shirt because it's a dual-function kind of thing, really. I mean some [referring to fellow NEA members] might disagree, but first, you know ten dollars on every sale is a lot of money to go to African relief, and, second, well, what you were asking about, I think, is that we need some black spaces on this planet to get it together, to be competent, at least half-civilized places. I'm not sure they can get it together very quickly, so we have to do it for them.

MWH: I still don't get it.

John: Okay, well, um, let me give you an analogy, right? So, let's say that I have a child, and he is misbehaving. Actually, this just happened not too long ago, so it's perfect. So my son doesn't want to clean up his room, he always leaves his toys out all over the house. So I've been trying to convince my wife to convert one of the rooms into a game room, you know, pool table and what not. She keeps saying no because my boy leaves his toys all over the place. She just thinks he should have his run just about all over the house, except my office, and he just does as he pleases. She knows I would throw a fit if he did that in my game room. So, it's in my interest to get him to clean up his stuff, to grow up and do as I say, so I started giving him some money every time he cleans up. In a few weeks, I bet you I will be able to get my game room, because he'll be better behaved. . . . It's the same situation with Africa. This campaign, if you do the research, is so tied into the bureaucratic strings that if certain African companies and governments don't act right, they won't get any money. It's the same thing practically. . . .

MWH: So the dual function you mentioned earlier?

John: Oh yeah, one, they get their own space so we have ours. Two, they learn a little obedience and responsibility along the way. And, really, there's a third; you know the whole political correctness thing, and I mean, I hate to play into it, but there are pragmatic considerations, and really, I mean, it's kind of hard to call me a racist with this shirt on.

His explanation makes clear the paternalistic motivation behind his support of the Red Campaign. Weeks later, several members of NEA bought Red T-shirts, and no less than a month after our conversation an article was printed in the NEA newsletter and posted on several white supremacist and nationalist websites about the white nationalist utility of supporting the Red Campaign.

During one day in the NEA Office, Charles, a twenty-five-year-old graduate student, showed me such a white nationalist website. Leaning on his desk,
he clicked on a site that loaded a picture of a malnourished brown-skinned
girl sitting on the ground, wearing disheveled, ripped, and filthy clothes; doz-
ens of flies swarmed and landed on her emaciated body. "This is a great photo,
I mean, it's really the same one we see all the time on the Sally Struthers com-
mercials or the Christian Relief stuff," said Charles. He continued:

> We're [NEA] not without compassion, . . . it's a functional relationship, really,
> we need Africa to be ready to take Africans, same with the Caribbean and
> South America. . . . We have to take over these areas to make sure they are up
> to par . . . Otherwise, they will keep trying to come here. Unless people un-
> derstand this pragmatic reality, we will keep having immigration problems.

The dominance of white paternalistic logic effectively rallied the support
of both WRJ and NEA around the Red Campaign. The campaign's patina of
a neutral and moral benevolence enabled divergent political groups to effectively use, and tie their identity to, the campaign. The campaign creates an
overly simplified way to exhibit interracial goodwill and generosity. White activists, despite nationalist or antiracist leanings, are juxtaposed as messianic
characters against the harsh realties of a postcolonial African continent mired
in both disease and dysfunction. Any possibility of cooperative solutions between equalized black African and white American actors is framed as impossible. Rather, a hierarchical relationship is reestablished and lubricated
with the allure of consumerist agency, as evidenced by WRJ member James's
previously mentioned comment: "Yeah, I rarely know how to help. This makes
me feel better."

For the white antiracists, supporting the Red Campaign meant they could
feel comfortable in "saving the Africans" via their support of companies like
Gap, Converse, Motorola, and Armani—which subscribed to the Red Campaign manifesto: "If you buy a (red) product or sign up for a (red) service, at
no cost to you, a (red) company will give some of its profits to buy antiretroviral medicine." Members often flattered themselves into thinking the purchase of a new cell phone or pair of sneakers was something more than engaging in a routine market transaction. Instead, conspicuous consumption came
to symbolize both their antiracist commitment and a moment of redemption
in which they momentarily purchased an escape from white guilt.

For the white nationalists, the Red Campaign enabled the reassertion of white intelligence, morality, and civilization through kindly actions of international service and commercialized commodities. NEA members labored quite hard to make sure that their attitude toward the Red Campaign created distance from the traditional image of white nationalism. Rather, their involvement appeared as a natural, even noble, step that any caring, globally attuned person with a conscience would take. Yet, the modus operandi of white paternalism was revealed via the metaphor of the African-as-child who needs to be bribed and controlled to solidify and protect future white gains.

The use of the Red Campaign demonstrates the reproduction of an "inspi(red) paternalism" that reflects the longstanding Eurocentric nature of development and discourse that assumes images of the superior and efficient white "donor" counterjuxtaposed against the inadequate, passive, unreliable recipient. "Saving the Africans," regardless of individual intention, is a loaded phrase. I certainly do not argue that there is something essentially wrong with, or inherently evil about, the Red Campaign. Rather, I suggest that the Red Campaign has been interpreted amid dominant and moral background rules that positioned members of differently racialized groups into the narrative of the capable redeemer and the inept redeemable. In the organizational contexts of both NEA and WRJ, the Red Campaign assisted actors to reproduce the dominant meaning of whiteness, particularly white masculinity, as a morally superior and competent savior.

Moreover, NEA's and WRJ's attraction to the Red Campaign cannot be divorced from the seductive and sometimes bizarre spectacle of white celebrity saviorhood that seems propelled by the epic intention to partake in a civilizing mission.[29] For example, supermodel Kate Moss put on blackface to grace the cover of the September 21, 2006, copy of the U.K. paper *The Independent*, which was temporarily renamed *The (RED) Independent* and "The Africa Issue," the proceeds of which would "help fight AIDS in Africa."[30] In another strange blackface performance in between mimicry and mockery, white celebrities like Richard Gere, Sarah Jessica Parker, Liv Tyler, and Gwyneth Paltrow donned face paint and beaded jewelry to the captions of "I Am African" in a 2010–2011 fundraising campaign for antiretroviral (ARVs) drugs for African nations. A white civilizing identity is also manifested in the spectacle of transracial and transnational adoptions à la Madonna, Angelina Jolie, Brad Pitt, and Sandra Bullock and in the recent portrayal of Afghani women that invites little more than "pity and a certain voyeuristic attraction."[31] Whereas the contemporary versions of white supremacy and colonialism explicitly disavow white desire for domination, a subordinate dark "other" is required for the production of a heroic white self.

Such popular cultural iconography mystifies a hierarchical relationship in which Westernized nations in the Northern Hemisphere regularly exploit the people and resources of the Global South. This relationship is glossed over by the image of well-meaning white celebrities swooping in to fix the problems of Africans by appropriating tokenized aspects of "African culture" (read: beads, face paint, and dark skin), while paradoxically claiming a kind of membership in a downtrodden group ("I am African") to rationalize their care for a group in which they temporarily stake claim. The exploitive, hierarchical, and unequal relationships between the races are both mystified and reproduced when dark-skinned people of peripheral nations and areas become symbolic objects and one-dimensional caricatures to be saved by white benefactors of the silver screen or by white "conscious" consumers of product(RED).

Hegemonic Whiteness: White Saviors

We are all accountable to others—not just in terms of fulfilling a promise to a friend or working at a job but in terms of adhering to the shared expectations and behaviors we associate with membership in salient groups, like our gender or our race. In this sense, Charles Cooley argued that "identity" is a "reflected or looking glass self" in which we see ourselves based on the images others have of us.[32] Furthermore, sociologist Michael Schwalbe writes:

> Often when we're called into account, it's as a member of a group or social category. And usually this is because we're not behaving the way someone thinks we should, as a member of that group or category. We are thus vulnerable to being ignored, discredited, shamed, or otherwise punished for behaving in a way that others deem wrong in light of who we claim to be or who they think we are. One way to put it is to say that identities carry accountability obligations.[33]

Hence, we constantly adjust and recreate our identities in relation to group expectations and social accountabilities.

Members of both Whites for Racial Justice and National Equality for All expressed frustration with the racialized codes of political correctness—what anthropologist John Jackson Jr. calls the "white man's newest burden."[34] Jackson writes, "The white man's new burden was guilt and shame for the moral failings about race. What used to be common sense was now a cancer, a deadly sin."[35] Alongside that frustration, and a palpable paranoia that they were unfairly painted as irrational racialists, these white activists creatively worked within the conventions and governing expectations of public discourse. The members of WRJ and NEA attempted to live out their lives and present their identities as people who cared about their activism and its relation to the world around them. They engaged in a great deal of impression management and identity work to accomplish an authentic, moral, and socially acceptable identity. In given interactions, a patriarchal dimension of their identity was also valorized and pursued. Failure to embody that dimension could result in members being "ignored, discredited, shamed, or otherwise punished."[36] Hence, pursuit of this dimension of a white racial self was rather obligatory if a member was to occupy the safe space of normality within the context of either organization.

It is important to realize that these obligations or "nets of accountability" help to reproduce racial inequality. I have already outlined how these understandings rationalize the inclusion and exclusion of certain racialized bodies in particular racialized spaces. When the routine ways that people do things together are interpreted not just as deviant *actions* but as markings of one's immoral, strange, or dysfunctional *identity*, then the mechanisms that reproduce an unequal society exist in the very meanings of our identities—in the very ways we go about reaccomplishing our sense of self. How we then go about making meaning of race is not simply an exercise in interpretation but is the very heart that circulates our social lifeblood. When a patriarchal white self is idealized as normal and proper, then it becomes the standard against which whites are judged as more or less worthy people and, in this case, as creditable white racial activists.[37]

7 Color Capital and White Debt

So yeah, well, as much as we, even myself personally, I mean,
[long pause] as much I might hate to admit it, . . . especially
not in public, there is just something cool, I mean, well, put it
this way, black people own the whole notion of "cool" . . . Yeah,
sometimes I do get jealous . . . I'd be lying if I didn't sometimes,
especially years ago, I mean, want to be cool like black people.
— **Steven, National Equality for All**

We were at this party a few months back, and normally, it's not
like there are a lot of black people that come in there, which is
messed up because they segregate, but you know, it's a problem
of racism . . . Anyway, these guys walked in, they were black,
and they started dancing, and we all formed a circle around
them and were clapping and cheering because they were just
amazing . . . Black people are so cool when they dance . . . I
wish I could dance like that.
— **Cassandra, Whites for Racial Justice**

The Souls of White Folk

Although *The Souls of Black Folk* is probably W. E. B. Du Bois's best-known book, he penned another essay entitled "The Souls of White Folk," in which he wrote:

> This assumption that of all the hues of God whiteness alone is inherently and
> obviously better than brownness or tan leads to curious acts; even the sweeter
> souls of the dominant world as they discourse with me on weather, weal, and
> woe are continually playing above their actual words an obbligato of tune and
> tone . . .[1]

Du Bois set an important trajectory for the research of whiteness as a social identity thought "inherently and obviously better." To Du Bois, a supremacist self-appraisal infected an array of whites—from overt racists to the "sweeter souls." To explain this widespread view, Du Bois argued that white racial identity sprang from identifying not as an enslaved worker but as a free and superior identity to those inferior persons of darker hues. Later, in *Black Reconstruction*, Du Bois wrote that, because white workers eschewed solidarity with nonwhite workers, they received a "public and psychological wage"—a set of symbolic and material privileges that nonwhites did not possess.[2] Moreover, Du Bois provided a robust overview of how the creation of whiteness as an identity couched in superiority was maintained by whites being "unconscious of any such powerful and vindictive feeling."[3]

Alongside this unconscious superiority, whites also possessed a paradoxical desire for contact with, and imitation of, nonwhites over whom they exercise power. Du Bois made clear that blacks were robust contributors to society, yet he distinguished among the different kinds of white usages of black offerings and practices.[4] For example, while Du Bois celebrated "Negro folk-songs as striking and characteristic," he lambasted white replication in minstrel shows as "debasements and imitations."[5] Hence, white racial identity and its performative interactions with nonwhite "others" developed in Janus-faced fashion—as both an identity superior to nonwhite otherness and as an identity dependent on appropriating that otherness.

The paradox of white supremacy and appropriation—what Shannon Sullivan calls "racist alchemy"[6]—has occurred in an array of historical moments, not just the obvious examples of white actors in blackface minstrel shows.[7] Racial appropriation was manifested in the Indian impersonators of the Boston Tea Party and within the Boy Scouts of America's "Order of the Arrow" movement.[8] During the 1920s, white socialites flocked to Chicago's black and tan jazz cabarets to consume black culture qua authenticity in the hopes that they would be released from the "bourgeois constraints of Victorian prudishness and sobriety."[9] And racial mimicry occurred in white consumption of the poetry of T. S. Eliot and e. e. cummings, films like *The Jazz Singer* (1927), the television and radio shows *Amos 'n' Andy*, and Shirley Temple's dance routines with Bill "Bojangles" Robinson. These practices were so well established that Norman Mailer commented on white appropriation of racial otherness in a 1957 article entitled "The White Negro: Superficial Reflections on the Hipster."[10]

Fast forward to the twenty-first century. We may still observe patterns of white racial appropriation in white consumption practices, interactions, and identity formation. One need not look far: from the branding of professional, collegiate, and high school sports teams with Native American caricatures to the increase of white tattooing of Polynesian tribal iconography, Kanji symbols, and Celtic bands.[11] The appropriation of race occurs in the use of stereotypical racial avatars in online and virtual interactions,[12] racial fetishism in private sexual settings,[13] white liberals' embrace of Rastafarian culture,[14] and white New Yorkers' attendance of "Kill Whitey" parties for the consumption of music understood as "black" and "freaky."[15]

In this chapter I delineate how the trend of white appropriation transposes itself among the everyday practices of both the white nationalists of NEA and the white antiracists of WRJ. I argue that a shared sense of white racial emptiness, a desire for racial otherness, and feelings of both white normativity and superiority together merge and constitute an unique economy of racial meaning. The production, distribution, and consumption of these meanings guide white racial identity formation and interaction. Such dynamics can be better understood via the conceptual framework of "white debt" and "color capital." *White debt* is shorthand for the feelings and practices associated with whites' perceptions that their racial identity is "bland," "cultureless," and "empty." *Color capital* is made up of the objects, discourse, and actors coded as non-white and that signify a primordial authenticity associated with the exoticism, carnality, and "soul." I demonstrate different levels of interaction in which these racially conscious whites have tried to obtain color capital toward the alleviation of white debt. These interactions serve as crucial elements of an ongoing process of white racial identity formation and help to reproduce essentialist, reactionary, and racist understandings of racial difference.

I offer a brief example here. Sean, a sixty-two-year-old part-time gardener and six-year member of Whites for Racial Justice, told me:

> It is difficult being in WRJ. . . . To many of us, being white is a part of the problem . . . Becoming less white is losing something but also about gaining something real.
>
> MWH: How do you become "less white"? What does that actually look like?
>
> Sean: Well . . . there is something more real, I think because of oppression and racism . . . that has made people of color more human. So, if I had to spell it out, being less white is being more like them. . . . There's something missing in white people.

Such an understanding of whiteness was remarkably similar to that of white nationalists. For example, a thirty-nine-year-old lawyer and five-year member of National Equality for All named Harry stated:

> Black people have their bright colors and their music or whatever . . . We have civilization that has lasted. It is unique and strong in that right. But because of many whites' approaches to white civility, they've made it dull, sold out its character, made it plain. In many ways that style transferred to blacks hundreds of years ago, . . . they stole many white styles and passed it off as "Af-

rican." Now we're in a situation that needs to reclaim our passion. Look at jazz, I love Miles Davis . . . so what if he's black, I'm filling in what was taken from me. The creativity of jazz is because of white people thousands of years ago. . . . Now we are at a point where white nationalism has to be more open to the authenticity of others.

These two examples were not aberrations. Rather, they were patterned and systemic meanings that helped members make sense of their own racial identity and how it should be performed in everyday life.

The Double Helix of Racial Logic

Before embarking on the examination of how racially conscious whites like NEA and WRJ members navigate the symbolic order of race, we should briefly examine how the mechanisms of white debt and color capital developed into the dominant cultural logics they hold today. Scholars point to two historically entrenched logics as definitive of the U.S. racial landscape: *assimilation* and *pluralism*.[16] Randy Blazak writes, "A nation as historically diverse as the United States holds many contradictions. . . . When it comes to race and ethnicity, we are even more schizophrenic. We cling dearly to the ideas of assimilation and its exact opposite: pluralism."[17] These two logics represent the double helix of the nation's DNA. With the simultaneous valorization of assimilation and pluralism, the paradoxical character of white racial identity slowly developed in embryo.

In the early 1800s, many shared the expectation that native peoples and immigrants should shed their language, values, and customs for burgeoning U.S. holidays, civic rituals, and the English language through its institutionalization in public schooling, common law, Protestant beliefs, and social services.[18] As this logic solidified into custom, law, and a policy of "Anglo conformity," it directly affected roughly 24 million immigrants between 1880 and 1920, many hailing from Southern and Eastern Europe.[19] While some European immigrants were stubbornly ethnicized as culturally out of place, other Europeans found themselves "white on arrival."[20] As the United States developed, the logic of Anglo conformity and assimilation underlay the U.S. Naturalization Law of 1790 that limited citizenship to "free white persons"; the Chinese Exclusion Act of 1882; the policy of "Kill the Indian, and save the man";[21] and the Immigration Act of 1924 that reinforced the primacy of select European immigration.[22] Today, scholars point to Anglo conformity as the genesis for the modern ideology of "color-blindness."[23] That is, as assimilation into whiteness was part and parcel of the national ideal, Anglo cultural practices were increasingly normalized as indelibly nonracial; they became neutral characteristics and behaviors to which *individual citizens* should aspire and adopt, rather than markers of a distinctive and privileged *racial group* at the center of the nation's founding.[24]

A strong counterweight to the idea of WASP (white Anglo-Saxon Protestant) assimilation was the notion of "cultural pluralism."[25] While some gently critiqued the Anglo conformity approach with the egalitarian notion that the United States was "God's crucible, the great melting pot," others went so far as to say that one should never relinquish prior acculturation.[26] The retention of distinct European heritages (for example, Irish or Polish) spelled the end of WASP dominance, while for others it represented a negative balkanization of Western heritage and legacy.[27] Some now suggest that resistance to Anglo conformity and the melting pot ideology was mounted first by "unmeltable ethnics" against the British foundations of American culture, then later by Americans of non-European origin against the Eurocentric basis of the U.S. social order.[28] As a variety of 1960s legislation passed into law, immigration policy was revised, and challenges to Eurocentric doctrines in education, family, law, and religion were mounted in diverse registers. Cultural pluralism morphed into the widely espoused ideology of "multiculturalism."[29] Ethnic and racial pride movements gained influence, and the implicit assumption that "whiteness" equaled "Americanness" was directly challenged.

From Logic to Identity: Whiteness as "Superior" yet "Cultureless"

The intermingled logics of assimilation and pluralism not only stratified different racial identities but created them; whiteness emerged as a superior yet normal, neutral, and "cultureless" identity, while nonwhites were marked with a strange admixture of stigmatized yet exotic "primordial ethnicity."[30] As people of color publically advocated racial and cultural pride during the civil rights movement of the 1960s, many whites argued that they had no seat at the "multicultural table."[31] Some interpreted this dynamic as a threat to the psychological health of whites. The U.S. Congress hastily passed the "Ethnic Heritage Act of 1974," which instituted nationwide educational programs with the expressed purpose of restoring whites' "lost" cultural heritage.[32] As pluralism took hold as multiculturalism in the 1980s, the cultural traditions of people of color were often framed as rich and unique contributions to society. Out of this backdrop, cultural critic bell hooks argues that people started interpreting nonwhite racial practices and styles as either dangerous and dysfunctional or as:

> a new delight, more intense, more satisfying than normal ways of doing and feeling. Within commodity culture, ethnicity becomes spice, seasoning that can liven up the dull dish that is mainstream white culture . . . fantasies about the Other can be continually exploited, and that . . . exploitation will occur in a manner that reinscribes and maintains the *status quo* [emphasis in original].[33]

Hence, white encounters with such "spice" were thought to alleviate feelings of "culturelessness." Given the widespread meanings of whiteness as culturally deficient and nonwhiteness as culturally enriched, it is important to observe how white racial identity formation is guided by this historically entrenched dynamic of pluralism and assimilation.

Levels of the Racial Economy: White Debt and Color Capital

I found that the members of National Equality for All and Whites for Racial Justice engaged in the appropriation of color capital toward the alleviation of white debt with patterned regularity and within distinct forms of social interaction. The historically structured schemas of white debt and color capital operate as stable processes that manufacture racial difference and white superiority, while converting people of color into essentialized objects of whites' desires. I highlight four dimensions in which this racialized exchange operated:

1. "Interactive Ties": The relationships, networks, and associations with nonwhites that result in a durable network of acquaintance and recognition.
2. "Embodied Dispositions": The aesthetic tastes, ways of communicating, styles, and performances associated with nonwhites.
3. "Material Culture": The objects and items symbolically coded as nonwhite that are in turn possessed, owned, and "consumed."
4. "Institutional Credentials": Officially sanctioned information associated with nonwhites.

Although each was defined by a different connection of white debt to color capital, all four were wedded to pursuit of an idealized form of white identity, a central resource in both NEA and WRJ members' lives.

Interactive Ties

This pattern describes how color capital operates via the relationships, networks, and associations with nonwhites that result in durable networks of acquaintance and recognition toward the elimination of white debt. It might well be thought of as the phrase often deployed in seeking to avoid the label of "racist": "I'm not racist; one of my best friends is black." While neither WRJ nor NEA members explicitly evoked this phrase, similar discourses were deployed to "fill in" their whiteness. Daniel, a thirty-two-year-old registered nurse with four years experience in NEA, told me: "Despite my politics, I have quite a few good black friendships." "So they know you are a member of NEA?" I asked. Daniel answered:

> Some do, some don't. I mean we disagree about some things, but who doesn't? But they're good black people; they have jobs, families, are intelligent people. We see each other a lot at the gym. I have lunch at least once a week with one of them. . . . You can't say I'm some redneck, ignorant racist now, can you?

So also, Will, a nine-year member of NEA, told me in an interview:

> I often try to hang out at a bar around the corner from my house . . . It generally has a lot of race mixing in it, . . . Now you know I don't agree with that or think that's the best for anyone, but it gives me an advantage.
>
> MWH: How so?
>
> Will: Because I have lots of black friends, I learn a lot about things I wouldn't otherwise know about, . . . In the end it shakes up what people think of white nationalists as "bigots" and whatnot. I know all the latest [black] music, sayings, and what their community is thinking about. I'm far from a dull white guy. . . . And I can use that information if anyone wants to equate white nationalism with racism. [laughing] It's like a "get out of jail free" card [laughing].

Both Daniel and Will's explanations illuminate that interracial social ties work like a form of capital that can credential them among others, particularly those that would label white nationalists as "ignorant racists."

Various members of WRJ also evoked such a discourse. Andre, a twenty-four-year-old graduate student, stated:

> I'm really excited about my neighborhood now . . . I have two black neighbors on either side of my house . . . We're an Oreo cookie! [said with a hearty laugh]. I guess I can't say I live in a segregated neighborhood anymore.

MWH: Did saying that before worry you?

Andre: Yeah, I mean, wouldn't it worry you? I don't ever want to live in an all-white neighborhood. I mean, especially around here, I wouldn't want to get made . . . I mean, it's just bad.

MWH: Go ahead and finish what you started to say.

Andre: It's nothing . . . I mean . . . okay . . . honestly [he takes a deep breath and is silent for some time]. I feel like others [in WRJ] would really give me a hard time about being in an all-white neighborhood. I just joined a while ago, and I don't want to mess up. Now I feel like I have *something to use*, like it's a medal or something. No one can call me out for that, I mean, in reality I really do have two black neighbors, and I'm great friends with them. It's safe, you know?

MWH: Safe where? Your neighborhood?

Andre: Well, yeah . . . but I was referring to WRJ.

A member of WRJ was expected to live an antiracist life, not simply show up to meetings. Andre's specific comments revealed that the expectation to possess close social ties with people of color often was felt as an intense pressure to conform. In following up the discussion with Andre, I asked him how having two black neighbors directly influenced his life both in and outside of WRJ. He responded:

I told you before that it affords me a bit of breathing room here [WRJ]. There's less pressure that I am not living up to the expectations. I really believe in what we are doing, and I think segregation is flat-out wrong, and so, I mean, that's good, you know . . . and I guess outside of WRJ I feel like I earn a bit of respect from others who think that we're just a bunch of crazy radicals. I use the fact that I have two black neighbors to show others that we live what we say; it earns me respect.

MWH: What earns you respect?

Andre: Oh, the fact that I have two black neighbors, I get an advantage from it . . . I mean, I brought [one of his black neighbors] by WRJ the other day, and it was great. He was asking me questions about what we did, and he seemed to look at me in a different light, and to the other guys [in WRJ] I became one of the "good" white people.

After I turned off the audio recorder, Andre further explained that he felt "cool" when he brought his black neighbor to meet his fellow WRJ members and that it reminded him of being in elementary school during "show and tell."

Andre's explanation that his friendship with his black neighbors is like "a medal," "affords breathing room," "earns respect," gets "advantage," and was like "show and tell" were all instructional. His developing friendship with his neighbors was a network of acquaintance that bought him recognition and status as "one of the 'good' white people." The impulse to gather diverse friendships and avoid residential practices of racial homogeneity was a result of the dominant interpretation of the logic of pluralism whereby diversity is an end in and of itself. Combined with the logic of Anglo conformity via color-blindness, Andre did not regard his relationship with his neighbors as a form of racial objectification. Rather, these logics provided Andre with a schematic map in which he could negotiate both the microdemands of local organizing in WRJ and the larger compulsion to inject positive meaning into the perceived emptiness of his white racial identity.

Such objectified familiarity with nonwhite people worked as an alleviation of white debt in both NEA and WRJ. Such a dynamic is illuminated no more clearly than in the comparison of the following two statements. As one guest speaker at an NEA event told a small crowd of members and those investigating the organization:

> White civilization has fallen off and been led astray, often by black and Latino people . . . At the same time, the passion and commitment of blacks is something we presently lack . . . We can reclaim our former glory and rightful place by building relationships and friendships with people of color. Become their friends; explain to them our agenda and how it helps both of us. Let them know we do not hate them; we only wish to separate. Take with you their passion for racial identity . . . and use your friendships with them as a valuable commodity . . . that will build a new white nationalism, a new white identity.

So, also, a WRJ member named Duncan told fellow members in a private meeting:

> I think what we need to do, as conscious, thinking, aware human beings who have decided to take a stand against racism, is what we can, or rather, *need* [his voice emphasizing the word] to do to stop racism in our own lives as well as take a stand against it structurally, is . . . well . . . to constantly ask ourselves, "How can I become less 'white'?" . . . Make friendships with people of

color, and I mean, really, guys, use those relationships, learn from them, become more of a human and less an oppressor, and build a new kind of whiteness up from the grassroots that can partake in multiculturalism as less of an exploiter.

As WRJ and NEA constructed differing worldviews and wished for a future of race relations that is quite contrarian, it becomes important to take into account that despite differences in the use of color capital within this social dimension, they served a similar function of the objectification of black and brown bodies.

Embodied Dispositions

This aspect of the white debt–color capital economy can be thought of as aesthetic tastes, ways of communicating, styles, and performances that are symbolically associated with nonwhites. Color capital is often reified as the stable properties of the individual self. For instance, the mastery of a particular language or dialect, styles of dress, bodily and facial expressions, and the aesthetic tastes for a certain music, art, literature, or sport are all constitutive of this pattern. The operation of color capital on this level was most noted via my ethnographic observations and recorded in my field notes. As I was invited into members' homes and other private settings away from the organizations' headquarters, I was better able to empirically observe how both groups shared many of the same tastes and dispositions for characteristics, products, and traits thought to naturally and essentially belong to people of color.

Whether it was the tattoos of Asian symbols that members of both groups possessed; their taste for the "magical realism" literature of various Latino authors and African American literary classics of Ellison, Morrison, and Hughes; their reverence for the jazz of Miles Davis, John Coltrane, and Charlie Parker; or even a desire for pornography that was almost exclusively dedicated to women of color—the two groups were united via collective aesthetic tastes of a racialized manner. As I began to notice these similarities, I asked members to explain their aesthetic tastes. It was during these question-and-answer sessions that the use of embodied color capital toward the elimination of white debt was revealed.

When I asked NEA member Laurence why he possessed (and prominently displayed in his living room) an extensive CD collection of black jazz, he replied that he simply "liked that type of music." When I pressed him as to what that "type" entailed, he replied:

Black jazz is not like white jazz. It's carnal and full of emotion. White jazz is more laid back—elevator music–like, softer somehow . . . Black artists have a soul and a . . . [long pause]. I don't know . . . they have something underneath the music, it's the rhythm or something. . . . Maybe it's because of discrimination or whatever . . . maybe after a few hundred years of reverse racism then whites will play jazz like that, but I doubt it. . . . There's a harsh quality to it, . . . it goes back to Africa and has been passed on genetically. Whites don't have it, so I listen to it. I just like it.

When I noticed a similar phenomenon of ownership of music almost exclusively performed by black artists in the homes of several WRJ members, I inquired why they had little to no music performed by white artists. Replies were varied, from "I just like that style," to "I don't know," to "I love black music." The WRJ member I call Blake told me:

I like hip-hop and jazz mostly, because the music is more real to me. I feel better when I listen to it, like I am more in touch with the human side of me. Even with the more hard-core rap music, I don't like as much of it, but it's like it really hits me here, you know [pointing to his heart], it's valid here.

MWH: So you like artists like Kenny G or Eminem?

Blake: Get out of here! [laughing] They are jokes, I mean, no, . . . listen . . . I like it because it's real, it expresses something I wouldn't be able to get otherwise. I'm not black, so I can't really get it, but I get closer to it when I listen to it, you know.

MWH: What do you mean by "it" when you say you really can't get "it"?

Blake: I mean, the black experience, I get closer to it with hip-hop, I guess that's why I like it. It fits with my whole life and being in WRJ.

Equating black music with soul, carnality, validity, and realness reveals many of the racist and essentialist features of WRJ and NEA that are embodied in the very dispositions of their members. In this sense, what might appear as individual choices and tastes are in fact indicative of what sociologists Eliasoph and Lichterman call a "group style"—how implicit, culturally patterned styles of membership and understanding filter the objects, people, and symbols that people encounter in everyday life.[34] Cultural understandings of bland whiteness and spicy nonwhiteness structured the interactions and belonging of these white actors.

In particularly disturbing instances, the actual fetishization of nonwhites as cultural objects for consumption by whites was illuminated. After I arrived at NEA headquarters for a meeting, I learned the meeting had been cancelled. Another NEA member named Joey—a thirty-six-year-old retail salesperson with three years' experience in NEA—also showed up for the cancelled meeting. Joey and I had a tense relationship throughout my study; he often expressed that I was a "race traitor." He thought that I had consciously turned my back on white nationalism and thus "the good of the white race." Hence, I was shocked when he invited me back to his place both to watch a basketball game and to interview him so I would "get white nationalism right." When we arrived at his place, Joey asked me to make myself at home as he turned on the television and left the room. As the picture from the TV came into view, I saw the title screen for a pornographic DVD that featured women of color. When Joey came back into the room, he blushed and said in a joking manner, "Is this one thing we can agree on?" Telling him I wanted to discuss not only his choice of pornographic material but also race relations and his membership in NEA, he agreed that I could record the conversation. "So . . . why do you watch this kind of porn exactly? I mean, why black and Latino women?" I asked. Joey responded:

I mean . . . yeah . . . I tried white porn for a while, but I just didn't get as much out of it. . . . Man, those black girls do some crazy stuff, they are so much more free and expressive. You think I'm crazy? Ask, uh . . . Nick and Erik [fellow NEA members], those guys love this stuff. We used to get together and watch it more often, but you know, it's the school year, and they're busy. But yeah, I like it because, [long pause] this is awkward, you know, talking about this. But I mean, yeah, they are just more sexy and voluptuous.

MWH: So, that's the kind of woman you are looking to settle down with one day?

Joey: Oh, hell no! I would only marry a white girl. . . . But I can take some tricks from watching that will sure liven up my ordinary sex life and whatever normal white girl I settle down with.

I never discovered other instances of explicitly pornographic material among the other overwhelmingly male NEA or WRJ members. However, I did witness a collectively shared "taste" for women of color as a way of improving the normality of white sexuality. As one WRJ member named Michael told me, "Black women have a way about them that is simply sexual. White women have been socialized to be prudes. That's continued because there is too much guilt associated with sexual expression. White civilization has been too up-tight; it has restricted sexuality. Black girls don't have that problem."

Both "racist" and "antiracist" whites equate blacks and Latinos with hypersexuality. The synthesis of sexist and racist narratives has deep histori-cal roots in our social structures but was also reproduced on the microlevel via both groups' desires and tastes. The approach of racial practice illuminates the simultaneous presence, and reinforcement, of power and structure along with culture and context. Both white identity projects of NEA (whose mem-bers explicitly advocated racial and sexual purity and interracial distance), as well as WRJ (whose members argued that interracial marriage and increased interracial contact is good and necessary), were reproducing white identity vis-à-vis sexuality as dull, boring and ordinary. To unabashedly draw from Marvin Gaye, the fetish of black and brown otherness is a kind of "sexual healing" for whites. Once nonwhites are transformed into a sexualized com-modity, their consumption is normalized and takes place as a seemingly harmless and even natural (and personal) disposition among varied whites.

Material Culture

The third dimension is framed by the objects and items symbolically coded as nonwhite that can be possessed, owned, and consumed by whites as a way of eliminating white debt. This is akin to the "crumbs" of reified and essential-ized nonwhite authenticity. Authenticity, as Walter Benjamin claims, requires "uniqueness."[35] That is, the authenticity of any given thing, that which distin-guishes it from anything else, needs a "distance" in a particular time, place, and history. The segregated space of NEA and WRJ that required "authentic others" to alleviate white debt and constructed nonwhite forms as bona fide, unique, and imbued with a special and essential power.

The dominant relational construction of whiteness as inauthentic and nonwhiteness as "primordially authentic" dictates much of the value of ob-jectified color capital.[36] Its value can be measured insofar as whites have a contextual ability to accumulate color capital and spend it within this social dimension to become "knowledgeable and worldly" people. One conversation with several WRJ members illuminates this dynamic:

> MWH: Since your organization is entirely white, do you ever feel like you are missing anything because of the decision to organize in this way?

Blake: That's funny. I mean, no offense, but we know a lot about things other than ourselves. That is part of the point of what we are doing. We are trying to re-create our whiteness, some even say "abolish it," don't they?

MWH: Yes, some do.

Blake: Yeah, thought so. So we are abolishing it through knowledge of black, brown, red, whatever cultures. That's the power of diversity; it remakes you less white and more human.

Bret: Very true. For me, I remember reading the *Autobiography of Malcolm X* and something about a white girl coming up to him asking what she could do to help black people and he replied that she should "go work with other whites," or when Huey Newton told whites to form their own White Panther Party—I feel like that is what we are doing. Maybe it's not as radical, but look, like he said [pointing at Blake], knowledge of difference is something I use . . .

Sean [interrupting]: That's the point right there, how many other whites even have read [*The Autobiography of*] *Malcolm X* or know who [Huey P.] Newton was? We are better people because we know about this stuff. You don't buy it from the mainstream, but I sure do spend it there.

MWH: What do you mean?

Sean: I mean, you can't get this knowledge of diversity through just going through the motions in an artificial way, you have to get, well, authentic things from people of color that really oppose racism. That stuff is not commodifiable; it's above that. It's real.

Samuel: I came to this organization because, I mean, I don't know if you feel this way, but I often wanted to be less white, like it's empty or has a hole in it or something . . . I mean, being in WRJ brings me in contact with lots of history about African Americans, music, styles, . . . I learned about César Chávez in our ed [educational] session a few weeks ago. And now I get to use that information, it's a part of me . . . The more I learn about blacks and Latinos, the more complete I feel . . . I know it sounds crazy, but no one can say I'm racist or boring.

For members of WRJ, the objects, styles, and knowledge symbolically coded as nonwhite were a common fixture in weekly "ed sessions." Often those discussions featured topics such as the difference in racial hair textures and the "process" by which black hair is made straight, why "black people wear baggy clothes," or how the hip-hop genre could be used as a window into the "soul" of black people. Likewise, for members of NEA, there was a subsequent push to learn about nonwhite history, styles, and political attitudes so that members could evade any claims that they were, as one member put it, "racially myopic" or put in a position in which their white nationalist beliefs could be blamed for an ignorance of, and hostility toward, nonwhites. Whites in NEA often spoke of their affection for, and knowledge of, nonwhite cultural products. I wrote the following in my field notes from one day at the NEA office:

> Sitting at main office table are [Derek, Ronald, and Samuel] discussing what's "good" about African American "culture." Ronald said jazz, food, and some art (paintings and sculpture) are beautiful. [Derek] said a Harlem Renaissance class he took in college—learned that black people are smart, but felt the class was propaganda/biased. [Samuel] agrees—states that he loves blaxploitation films because they are funny. [Ronald] comments on skill of Miles Davis, Charlie Parker, other black jazz musicians. They begin all speaking about knowledge of black athletes (esp. basketball, football stars). [Samuel] says he loves talking with black people at bars about these topics because it shows he doesn't think all black people are bad. He comments that he loves doing this in mixed racial crowds and then getting the white people alone later to talk about NEA. He states: "They can't understand us as racist then."

The supposed affection and even reverence for items coded "black" among white supremacists is a paradox of modern race relations. Such findings illuminate that varied, diverse, and even progressive behaviors among whites must be analyzed within the context of their meaning and the cultural logic of the group in which such discursive strategies are enacted. As Paul, a five-year member of NEA, told me in an interview:

> I admire black people. I do. It's not like we're hate-mongers. They have a style and substance to them that is admirable . . . We can learn from black power, black pride, whatever. When they say that "black is beautiful," well, "white is beautiful" too. We have to take this strategy . . . Well, that's not it . . . It's not like this is a strategy, it's their natural style and flair.
>
> MWH: What do you mean exactly? Can you give me some examples?
>
> Paul: Yeah, okay, look at the, uh, okay, the black power movement and how that was transferred over to actual items like black leather jackets, afro combs, berets, and other things that became romantic icons for their agenda. We don't have that. People think whites are boring. [laughing] I mean, some-

times we're pretty plain. But when blacks talk and organize, they do it with a charismatic flair that is natural to them . . . Anyway, we have to take this kind of natural style or flair or whatever and fill in the gaps in how we organize and speak about white nationalism. Don't get me wrong, I don't mean like, you know, pollute things, but . . . take what works and fill in the holes.

Whites in both WRJ and NEA understood that the co-optation of objectified color capital could afford them distinct advantages in their own personal lives and racial identity as well as for the strategic goals of their antiracist or nationalist agenda.

Institutional Credential

The fourth aspect of the economy of racial meaning is ordered by formal records and/or qualifications that are sanctioned by a particular organization, association, and/or institution. Several members of the antiracist WRJ organization possessed associate or bachelor's degrees in social scientific or humanities disciplines in which they studied race relations or some particular aspect of ethnic studies. The holders of these degrees were often praised for their expertise and knowledge of otherness that symbolically distanced them from the empty form of whiteness. Moreover, I was surprised to find that two NEA members attended classes at Howard University (a premier historically black university). Their attendance served to credential their activism and their racial identity. As George, a thirty-eight-year-old accountant and two-year member of NEA, told me, "I learned a lot about black history there [Howard University]. I got an insider view, if you will, of things. It's effective here . . . lot of folks see me as an expert on race relations now, simply because I went to Howard." I replied, "So you'd say you got a good education there?" "I didn't go to get an education, I had that already," George said.

Official academic credentials were not the only forms of color capital in circulation in this dimension. Both groups offered training courses and certificates in various aspects of racial consciousness and awareness, black history, and race relations for anyone willing to devote the time to take the course. Those members who completed these courses were often afforded a higher level of status because of their credential—understood by others as an important element in white racial activism. Such "official" knowledge of black history and race relations was frequently used to "fill in" a perceived emptiness of whiteness.

During one discussion of an upcoming public event organized around the celebration of "diversity" and "multiculturalism," at which WRJ was planning to display an information table, I observed the following dialogue:

Wayne: All right, it's getting late . . . it's not like we have no clue as to how to organize this—talk to Andre, he wrote a paper on the Klan when he was in school.

Mark [interrupting]: Very true, didn't Blake write some paper last year on white supremacy and . . .

Christina [interrupting]: He has a degree in psychology, studied racism mainly, I think, no, wait, it was a thesis on multiculturalism.

Michael: Simon majored in English. I think he wrote something about colonialism or something.

Mark: No, that's not quite it, it's not about black or Latino oppression. He might know . . .

Wayne [interrupting]: All right, we need to make sure Blake and Simon are at the event, agreed? [members nodded in affirmation]. I think they're examples of what we are talking about, you know, that it's important to learn and dedicate yourself to the struggle. . . . Ah, we can present them as "panel experts."

Colin: Oh! Ask them to bring their diplomas, and we can set them on the table. . . . We always get criticism as being hippies or what not, that should, you know, throw them off . . .

Mark: That could come off a little pretentious, but it would buy us some legitimacy.

As the members continued to discuss what members possessed the "right" forms of color capital to credential the group as authentically "antiracist," Mark turned to me and in a whispered tone asked, "Didn't you write your thesis on the Black Panther Party?" "Yes, I did," I replied in an equally hushed tone. "Well," he continued, "they should be asking you what to do. You're like the least white person in here." Overhearing Mark's comment, Christina giggled and said, "Yeah, so true."

I include this reflexive moment of research in which my color capital was brought into the economy of racial meaning at WRJ; my possession of that credential temporarily alleviated my white debt. On this level, the exchange of color capital often structured WRJ activities and assisted in members' active meaning making as to what members qualified for which specific jobs.

Within the scope of an activity dedicated to the valorization of multicultural-ism—in which they felt their commitment to a politically just and efficacious antiracist position was in jeopardy—color capital became a valued resource toward organizing the event and validating their identities as authentically belonging.

A similar dynamic exists among NEA members. As Steven, a twenty-eight-year-old banker with four years in NEA, explained:

> It's not like we think we need anything, but, at the same time, people need tangible things . . . [long pause] That's very real to people. I myself, I mean, I went through our courses, went to the sessions like "The African Mind" at the conferences and what not. I was lacking crucial information on others that someone in my position needs to be able to defend his position. White identity politics are a tricky matter . . . I guess you could say my presentation of whiteness was lacking. . . . Going through the courses gives me credential that I can sell.

These interactions and discourse demonstrate that credentials are not simply static objects with fixed meanings but are symbols that hold changing sig-nificance in their moments of usage. The shared economy of racial meaning is dynamic and shifting. Unlike a dollar or an identification card in one's pocket that is relied on (because of its structured and stable value) to have a spe-cific worth, purchasing power, and effect on its presentation to another, these white actors had to make a case (in the lived moment of social interaction through that actor's performance) that one's particular institutionalized color capital has a value and significance that alleviates white debt.

Magnified Moments of My Misconceptions

To illustrate how the exchange of color capital is a cultural process that resists capture as either static commodity or intentional process, I offer the following "magnified moments."[37] These interactions highlight several instances when I attempted to exchange color capital for status and credential but found my sup-posed commodity "null and void" (further increasing my white debt in the eyes of others). The exchange of color capital is not automatic or consciously rational. Possession and exchange of color capital operates according to an implicit and sincere logic—a practical sense of dispositions and one's social location.[38]

As I became immersed in the ethnographic location of both sites, I tried to closely imitate observed behaviors to see whether I would be received in the same manner. For example, during the month of February (black history month), NEA members actively expressed how their knowledge of black history and culture was more extensive than that of the "average African American." After I noticed NEA members Chris and George engaging in an informal game of one-upmanship regarding their knowledge of black civil rights leaders, I joined in their conversation. Based on their competitive display of color capital, I attempted to "compete" with them. After a few minutes of engaging in this conversation Chris suddenly gave a deep sigh, placed his hand on my shoulder, and told me, "You should really get to know more about your European roots. You are too wrapped up in black culture . . . 'Gothi Seauton.' You know what that means? 'Know Thyself.'" To Chris, it was not that I possessed too much color capital but rather that I was too far removed from my whiteness, and because I did not "know myself" I was understood as inauthentic and even further in white debt.

My attempt to "exchange" some of my supposed color capital with WRJ members resulted in my chastisement for reproducing what members were "trying to fight against." I observed WRJ members talk about the decorations in their homes as more than aesthetic choices and as political decisions that advertised their antiracist position. One member spoke of the Malcolm X posters in his living room as "intentionally placed to make guests feel a little uncomfortable," while another WRJ member spoke of a small library of books on African colonialism that his family kept next to their living room couch. After watching these interactions, I tried to imitate this use of color capital. At one WRJ meeting I told members that I had recently purchased a copy of Frederick Douglass's book *My Bondage and My Freedom*. I told them I was going to display the book on my coffee table so that "people would know my political position; know I'm not a racist." WRJ members were quick to rebuff me:

> James: Uh, that's great . . . you should really think about why you're doing that. Books like that are not so that you can feel better about yourself or prove to someone that you're better than him. I mean, as whites we are all racist to a certain degree; so, I mean, take what I'm saying with a grain of salt, but that is part of the problem, it's . . .
>
> Philip [interrupting]: Read Douglass to make yourself a better person, not to artificially prove something to someone; I mean, it's a little disrespectful to use a book like that, the memory of Douglass, so that you as a white person can feel better . . .

James: It's against the point, don't objectify it . . . I know you're looking for
something . . . You're needing something you lack.

Mark: Don't reproduce the stuff we're trying to fight against, okay? Do you
get it?

In *Real Black*, anthropologist John Jackson Jr. makes a distinction between racial *authenticity* and racial *sincerity*.[39] Whereas discussions of racial
authenticity presuppose a kind of hierarchical relationship between "subjects
(who authenticate) and objects (dumb, mute, and inorganic) that are interpreted and analyzed from the outside," racial sincerity "presumes a liaison
between subjects—not some external adjudicator and lifeless scroll."[40] That
is, simply examining the construction of nonwhite culture as somehow primordially authentic may gloss over how white subjects cooperate to perform
a sincere self to both themselves and others. It was not enough to imitate the
patterns I observed. As evidenced by these previously mentioned failures,
I ossified complex and subtle racial dynamics into a reductionist subject–
object economic transaction (of debt and capital, respectively). I lost touch
with the nuanced and finely tuned intrawhite dynamics in which constructions of white debt and color capital circulated. My supposed capital proved
unfungible in that moment of interaction, not because my knowledge of black
history or Douglass's text were incapable of conversion into racial commodities but because my performance was received as trite, forced, and insincere.
The reader should take note, then, that my delineation of white debt and color
capital is merely a heuristic tool that opens a window to the world of modern
racial appropriation across the white political spectrum. One should take care
not to reduce social processes into an a priori script that floats above the heads
and real-life concerns of the actors involved.

Hegemonic Whiteness: White Appropriation

The cultural contradictions embedded in the contemporary meanings of
whiteness enable diverse strategies of action—whether apolitical, nationalist,
or antiracist in orientation. And while these strategies manifest in sundry ideological goals, they remain intertwined with rather robust logics that reaffirm
and rationalize white dominance, normativity, and agency.[41] NEA understood racial differences as biologically determined and interpreted nonwhite
styles as the natural outgrowth of nonwhite carnality, eroticism, and physical
prowess; WRJ comprehended racial differences as the product of cultural and

historical forces and construed nonwhite performances as potent styles full of life, virility, and spice. In both scenarios, the symbolic order of dominant racial meanings was reproduced. Among NEA members, tales of nonwhite virility were accompanied with nostalgic narratives of whites' prior control of such skills coupled with accusations of their unfair theft. Such a tale helps to rationalize white control over interracial relationships and further entrenches the association of nonwhites with criminality, immorality, and lack of intellectual acumen. Among WRJ members, the expectations that people of color are more culturally attuned to music, food, dance, and racial authenticity encouraged whites to approach interracial relationships as appropriators and exploiters. It is perhaps this rather robust and structured pattern that led Frantz Fanon to write, "To us, the man who adores the Negro is as 'sick' as the man who abominates him."[42] Fanon's words drive home the point that, regardless of the best or worst of intentions, the objectification of people of color as objects to be owned and/or controlled by white desire is a "sickness"—a form of racism embedded in white supremacist desires for contact with, and control over, dark "others."

Still, some might argue that there is great difference between the white racist consumption of minstrel shows in the nineteenth century and modern white fascinations with Native American jewelry or black jazz, for example. That difference is not one I wish to dispute. My attention is not focused on the essential meanings of the objects or practices in question (a fruitless strategy, anyway, given the social construction of meaning), but on the structured patterns of white racial meaning making that generate feelings of white debt and desire for color capital. In a white-dominated culture and society structured by the intertwined logics of Anglo conformity qua color-blindness and pluralism qua multiculturalism, the interplay of white debt and color capital can mean different things depending on the contexts in which they are enacted. Both a white nationalist and a white antiracist usage of color capital earns status—and temporarily alleviates feelings of white debt—whereas when people of color wield their capital they are not afforded status but are objectified. Hence, ideals about love, sexuality, knowledge, aestheticism, and power are racialized; they are embedded in racialized assumptions that allow for white appropriation and usage while demonizing or romanticizing their association with people of color. Such a multileveled dynamic demonstrates the ways in which white racial identity is simultaneously constrained and enabled by the cultural understandings of racial authenticity and sincerity.

These conventions guide the pursuit of another idealized dimension of whiteness: white appropriation. The ideal performances of whiteness were marked by the realization of cultural blandness or emptiness (white debt) and the controlled and rational pursuit of color capital to temporarily alleviate those feelings. As the contemporary manifestation of white supremacy shuns any overt or explicit desire for racial domination and control, a potent nonwhite "other" is required for the production of a fully human white self. Members constructed a nonwhite identity full of virility and spice that could be admired, imitated, and appropriated as a simulacrum of their own fantasy. In that sense, the more white racial actors—whether members of WRJ or NEA—appropriated and controlled aspects of nonwhite culture, the more well-rounded, cosmopolitan, and completely human they became in the eyes of others with whom they interacted. Such an ideal is not easily pursued. This dimension of the hegemonic ideal exists in a tenuous space in between *mimicry* and *mockery*. While this dimension of hegemonic whiteness depends on the imitation of nonwhite cultures thought authentic and virile, such practices of appropriation can easily slip into a kind of mockery in which the white user is understood as fake, trying too hard, or socially inappropriate, if not blatantly racist.[43] If examined in this light, the genocide of Native Americans alongside the white attraction toward "dream-catchers" or silver and turquoise jewelry is not an atypical paradox or blip on the radar screen of an otherwise harmonious U.S. culture but reveals how the simultaneous love of racialized material objects and killing of their racialized human subject-creators is a strange sort of racial necrophilia.[44]

8 Hailing Whiteness

If I don't understand it, what use is it? . . . People can do what they want to, but what good is rap music if I can't relate?
—**Adam, National Equality for All**

I'd be lying if I told you I never get upset when black people say "It's a black thing, you wouldn't understand." . . . I get it, but I should understand, I really should, you know? . . . If I don't, how are we doing to get anywhere?
—**Michael, Whites for Racial Justice**

"Hey, You There!" Hailing an Omnipotent White Subject

On a warm summer afternoon in Fairview, I sat in the passenger's seat at a red light with Jerry, a thirty-eight-year-old music teacher and seven-year member of Whites for Racial Justice. Because his air conditioning was broken and we were sitting in direct sunlight, I rolled down my window to seek relief. "Sorry," he said. "I keep meaning to get the AC fixed." As we were waiting for the light to change, a black SUV pulled up beside us, sitting on spinning rims so large they resembled chromed Ferris wheels and playing music at a volume that shook the car with the bassline. Jerry made a noticeably deep sigh and rolled his eyes. As the light turned green we took off like a rocket, leaving the mobile boom box behind. After a few moments Jerry said, "I can't stand rap music. I never understand all of the words. When I do, they're about killing, and drugs, or women, you know? Or at least about something kind of silly and irrelevant." Knowing Jerry harbored an admiration for Bob Dylan, I said, "Well, some folks have said the same about Dylan, you know? That his lyrics were about drugs or about 'silly and irrelevant' things, too." "That's entirely different!" he exclaimed. "At least Dylan is, you know, pertinent and, and, what I like. [long pause] Rap music is just, it's just noise. It doesn't speak to me." Seeing that Jerry was quite adamant about this distinction, I attempted to defuse the situation: "Well, to each his own," I said. His reply surprised me. "No! It's more than a matter of choice. Rap doesn't offer much, socially, that is. It's just like, entertainment. Smoke and mirrors. It's like, I mean, look, if blacks want to be respected in their art, then they should go back to jazz and blues. Rap's a bunch of noise."

Given Jerry's profession as music teacher, one might dismiss his comments as either individualistic taste or the result of his specialized musical acumen and training. However, Jerry's critique of rap lyrics was not merely the reflection of individual aesthetic judgment or educational preparation; rather it illuminated the pursuit of a white racial ideal shared among and across WRJ and NEA members.

In this chapter I discuss the processes by which WRJ and NEA members have come to feel either entitled to, or dismissive of, racialized knowledge—such as the meanings and significance of rap lyrics (coded "black" in Jerry's mind). I argue that whites' feelings of entitlement and trivialization are not racially neutral judgments and interpretations but help constitute white racial identities. NEA and WRJ members pursue the same white racial ideal that invariably relies on either entitlement to, or trivialization of, knowledge deemed racially important and significant. In our contemporary moment replete with contradictory messages about race, racism, and equality, whites' desire to know, understand, and control the racialized knowledge around them together exists as a social imperative. Especially for whites who deem themselves knowledgeable and conscious "antiracists" or "nationalists," making "truth claims" about race is an all-important endeavor.[1]

NEA and WRJ members alike often expressed negative emotions ranging from slight disgust to overt hostility when they interpreted themselves excluded or marginalized from understanding the dynamics, purpose, and/or nature of racialized knowledge. As they were self-proclaimed "experts" on race relations and had dedicated their lives to racial activism, such feelings are somewhat understandable. After all, how many among us would be upset if we were denied access to, could not understand, or were unable to possess, some aspect of life thought crucial to our careers, family, or personal life? What makes this observation revealing about the dynamics of white identity formation is that both groups did not just illustrate an interest in understanding topics surrounding race but also displayed entitlement to full understanding and control of the knowledge in question. When disallowed this prerogative, members reacted in harsh and vehement ways, often attacking the perceived source of the disallowance or trivializing the knowledge as unimportant.

The concept of "interpellation" helps us understand this conflict.[2] Interpellation is the process by which a society's dominant narratives and practices address or gain the attention of an individual. In recognizing the dominance of a particular story or practice, and adjusting one's speech and actions accordingly, we are then produced as a particular type of individual subject to that ideological formation or expected performance. Louis Althusser explains interpellation with a metaphor:

> There are individuals walking along. Somewhere (usually behind them) the hail rings out: "Hey, you there!" One individual (nine times out of ten it is the right one) turns round, believing/suspecting/knowing that it is for him, i.e. recognizing that "it really is he" who is meant by the hailing. But in reality these things happen without any succession. The existence of ideology and the hailing or interpellation of individuals as subjects are one and the same thing.[3]

This dynamic relates to the racial identity formation of WRJ and NEA members. These members anticipated being hailed by the racialized knowledge they encountered in everyday life. Members expected to be hailed as all-knowing subjects of racial information. When members were hailed by racial knowledge they did not understand or practices with which they were not accustomed, they framed the hailing as irrelevant to them and/or temporarily occupied a deficient or subordinated form of whiteness. Such a disconnect required substantial racial identity work and repair—NEA and WRJ members either lashed out at those preventing their access to knowledge or they framed the racial knowledge in question as trivial.

The processes of becoming a hailed subject and already being a subject are intertwined and continually ongoing. We are "always-already" hailed by racial narratives and knowledge. NEA and WRJ members had to continually rebecome the white racial subjects that they already were. Because they were preconceived as knowing, entitled, and authoritative subjects, their hailing reproduced their identity as such. And as active agents in this process, they labored to reproduce the conditions that hailed them because they were expected and normative. Hence, the ideal or hegemonic white subject is always-already in formation by way of intraracial distinctions against whites who do not possess access to, and control over, racialized knowledge.

Rap Attack

The example of Jerry's distaste for rap lyrics presented in this chapter's opener exemplifies much of today's apprehension and fascination with rap. From Ice-T's 1992 song "Cop Killer," which brought condemnations from then-President George H. W. Bush, then-Vice President Dan Quayle, and Tipper

Gore and the 2002 controversy in which political commentator Bill O'Reilly called for people to boycott Pepsi products due to the company's sponsorship of the rapper Ludacris to the 2008 storm over the Nas's tentative album title "Nigger"—decried by both the political left and right. For many white Americans, rap music is a potent cultural force. Yet its meanings are anything but one sided. For some, rap represents all that is wrong with a nation in the midst of civic and moral decay. For example, best-selling conservative author Bernard Goldberg decried rap music as little more than "cultural pollution."[4] For others, rap music holds appeal for its exposure of a subculture immersed in poverty, racism, and violence. Chuck D (front man for the rap group Public Enemy) said that rap music is "the CNN of the street."[5] These disparate voices share an astonishing premise: Nearly every time a rap album hits the marketplace, the future of American civilization seems to hang in the balance. I offer a different analysis. The interpretation of rap music may not actually illuminate the nation's future prospects; rather, how whites encounter racialized knowledge and culture (like rap music) may shed light on the meanings and reproduction of white racial identity.

At the conclusion of a particularly long WRJ meeting, Malcolm seemed to notice a general malaise among the members in attendance. It was early March, and WRJ was recovering from black history month (February). February was one of the WRJ's busiest times due to frequent programming, guest lectures, and speaking engagements. Trying to energize the group for the next week's meeting, Malcolm asked his fellow antiracists to consider the ways popular culture demonizes black people. Following an exercise from an antiracist education textbook on the ways to better understand "institutional racism," Malcolm told members to take time before the next meeting to bring in some object commonly associated with blacks. He told members to bring in an object that they think is "commonly used to label blacks as stupid, deviant, or inferior." After he completed reading the assignment, one member asked for an example. Malcolm replied:

> Okay, well, like maybe, I mean, I was going to bring in a pair of baggy jeans, because they are often, you know, associated with young, uneducated, black men. . . . I've been hearing the news reports about how schools are starting dress codes to ban clothes like that because they think it's gang related, but, I mean, I see a lot of the white kids around here dress like that. I don't think that the [local] school district is going to start banning baggy jeans, so [laughing],

I think that is a good example of how some rather mundane aspect of popular culture becomes used by an institution to discriminate against blacks.

As the next WRJ meeting approached, I wondered about the objects that members would bring. As the time of the next meeting arrived, members seemed excited to talk about their "homework." I rarely saw such animation from members. Such energy seemed related to the assignment, which focused much of their regular abstract discussions and storytelling emphasis on a physical object.

After discussions of a rap music CD, a pair of baggy jeans, a baseball cap, and a dictionary (to emphasize the distinction between "Ebonics" and "standard white English"), I noticed that Colin was without an item. When it came time for him to speak, he told the group that he had reservations with the assignment. Asking me to turn off my audio recorder while he spoke, he said that he felt disconnected from the experience. In referencing a rap album that another member brought, Colin stated that he "didn't understand half of the lyrics" and that even among the ones he did, he didn't "see the point." While he made sure to emphasize that he understood the reason behind WRJ's exercise—to understand how mundane objects can be used against nonwhites— he also made clear his point: Blacks were unintentionally facilitating their own social marginalization. Again returning to the rap album as an example, he stated, "Whites wouldn't be so scared of rap if it was about something they could relate to."

Many members shook their heads in agreement. One by one, and akin to a slow confrontation with Malcolm (as facilitator of the exercise), members expressed how frustrated they were with trying to "understand" nonwhite (especially "black") culture. After being allowed to turn on my audio recorder, I captured the following exchange:

> Blake: No, no, no, I totally disagree with what you're saying. There is just something's that are just . . . closed off to understanding among some whites. . . . whether we're talking about those songs or how they dress or whatever. . . . [taking a long pause] I'm all for diverse expressions, I did lots of crazy things when I was younger, but blacks are not making it any easier for us to understand their plight, you know. If they want to make songs about the ghetto or whatever, they have to be understandable. Colin's right, if they want us to unify, then make it just a little easier to understand what they are talking about.

Duncan: Yeah, but I mean, it shouldn't be about them, I don't know, just something else, so it's easier . . . so it's easier for us to just get it.

Colin: I'm not saying that. I'm saying that it's got to be a bit more cooperative and less angry sometimes. Rap music is angry, and it scares whites, and, I mean, that's good for lots of them, but for us, I mean, what's the point? How is rap music going to help me be a better white person or help get rid of racism [said with sarcastic chuckle]?

Blake: No, no, I get what you're saying. That makes sense.

. . .

Duncan: I just don't understand what the point of those lyrics are. What good do they do?

When cultural objects coded nonwhite (especially black or Latino) function as autonomous, self-supportive, and unrelated to a seemingly white world, some may decode them as an alienating force and substance. Despite the antiracist motivations of WRJ, the members' dialog reveals a specter of (post)colonial attitudes toward blackness. When the rap album (coded as black) refused to interface with the members of WRJ (through either seemingly unintelligible lyrics or subject matter deemed inconsequential or irrelevant), it was subjectively felt as an aggressive form of alienation. When cultural objects and practices do not hail (interpellate) the white actor as an omniscient subject, a sense of frustration often builds. Many WRJ members questioned why the object in question did not adhere to the common (read: white) ways of communicating or understanding. Accordingly, many took direct offense that a marginalized people qua object would choose alternative ways of communicating. Given this background, I argue that one can be offended only if one expects (or feels entitled) to be hailed as the "always-already" all-knowing subject of the discourse at hand.

Among some members of National Equality for All, I noticed a similar desire to be hailed as an all-knowing white subject. One day in The Office, members somehow stumbled onto the topic of rap music, which, according to their offhand comments, was created entirely by black male artists. Some made statements that they enjoyed some rap music (see Chapter 7 on "color capital"), but many expressed hostility and frustration that they did not see much of the point of rap music specifically or in hip-hop generally. From my field notes I recorded the following: "Nick and Mason discussing rap music and hip-hop. Feel most nonsense. Frustrated at not understand point/ purpose. Mason mad when doesn't understand rap."

Later that day I had a chance to interview Mark, a thirty-three-year-old NEA member. I asked him about his earlier statements on rap, to which he responded:

> Well, I mean, I listen to some rap, I like it if it's got a good beat. I mean, a lot of others don't, but I like some of it, and I mean, like I was saying, I mean, it's okay, but some of it is just angry or even, I mean, just way out there. So I don't even understand half of it, or even when I do I have no idea what they are talking about. Honestly, I don't know how half of the stuff sells, I mean it must because they keep on making it.
>
> MWH: So, you seem a little upset when you don't understand it?
>
> Mark: No, not upset, I mean, it's frustrating not understanding what half of it is talking about. . . . I guess in the end, some of it [rap] is okay, but if I can't understand it, and I'm a smart guy, it's really a waste of space. . . . I guess I don't like it if it is too angry, either.

Mark's comments demonstrate how those aspects of rap deemed incomprehensible are framed as a "waste of space" for not only himself but for others. As such a genre does not hail some white subjects in terms with which they are comfortable (as controllers of racial knowledge), the genre itself is framed as unnecessary and/or hostile.

For some, rap hails a subject position foreign to some whites. That is, WRJ and NEA's minute attraction to rap seems generated by its difference rather than its content. By standing as a reflection of qualities thought exotic and carnal, rap holds value. But when members try to interface with it as more than a symbol of potent "otherness," their inability or unwillingness to understand its nuance enables a kind of racial frustration. Rap becomes not a heterogeneous art form but a white racial pariah that is significantly out of place and thus trivialized.

Stepping into Whiteness

There were many indications of white entitlement and nonwhite trivialization that I observed throughout my study of NEA and WRJ. To demonstrate how these social relations manifest in everyday interactions and were altered by my presence as an ethnographer in the field, in the following paragraphs

I detail how my own identity and knowledge became a source of potential interpellation and trivialization.

Weeks before WRJ members were tasked with bringing in an object to explain its racial significance, the group met to discuss an upcoming black fraternity and sorority (or Black Greek Letter Organization ["BGLO"]) step-show. Many months prior, the step-show had been organized by a local chapter of the National Association for the Advancement of Colored People (NAACP). Along the way, the NAACP approached WRJ about cosponsoring the event—evidently in the hopes of expanding the advertising and audience demographic at the show. The two organizations worked together to publicize the event at which not only would step-show entertainment be provided but several college scholarships would also be awarded to deserving local high school seniors in predominately black high schools. While WRJ members knew full well that the NAACP, the event, and the scholarships were a big deal known by many, few members were familiar with tradition of BGLO stepping. As they discussed the topic, it was clear they knew little to nothing about either the black fraternal tradition in the United States or their trademark step-shows. After a few minutes, I interjected that I had some knowledge of BGLOs and the tradition of stepping because I was a member of a BGLO and participated in competitive step-shows during my undergraduate years.[6]

On my disclosing this information, WRJ members became very excited. I was immediately seen as an example of what white antiracism could accomplish—a white male allowed membership into the rather closed and secret brotherhood of a black fraternity. To these members, I hadn't just crossed the color line, I had smashed it. "Oh my gosh!" said Cassandra. "Was it like in *Revenge of the Nerds*? Did you and a bunch of white guys join a black fraternity?" "No, it wasn't like that," I replied. "I was the only white guy on my line, or uh, pledge class. But my chapter has had a few white guys pledge over the years." "How, I mean, why, I mean, so like, what made you want to become, I mean, did you always want to be, . . . sorry! Okay. So, why a black fraternity?" Andre asked in rapid-fire fashion. "Did you get hazed? I bet you got hazed," Wayne said bluntly.

I tried to answer everyone's questions, one by one, as they were raised. I addressed the history of racial segregation in the Greek-letter system, differences in traditions and new membership intake procedures, questions over the controversies surrounding hazing and pledging, and finally stepping. "Yes, I competed as an undergrad. My chapter won several step-shows. We're all quite proud." Suddenly, Malcolm asked if I would teach everyone some of my fraternal steps, and everyone else started cheering me on to do so. I politely refused, citing the rationale that BGLOs are extremely particular about teaching steps to nonmembers. I continued by stating that many BGLOs have a feeling of possession over certain steps as they carry symbolic meanings that are representative of fraternal ideals and traditions.

I was not prepared for WRJ members' responses to my refusal. I was rebuked for being "close minded" and chided for not engaging in what was being considered my "duty" to teach them as I was allowed to attend WRJ meetings. Patrick stated:

> Are you being serious? You're really not going to teach us? That's a bit close minded. We're trying to learn about different cultures and experiences. . . . We have been letting you come here for quite some time. I'll be honest with you, Matthew, I'm a bit hurt and offended.

Cassandra told me, "I think that's unfair of you. We all come here out of duty to fight against prejudice. You have a duty, too, you know, not just to us, but to the cause."

At this point I felt as though I was experiencing a case of déjà vu. Approximately two years earlier an almost identical dynamic had occurred in a pilot study for this research.[7] In a study of a majority, but not exclusively, white antiracist organization I called "Reformed Relations," I was asked to teach them how to step, after which I replied that I did not feel comfortable doing so. I wrote about the subsequent interaction in which two white members confronted me about my choice not to teach them a step routine:

> Jane stated, "I can't believe you won't teach us . . . it's just stepping . . . that's kinda inappropriate don't you think? I mean, we're trying to learn more about different cultures . . . it's like a duty to teach others about things they don't know." In an attempt to defuse the situation, I responded that I would be more than happy to teach them whatever I knew *about* stepping, but not the act itself. I explained that if they learned specific fraternal steps, such an action could be perceived as a flagrant act of disrespect or even *theft* among my fraternity brothers and resultantly, would be counterproductive to the goals of their organization. To this Natalie replied, "See, that's part of the point, I know you are here to research race and whatever, but we can teach you some

things too. You're being *exclusionary* [my emphasis] . . . what's the harm in us just learning, especially if it's like learning a new dance step or whatever?"[8]

The similarities between "WRJ" and "Reformed Relations" gesture toward an important facet of white antiracist logic. Knowledge that is exclusive to nonwhite racial groups, whether grounded in specifics traditions of stepping or larger epistemological worldviews, is often framed as self-segregating and exclusionary. Many white members, by virtue of their membership and self-conception as "moral" and "antiracist," simply feel entitled. The sharing racialized knowledge is understood to break their own walls of exclusion. Conversely, harboring such knowledge is seen as an act of racism—an individual wrong choice that supports the racist order and hierarchy.

Such a dynamic is not simply a psychological one, as it is inextricably intertwined with the "ongoing accomplishment"[9] and "interpellation"[10] of white identity. Members of both WRJ and NEA expected to be hailed by whatever nonwhite cultural form, idea, or tradition they encountered. They desired unmediated knowledge of, and access to, that knowledge. A dimension of their white racial identity depended on such access. When culture coded as "black" functions in explicit and distinctive ways that exclude or marginalize white people—which does not have to be about antiracist or racist politics in distinct terms—the lack of the expected interpellation feels like belligerent alienation. As a result, some implicitly trivialize the knowledge or the person blocking their access. When WRJ members did not understand the import of stepping, they took it as a direct offense that there was an aspect of racial life to which they would not be privy. WRJ members were offended simply because they assumed their identity, or ontological presence, was a guarantee in and of itself as an all-knowing racial subject with unlimited access. When I stood in their way, I became "selfish" and "part of the problem."

While I doubt that the members of NEA would have expressed hostility if I had refused to teach them about the intricacies of BGLO stepping, they still expressed anger and frustration when not hailed as competent, knowledgeable, and controlling white subjects when it came to issues of nonwhite cultural production. At one of the first meetings I had with members of NEA, I was confronted about my status as a white male who was affiliated with, in the eyes of NEA, "troubling" things. It turns out that a quick Internet search of my name revealed my affiliation with the Association of Black Sociologists, my writings on the Black Panther Party, and my membership in Phi Beta Sigma fraternity.

In asking about my membership in Phi Beta Sigma, most members revealed that they were uninformed about the most basic of knowledge concerning the black fraternal tradition. As I answered some of their questions regarding various aspects of BGLO history and culture, they seemed interested but perplexed as to why I had joined. Explaining that my choice to join was largely personal and based on the political and ideological goals of the black fraternal system, NEA members questioned some of the secretive aspects of Greek-letter societies:

> David: So, what's with all the handshakes and passwords and secret meanings behind things?
>
> MWH: That's for the membership. Sometimes it's used as a way of identifying the validity of membership. Some of it is for other things that I just am not going to tell you.
>
> David: And why won't you tell us?
>
> MWH: Uh, well, really, it's none of your business. That information is for members.
>
> Albert: So how do we not know that you are secretly doing things, or, I mean, let me rephrase: How are we supposed to know whether black Greeks are a threat? . . . If they are so secretive about their membership, I mean, I don't think you are, but you could be a spy for them, especially if they are as politically active as you say.
>
> MWH: Well, I think you would run into this problem with any Greek organization, as they all have secrets. There are lots of organizations like this. Were any of you in fraternities in college?
>
> Charles: Yeah.
>
> Nick: I was.
>
> MWH: So, what is the difference exactly? I mean, anyone that doesn't agree with your mission could be a spy for a fraternity, although I highly doubt that such a thing is occurring.
>
> . . .
>
> Derek: If their history is true, that they came about because of white discrimination against blacks, . . . they should want to be more open and not

discriminate like they were treated, unless they have some political goal that needs to be kept secret.

Although the U.S. Greek system is veiled in some secrecy, as are various societies like the Masons, Elks, and Shriners, such secrets are not lumped on one side of the color line. The U.S. Greek system is immersed in exclusion and knowledge that often functions as a network system for employment and opportunities, a form of cronyism. To NEA's membership, however, the black fraternal system posed a threat as an autonomous system that is unconcerned with sharing its "secrets" with a largely white world.

In a follow-up conversation with David, I asked why such retention of knowledge by BGLOs would be so threatening:

> MWH: So, there's what I am trying to understand. The U.S. Greek system is still very segregated. I would think this would be perfectly fine with you and align with your goals, but you seemed upset by some of the things I said.
>
> David: Yeah, you're right. Some of things you said were upsetting, but not because of our separation. That is fine and going in the right direction. . . . I was upset that the information they have is not open.
>
> MWH: . . . So what about the secret information that white fraternities and sororities have that they are not going to share with you either?
>
> David: That's different. That's not a threat. We have to understand our threats. If it's not a threat, then they would have no problem including us.

As David explained, BGLOs were seen as more threatening because they controlled knowledge that was cordoned off from white mainstream understanding. Because NEA members were far from being interpellated as omnipotent subjects by the institution of black Greek life, the institution was deemed a menace to white authority.

Hegemonic Whiteness: All-Knowing Actors

Racialized expectations, feelings of entitlement, trivializing judgments, and their relationship to white racial identity are tricky things to uncover and connect. It's like trying to see the very lens through which we are supposed to look. Polished and cleaned to near invisibility, lenses instead provide a specific way of seeing. Feelings of racial entitlement and judgment are not directly observable. They hide in plain sight. Hence, for many whites who encounter rap music as either vague or nonsensical or see BGLOs as dangerously secretive and closed off, these judgments are understood as rational and nonideological "facts."

For WRJ and NEA members both, the process of white interpellation took place in varied, but coherent and predictable, forms. When not positioned, or called out to, as knowledgeable and authoritative white subjects, members expressed a great deal of displeasure with their particular situation. Such a dynamic reveals another dimension of hegemonic whiteness—idealized white racial identities are to be constantly hailed as nearly all-knowing subjects of racial knowledge. White members evoked a narrative and drew boundaries that reinforced their pursuit of this ideal. Rather than admit their lack of knowledge qua inferior white racial identity, mundane (yet racialized) aspects of social life that refuse to interface with NEA and WRJ members were trivialized.

Few members of either group, as actors whose racial identities are tied to being competent and expert activists on race relations, admitted or acquiesced to racial ignorance. When members did, they were perceived as amateurish or sophomoric in relation to the subject at hand. Personal rivalries, petty disagreements, and battles for organizational positions found expression in these intraracial demarcations. After NEA member David both admitted his ignorance concerning BGLOs and failed to convince me to open up about the secret intricacies of black Greek life, his fellow members chided him for weeks and began openly joking that he was a "nationalist-lite." Conversely, weeks after the WRJ discussion of rap music, Andre attempted to convince fellow members of the "artistic merit" of rap music during lunch. Compelled to pursue the white ideal, members could not discuss rap music as "artistic" and so proceeded to denigrate it and Andre for his stance. "Go ahead, Andre. Bust a rhyme at the next recruitment meeting. I bet people will think we're really *cool* [said with emphasis] white folks then," said Duncan.

In the case of both NEA and WRJ, racialized knowledge—especially concerning nonwhites—is presumed transparent and knowable to whites. If they don't understand it, then it isn't worth knowing because it isn't valid racial knowledge. In the aforementioned examples, rap became either too hostile or superficial, and the black fraternal tradition became too secretive and exclusive. Members' belief in an almost unbounded capacity to know ironically binds them to the pursuit of a particular kind of white racial identity. Interpellation works when people hear and recognize their categorical place in a social and cultural narrative. The continued implicit and "commonsense" correlation and conflation of whiteness with the normal, natural, and superior effectively interpellates, disciplines, and rewards white subjects who can successfully navigate the dialectical detour through either entitlement or trivialization: Whites are interpellated either as knowing subjects of the racial world or as designators of unknowable objects. A recognized social failure to occupy either position results in the reproduction of intraracial boundaries and narratives. Those whites viewed as ignorant of important racial phenomena or as hoodwinked by unimportant racial knowledge took on a "lesser-than" status in the context of the discussion. The process of interpellation was constant and always in process. White racial identity and the pursuit of a knowledgeable white subject position is an "always-already" accomplishment from one situation to the next.

9 Beyond Good and Evil

*We have our beliefs, and we stick to them. . . . I can't disregard
the love for my race any more than I could just stop being
white. It's natural. . . . Being around others in NEA affects how
I think about race and, I guess, like you have been asking, how
I see my race. There's an expectation there to defend your race,
and I'm glad that I have been taught it.*

—Mason, National Equality for All

*Yeah, I'm white, that's the reality of it. We try to fight the
system, . . . but at the end of the day, when I'm at the grocery
store or whatever, people see me as a white man. All that I do, it
feels, sometimes, like it's pointless. I couldn't ever, morally, give
up. . . . I'm trapped in my whiteness, and I know it affects what
I think and how I feel . . . It's who I am.*

—Bret, Whites for Racial Justice

IN 1886 FRIEDRICH NIETZSCHE PENNED ONE of his most prescient works, *Beyond
Good and Evil*. Early in the text he wrote, "It might even be possible that what
constitutes the value of those good and respected things, consists precisely
in their being insidiously related, knotted, and crocheted to these evil; and
apparently opposed things—perhaps even in being essentially identical with
them."[1] Nietzsche's prose admonishes us not to assume the stable existence of
moral dichotomies and bifurcated social worlds. Whereas two things might
appear as distinct polarities, their existence could be "essentially identical."

White nationalists and white antiracists certainly possess many divergent, if not antithetical, political attitudes. Yet they also remain bound to
similar understandings of racial categories that remain laced with racist,
reactionary, and essentialist schemas. NEA and WRJ members' words and
actions together provide fairly lucid displays of hegemonic whiteness even
if all their members do not do so easily or candidly. Often understood as
little more than "commonsense" interpretations of the world, these schemas
structure the pathways by which these antagonistic groups make meaning
of the racial order and where their white racial selves fit within it. Through
practices of inter- and intraracial "othering" to define and pursue different
situational dimensions of an ideal white self, these actors well demonstrate
how white nationalism and white antiracism may be "insidiously related,
knotted, and crocheted."

Blinded by the White?

Despite the empirical delineation of similarities in white racial meaning making, finding correspondence between the dominant bookends of contemporary white racial activism may prove an irritant. Some will resist this understanding because they believe race is "declining in significance." From this point of view, race is only a "confounding variable" that distracts from the very real dynamics of class inequality, resource-based analysis, or political antagonisms endemic to the latest battle waged within the culture war.

For others, race does matter. But speaking of white similarities across a racist and antiracist divide remains an untenable proposition. In this line of reasoning, whiteness is too heterogeneous and politically fractured a category to yield any type of meaningful social cohesion. Hence, many speak of *whitenesses*—emphasizing the plural over the singular. White racial identities are certainly and irreducibly diverse. While this emphasis might sensitize us to crosscutting differences and inequalities, it can obscure commonalities held across outwardly different white racial identities. This approach can too easily foster the reification of types of whiteness thought to occupy distinct positions along a stable political spectrum.

And, still, others will assert that I approach these two groups as if their differences matter for naught. It is certainly important that some whites choose an "antiracist" path whereas others take up a decidedly "white nationalist" position. Whiteness is no monolith. Many whites today stake their claim in decidedly different political agendas and work toward very different versions of tomorrow's world. As sociologist Howard Winant writes, "The contemporary crisis of whiteness—its dualistic allegiances to privilege and equality, to color consciousness and color-blindness, to formally equal justice and to substantive social justice—can be discerned in the contradictory character of white identity today."[2] And while this contradiction and supposed bifurcation grows between differently politicized white organizations, something else is afoot. Differently oriented whites—like those in NEA and WRJ—do not make their choices, interact, or build a sense of their racial selves within entirely different social worlds but within a larger space of interaction and common meanings. They share the world in which they fight. They are together influenced by the ideas, unequal resources, and patterns of interaction that historically benefit and privilege whiteness. They are neither victims of false consciousness nor do they possess a magic pill to take that would transport them outside of society, history, and ideology.[3]

Resistance to viewing white systemic advantages, routinized practices, and shared interests across supposedly divergent political orientations and contextual divides may also stem from the dominant racial problématique of our time: White racist and reactionary actions are often thought the result of cognitive prejudices, bad intentions, and attitudes based on ignorant and/ or irrational beliefs. Hence, the implementation of standard social scientific measures of racial prejudice—generally of the survey methodology ilk—yield a picture of white nationalist groups like NEA and white antiracist groups like WRJ as two opposed and antagonistic sets of people. And, in many ways, they are very different when it comes to overt racial attitudes and policy positions on racial "hot button" topics. However, my approach does not center on the analysis of white racial attitudes but examines how white racial identity is remade in the everyday interactions of these actors.

The individuals in this study hold an array of positions in society: from police officers, lawyers, graduate students, and plumbers to nurses, accountants, waiters, and bankers. Twenty-four (53 percent) identify as either democratic or independent in political leanings, twenty-three (51 percent) hold a bachelor's degree and twelve (27 percent) hold an advanced degree, and thirty-five (78 percent) are middle or upper class. My research disputes the convenient notion that white racial identities represent a fractured and heterogeneous collection in which only conservative, uneducated, and lower-class white men hold privileged positions underpinned by racist views. In the *Annual Review of Sociology*, Monica McDermott and Frank Samson wrote, "Navigating between the long-term staying power of white privilege and the multifarious manifestations of the experience of whiteness remains the task of the next era of research on white racial and ethnic identity."[4] In this vein, *White Bound* accounts for the structured linkage of white racial identity and racist worldviews across diverse, even antithetical, social locations.

Dimensions of Hegemonic Whiteness

In Chapter 1, I briefly reviewed the notion of hegemonic whiteness. I wrote that, in any given setting, an ideal of whiteness emerges alongside many other ways of "being white" that are complicit, subordinate, or marginalized in relation to that ideal. Among NEA and WRJ members both, this ideal grounds itself in the everyday reproduction of, and appeal to, both inter- *and* intraracial distinctions. In specific, hegemonic whiteness is formed through a process of marking the meanings of "whiteness" as (1) essentially different from and superior to those marked as "nonwhite" and (2) through marginalizing practices of "being white" that fail to exemplify those differences. Within the contexts of both NEA and WRJ, these distinctions rested on racist and reactionary understandings and assumptions of racial differences and characteristics. Together, they functioned as a kind of implicit ideal against which one's worth, behavior—and ultimately one's identity—were measured.[5] While very few whites may actually attain or measure up to the ideal white racial identity, those who hold a dominant status have greater ability to define the standards and distinctions. To successfully pursue this ideal, one must continually engage in inter- and intraracial boundary work in order to demarcate both nonwhite "others" and specific "lesser" forms of whiteness.[6] Together, these in- and out-group distinctions validate race theorist Michael Banton's assertion: "Relations between groups identified by skin colour . . . have features in common that are independent of the particular kind of feature that designates the group. Expressed succinctly, inter-racial relations are not necessarily different from intra-racial relations."[7] Hence, members of both groups valorized certain performances of whiteness that they strove to attain but of which many fell short. This resulted in a great deal of variation in white racial identities, but it was a variation cohesively bound by the pursuit of the ideal.

In Chapters 4 through 8, I empirically demonstrated that the white ideal is not one dimensional. Inter- and intraracial boundaries are not written in stone. How they are redrawn or emphasized depends on the situational dilemmas at any given point. The careful reader will have noticed that these distinctions can take different forms at different times. In any given social relation, white hegemonic status can be defined in relation to people of color and their supposedly "dysfunctional" pathologies (Chapter 4), by successfully claiming an embattled victim status (Chapter 5), by framing oneself as a kind of messianic "white savior" to people of color (Chapter 6), by claiming possession of "color capital" through interracial friendships (Chapter 7), or by exhibiting entitlement to racialized knowledge (Chapter 8).

These various dimensions are not static traits or individual attributes but exist as a patterned and robust set of social relations. These social relations play a critical role in perpetuating social inequality in the absence of formal laws and policies that stratify resources in "postracial" America. While these processes are certainly not the only ones that exist, the meanings of race act as an organizing force in everyday social relations. By "social relations," I refer to situations in which actors makes sense of themselves *in relation* to others in order to comprehend the situation and act accordingly; for example, when a child recognizes his or her expected subordinated identity in relation to a parent and acts accordingly (consciously or unconsciously) to receive praise and status as either a "normal" or "good" child . . . or conversely rebels against the parent and then navigates the consequences of explicit punishment and implicit judgment. Even when people act alone, social relations are at work when they imagine how others will evaluate them and their actions. Racist meaning making and identity formation live in social relations.[8]

Dimensional Reach

The everyday use of racist meanings as a basic resource for structuring social relations is widespread. These meanings are not confined to explicit discussions or encounters associated with racial identity or race relations. Rather, the racially segregated and hierarchical character of American life normalizes racist meanings amid an array of whites and situations. Bonilla-Silva and Embrick write:

> The racial universe of whiteness in which whites navigate everyday fosters a high degree of homogeneity of racial views and even of the manners in which they express these views. Despite the civil rights revolution, whites, young and old, live fundamentally segregated lives that have attitudinal, emotional, and political implications.[9]

Evidence suggests that whites possess similar and shared definitions of social relations and their identities relative to those situations. Shared understandings of racial categories provide whites with a common knowledge for how to make meaning of their own racial identity and how they should relate with others. Because there are infinite contexts and situations in which people find themselves, the dominant meanings of white racial identity—as primary categories—provide a way of navigating everyday life regardless of context. Racial categories (like that of gender, age, and some socially perceivable markers of class or sexuality) transcend contextual limits and local definitions of the self and "others." Shared understandings of race allow one to act quickly within the structural constraints of quick and unexpected interactions. The primacy of social categories like race, then, enable the process of self–other interactions by affording what Cecelia Ridgeway calls "an all-purpose starting place, an initial frame for figuring the other out, whether we encounter that other in a familiar institution or in an utterly unfamiliar context."[10] The dimensions of an ideal white racial identity are far reaching and shared schemas. These dimensions are what we can call "transposable": "To say that schemas are transposable, in other words, is to say that they can be applied to a wide and not fully predictable range of cases outside the context in which they are initially learned. . . . Knowledge of a rule or a schema by definition means the ability to transpose or extend it—that is, to apply it creatively."[11]

By arguing that racial schemas or meanings transcend context, one could too easily reinstall a view of culture as free-floating norms and values to which actors latch on and apply befitting their utilitarian needs.[12] Rather than take this misstep, I think of dominant racial meanings as powerful, implicit, and far-reaching scripts and expectations to which people are socially accountable as members of particular racial groups. While meanings are certainly situational, they are never disconnected from extralocal concerns.[13] Rather, the relationships between actors in any locale or context depend on a larger "net of accountability" that is shared with people outside of the particular organization or setting.[14] While actors in divergent settings certainly navigate the meanings of race in different ways, dominant expectations constrain and enable actions in similarly recognizable patterns and in ways that produce similar performances of white racial identity. The dominant racial meanings that guide white racial identity formation are not simply local matters but are a changing configuration of inter- and intraracial boundary-making practices that occupy the dominant position across varied social relations.[15]

The far reach of these dimensions provides the grid or net that binds whites to expected actions and creates a multidimensional yet coherent sense of white racial identity. The dimensions—constructed from the ongoing accomplishment of inter- and intraracial distinctions—enable whites to explain and justify their actions in ways that appear normal and even racially neutral but that preserve the privileges implicitly associated with whiteness and exploitive social relations that often benefit whites. This net of accountability structures an array of situations. Michael Schwalbe argues:

> Often when we are called to account, it's as a member of group or social category. And usually this is because we're not behaving the way someone thinks we should, as a member of that group or category. We are thus vulnerable to being ignored, discredited, shamed, or otherwise punished for behaving in a way that

others deem wrong in light of who we claim to be or who they think we are. One way to put it is to say that identities carry accountability obligations.[16]

These dimensions of hegemonic whiteness serve as widely accepted "moral and normal" characteristics to which many are taught to aspire and that are reproduced in everyday accountabilities to others. Amanda Lewis writes:

> Hegemonic whiteness thus is a shifting configuration of practices and meanings that occupy the dominant position in a particular racial formation and that successfully manage to occupy the empty space of "normality" in our culture. Collectively, this set of schemas functions as that seemingly "neutral" or "precultural" yardstick against which cultural behavior, norms, and values are measured . . . It is also something people may well have only partial access to and that regularly is contested. For example, colloquial references to blacks "acting white," to Jews being "too Jewish," and to whites behaving as "wiggers" all are examples of people partially crossing borders in and out of hegemonic whiteness, with varying degrees of reward or penalty. Undoubtedly, hegemonic whiteness is not merely an ideological or cultural artifact but carries material rewards.[17]

I do not argue that all whites engage in the practices of inter- and intraracial othering at all times. Rather, my argument is that whites, by virtue of their membership in that racial category, are not immune to the pursuit of the white racial ideal. Political orientation does not provide escape from social expectations. Membership in an antiracist organization or living as an apolitical "racially unconscious" white does not exclude one from the grids and nets of accountability. This "racial contract" thus compels consent "to the extent that those phenotypically/genealogically/culturally categorized whites fail to live up to the civic and political responsibilities of Whiteness, they are in dereliction of their duties as citizens."[18] It is not that NEA or WRJ are atypical—it is quite the opposite. These two groups demonstrate patterns of racial meaning making that more and more white Americans might share. Accordingly, when Erich Gliebe, former boxer (under the name "The Aryan Barbarian") and present leader of the white supremacist group National Alliance, recently stated that "most white Americans agree with our message," he might not have been far off.[19]

From Dimensional Reach to Social Inequality

I have outlined how five key dimensions of an ideal white racial identity are widely shared and bind whites to their pursuit. Yet, practices of inter- and intraracial boundary making do not just guide whites' sense of self relative to others but reproduce already entrenched social inequalities. White racial identity formation is (re)produced and (re)articulated in relation to rationalizing and dictating where one lives, with whom one interacts, what job one holds, and what power one wields. These dimensions are not abstract or happenstance positions but are detailed practices that labor to defend white racial group privilege without any conscious or planned cognitive component. When widely shared beliefs about difference racial groups conflate with beliefs about racial inequality (for example, blacks are poor because they are lazy; whites get jobs because they are rational; Latinas are inherently overly sexual and have too many babies; and so on), then the usage of racial meanings serves to naturalize unequal material conditions and to reproduce the unequal statuses associated with different groups.

Race affects all our lives. The racialized social order serves as a basis for inequality among various people. Social scientists have along agreed that stratified and institutionalized control over resources forms and reproduces racial inequality. Even a cursory and whitewashed view of U.S. history demonstrates the formation of a white supremacist nation in which full citizenship, legal rights, and social privileges were reserved for propertied white men of specific class, religious, sexual, and cultural orientations. In theory, then, when the institutional systems that stratify access to resources change and relax, then the racial hierarchy should crumble or at least flatten out. Yet the collapse of white supremacy has not occurred. This presents a puzzling dilemma. How, in an era of "posts" (post-racial, post-Obama, post–Civil Rights) does the salience of race and the linkage between white racial identity and racist worldviews persist? What is the structure of white racialization? In specific, *how* does white racialization occur in specific social situations?[20] To answer these questions, one must uncover the precise social mechanisms and processes of white racial identity formation and meaning making. The previous chapters supply an answer by comparing two groups assumed incomparable and delineating the pieces of this structure of white racial identity formation as it reproduces racist worldviews.

The recognition that there are multiple dimensions of the hegemonic ideal to which people are more or less accountable does not mean that some whites remain unaffected by the dominant expectations of membership in the category "white." We must reject the one-dimensional assertion that whiteness is synonymous only with systems of privilege, regimes of terror, ideologies of white supremacy, and an unconditional, universal, and equally experienced location of power. We must also discard any assertion that whiteness is either decoupled from global systems of inequality or that it is not a social "group" that shares both symbolic and material similarities across varied contexts.

Given this realization, we might recast the characters of National Equality for All and Whites for Racial Justice. Often understood as outliers on the margins of America's racial drama, perhaps these two groups actually magnify the dominant meanings of whiteness today. NEA's focus on "color-blind" approaches reflects a commitment to formal racial equality. In some ways, the logic behind color blindness is understandable; downplaying or ignoring racial distinctions could limit the potential for bias and inequality. [21] That logic is widespread among many whites today, not just those who espouse variants of white nationalism. Regardless of overt political orientation, the denial, avoidance, and distortion of race serve to buffer and protect white privilege and superiority.

In distinction, WRJ evidences a commitment to civil and human rights for people of all racial and ethnic backgrounds. This logic is seen among an array of whites who attempt to live "color-conscious" lives. These whites often try not to engage in racist practices and support, more than prior white generations, interracial marriages and desegregated schools and neighborhoods; acknowledge the role advantages they have beneficiaries of a white supremacist nation; and often speak in glowing terms of "diversity" and "multiculturalism." Yet, a fetishization of nonwhites, a view of "otherness" as essentially potent or exotic, and/or a tokenized approach to interracial interactions that safeguard one's own supposed lack of racism ("But one of my best friends is black!") can also reproduce the very same white privileges as color-blind logic.

When spotlighted on center stage, white attractions to both color-blind and color-conscious logics not only reveal themselves as dichotomous worldviews that magnetize various whites toward antagonistic political agendas but represent the heart of white racial identity and power today. Whites are bound to, but not overdetermined by, the dominant meanings of white racial identity. These meanings assist whites in meeting everyday accountability obligations across an array of settings and contexts, while also reproducing access to resources and power. As such, National Equality for All and Whites for Racial Justice are not outliers but are fundamental reflections of whiteness today. So, when looking for the consummate white opponent—the prejudiced boogeyman who represents all that whites do wrong—perhaps we have met the enemy, and he is us.[22]

What Is to Be Done?

I do not seek here a final or definite word on white racial identity formation. Rather, I build on a handful of studies that employ the concept of "hegemonic whiteness."[23] I use the preceding pages to take the unrefined concept and provide the empirical and theoretical edifice to make it a testable theory.[24] As presented, future scholars can certainly seek to falsify the presence of the aforementioned dimensions, measure their salience, delineate their frequency, and illuminate their role in the reproduction of white privilege and supremacy within the scope of everyday meaning making and white racial identity formation. These dimensions afford a theory that neither flattens out whiteness as one dimensional nor assumes that the ideal and subordinated forms of whiteness do not vary across different settings. My approach refuses to disconnect power and racism from the mechanisms of white racial identity formation.[25] Each of the dimensions of hegemonic whiteness labors to rationalize and legitimate a dominant white subject position. These dimensions are not qualities or characteristics inherent to individual whites but are aggregate social forces that constrain and enable their lives.

Future use and refinement of this theory should resist a reading of the dimensions of hegemonic whiteness as merely an account of styles or performances. Rather than solely highlighting the ways in which white racial identity is lived out, I remain concerned with the greater implication of white racial identity formation: How white people understand racial identity can create path dependencies of action and order in which white racial dominance is reproduced under the best of intentions and political motives. Meanings matter. Whiteness is not just what white people do. Such a tautological misstep would reify the white body as the location of whiteness. Rather, the processes that produce white people as such can be applied to or taken away from certain people (this is evident with just a cursory glance at the history of racialization in the United States alone). By recognizing that racial meanings are irreducible to the bodies they inhabit, we can gain purchase on how processes of racialization continue to shape how rights, resources, and rewards are (re)distributed.

In addition to the formal academic implications, I wish to conclude on a practical note. By speaking of the "hegemony" of idealized forms of white racial identity, I draw attention to the unsettled power of whiteness. While the members discussed herein are indeed "white bound" (in the double meaning of attachment and pursuit), their bonds are soluble and their course amendable. *Counter*hegemonic practices are not only possible; they occur. The previous pages are rife with examples of NEA and WRJ members either purposefully resisting or failing to adhere to the expectations that others hold of them as members of the white racial category. Yet race is a primary category of social recognition. The confusion and anxiety generated by the strong desire to racially catalog others demonstrates that race—as a *system* of disparate meanings and as a *system* of unequal social relations—is not going to disappear, at least anytime soon. So, rather than simply pretending to be "color-blind" or pining away for a utopian day in which race suddenly stops mattering, it seems germane to explore how we might contest the correlation of different racial groups with essentialist characteristics and status beliefs and challenge the formation of contexts and movements that make such correlations easier to formulate. Accordingly, the questions arise: How can we weaken the "nets of accountability"? How might we provide support for beliefs and practices that do not collude with white supremacist logic? How do we encourage new identity formations predicated on difference without hierarchy? There are no easy answers to these questions, but I believe there are some pragmatic and tangible steps we can take.

First, it is important for scholars and laypersons alike to provide strong counterhegemonic evidence for each of the dimensions listed. The beliefs in black pathologies and white saviors must be exposed for the myths that they are and the inequalities that they rationalize. These racist underpinnings to white racial identity formation are robust and, as shown, widespread. They will not change suddenly. Advances and alterations in the patterns of racial dominance and exclusion do not necessarily equate with the decline of racism. For example, when the Obamas entered the White House in 2009, they did not change the dominant meanings of blackness in relation to whiteness. Instead, their meanings became slippery within a white supremacist logic: At one moment Barack and Michelle were framed as powerful *exceptions* to blackness (when discourse turned to their supposed "positive" traits that resembled an ideal whiteness), and at the next moment they were seen as unfortunate *examples* of a dangerous and deceitful racial group (when talk shifted to alleged "negative" characteristics that threatened whiteness). Hence, we must engage in a concerted effort—endeavors already underway—to demonstrate how racial meanings alter and shift to support unequal relations of power. Making these strategies apparent and topics of important conversation is an uphill battle, especially considering our contemporary moment in which talk of race is often seen as impolite or ideological.

Second, and because academic concerns do not exist in an apolitical vacuum, the marshalling of social scientific evidence needs to be connected to a new civil and human rights activism. As shown, resisting the standard expectations of hegemonic whiteness is fraught with danger and penalties. We need communities of intellectually informed folks who will safeguard those who resist the nets of accountability and are then deemed "less than" and somehow socially "spoiled." A new movement will work to reframe deviations from the "ideal," not as "alternative" identities and practices but as necessary and moral imperatives crucial to the livelihood of democratic praxis, substantive justice, and materially observable equal opportunities. We must engage in informed struggle against legal, policy, and de facto practices and logics that promote racial inequality. "We need, in every community," as Baynard Rustin said, "a group of angelic troublemakers."[26] Such angels would illuminate and make unworkable—through either votes, tax dollars, or direct confrontation—police profiling, lending and employment discrimination, unequal health care access, and an array of institutions that directly stratify life quality and longevity by racial, gender, and class status. Yet this will not happen without some kind of safety net. Opposing white supremacy has consequences, and there must be a movement that provides protection and buffer for the formation of new racial identities.

These two steps are not beyond the pale. Conversely, they are not preordained. The long march of history is not linear. The stream of time cuts peaks and valleys alike. I am repeatedly astounded by the naïve faith that racial equality will magically occur if we just play nice. If history shows us anything, it demonstrates that the social dislocations and turmoil produced by periods of cooperation and struggle are often followed by moments of stasis, if not concerted backlash. After the formation of the United States, the Reconstruction era, the Great Depression and the Great Migration, and the civil rights movement of the 1950s and 1960s, the hard-won steps toward racial equality were rolled back, diminished, or eviscerated. Today, in the age of Obama, another backlash is underway. Ironically, this reaction gains traction under the banner of progress and multiculturalism. Many now adopt a concept of a neoliberal and hyperindividualist "diversity" in which racial equality is increasingly understood in terms of a Horatio Alger narrative. This illusion of inclusion—the elevation of select nonwhite faces to high places—gives more photo opportunities than equal opportunities. Rather than praising select individuals for their triumph over the vestiges of Jim Crow, the recognition of our contemporary backlash requires a collective consciousness in which we call out and resist James Crow, Esquire—we must admit that our social order unfairly structures differently racialized bodies and creates racial identities bound to that order. Talk of diversity without talk of power is hollow speech. Lest we forget, there was diversity on slave ships. Plantation owners elevated select dark faces to supervisory positions. In looking backward, few would say such systems were equal or progressive. One can only wonder at how future generations will interpret our era. Racial equality is not guaranteed, nor are we fated for enduring white supremacy.

Before I began the research for this book, I was concerned that my analysis would wind up as an academic treatise on white racial identity formation. I feared that my future book, now manifest in these pages, would contain relevancies about "hegemonic whiteness" of interest only to ivory tower puzzle solvers. Now, at the conclusion, I emphasize the pragmatic weight of my spilled ink. For true racial empowerment and self-determinism to take place, we must have knowledge of, gain the collective volition to resist, and then act on the racist social order that binds an array of white political projects and identities to a similar trajectory of supremacy. Knowledge, volition, and action remain vital given the social climate we all inhabit. Now is a time of increased white backlash against recent civil and human rights gains, the dismantling of the Keynesian welfare state, an array of white racial victimhood narratives in popular culture, the continued embrace of "dysfunction" and "pathology" arguments to explain away social stratification, the racialized surveillance by police, immigration, and national security profiling, the juggernaut of the prison-industrial complex that transforms black and brown bodies into capital, and the U.S. struggle to dominate darker-skinned nations on the "underside of modernity"—from the Middle East to South America. These all exist under a banner that proclaims we have reached either a "postracial" or "color-blind" era. These conditions, and many more not mentioned here, represent the continued need to interrogate how white racial identity projects, even under the best of individual intentions or political imperatives, help reproduce white supremacy.

Appendix A
A Primer on Nationalism and Antiracism

White Nationalism

Sociologists often subsume white supremacist and white hate groups under the umbrella term *white nationalism*.[1] White nationalism applies to the Ku Klux Klan (KKK), neo-Nazis, militia movements, variants of the Christian Identity Church (CIC), and more "refined" political organizations like the National Association for the Advancement of White People (NAAWP).[2] White nationalism encompasses a large array of ideologies and practices, yet many dispute white nationalism's conflation with, or reduction to, white supremacy. "White nationalism" proper is a movement to create or maintain a separate white nation-state, whereas "white supremacy" relies on social Darwinist, biological, or theological doctrine to rationalize a belief in inherent racial differences and hierarchy. However, many find such distinctions quite dubious, as a great deal of social scientific analysis indicates a large overlap between the two camps in terms of membership, ideology, and practical cooperation.

While some might dismiss these groups as fringe or radical outliers, there is some evidence that their membership and/or influence is growing. From 1992 to 2000, the number of hate groups (largely white in membership) increased from 300 to 602, and by 2010 there were 1,002 hate groups. That is a 7.5 percent increase from the 932 groups active in 2009 and a 66 percent rise since 2000.[3]

In broad strokes, white nationalism can be traced to eighteenth-century European philosophers and naturalists such as Hume, Kant, Linnaeus, and Georges-Louis Leclerc. These figures engaged in a collective promotion of racial supremacist doctrine as various European powers colonized the globe.

Predominant features of European "settlement" included the naming and exaltation of whiteness as a proxy for morality, leadership, and intelligence. As the United States took shape, many of the founders expressed white nationalist sentiments. Thomas Jefferson wrote:

> Nothing is more certainly written in the book of fate, than that these people [white and black] are to be free; nor is it less certain that the two races, equally free, cannot live in the same government. Nature, habit, opinion have drawn indelible lines of distinction between them.[4]

The institution of U.S. slavery helped formally segregate racial groups hierarchically. Once the partial abolition of slavery occurred and some became increasingly insistent that the nation's claim of "life, liberty, and justice for all" should apply to all people, an intense backlash resulted in a number of white nationalist organizations (such as the KKK). Politically, socially, and economically, white nationalism was an integral part of everyday life throughout Reconstruction (1866–1877) and into much of the Jim Crow era (1877–1965).

White nationalism has radically changed its tone and timbre in an attempt to remain relevant. Today, nationalists widely shun their affiliation with formal white supremacy and hate-filled rhetoric. White nationalist organizations are diverse in number and kind, from the Council of Conservative Citizens and the National Alliance, to various other neo-Nazi, KKK, and Christian Identity organizations. Even social networking websites modeled after Facebook such as NewSaxon.com, an "online community by whites for whites" have recently surfaced. Also, the Stormfront website (started in 1995) received so many visits on the day after Barack Obama's election that it crashed. More than 2,000 people joined Stormfront that day, a dramatic rise from the previous average of eighty new members a day.[5]

White nationalism holds several key tenets. The first is the formation of a white-controlled and/or segregated nation. Some white nationalists support white separatism based on the already entrenched de facto racial segregation that exists today. Other forms of white nationalism argue for a far-reaching racial segregation of all social institutions akin to the legalized Jim Crow policies of the United States pre-1965. Both proposals suggest the separation of the races by white and nonwhite (as well as white "race traitors" who fail to support the goals of white nationalism).[6]

A second tenet of white nationalist thought is their collective shunning of the titles "racist" and "supremacist." As Michael H. Hart, a retired professor of astrophysics and influential white nationalist, states, "I, like most other white separatists, resent being called a white *supremacist* [italics in original] . . . I have no desire to rule over blacks, or to attempt to rule over blacks, or have someone else rule over blacks in my behalf."[7] White nationalists generally adopt this position so as to downplay accusations of supremacy and to emphasize white "culture" and "heritage."

Next, many white nationalists argue that their political program is salient because the nation is quickly becoming less white. White nationalists seem most threatened by a statistical projection of the U.S. Census Bureau—by the year 2050, whites will be close to or less than half of the demographic makeup of the nation.[8] Because many white nationalists believe that white culture created modern civilization and social order, they hold that the "darkening" of the United States will result in catastrophe (as they often assume people of color to be morally and intellectually inferior).[9]

Fourth, many white nationalists claim they are victims of "reverse racism." For example, white nationalists might argue that policies such as affirmative action provide unfair preferential treatments that institutionalize racism against whites.[10] Such arguments hinge on the presentation of a victimized white self and the use of traditional civil rights rhetoric. Mitch Berbrier compared the discourses of white nationalists with that of gay and deaf discourse to demonstrate how white nationalists frequently map their rhetoric onto a framework historically used by "minorities."[11]

Fifth, white nationalists often hold divergent views of history, especially in regard to the trans-Atlantic slave trade and the Holocaust. White nationalists often reject the idea that whites had a controlling or beneficiary role in the slave trade and either reject any belief that the Holocaust occurred or claim that the event has been vastly exaggerated to vilify select heterosexual and Christian whites.[12]

Sixth and lastly, white nationalists define the term *white* in a specialized way. For white nationalists, being white implies specific European ancestry as well as identification with select and glorified aspects of European culture. However, many white nationalists do not accept all descendants of European immigrants and would most likely question the whiteness of Eastern Europeans. They generally draw from certain nineteenth-century racial taxonomies. They rely on various race theories (for examples, Nordicism and Germanism, which define different groups as white by excluding Southern and Eastern Europeans; or Pan Aryanism, which defines most Europeans as Aryan-origin whites). All these definitions of whiteness exclude very large populations commonly understood as "white." These definitions effectively redefine the racial category by excluding those they do not want within their ranks.[13]

While such an ideological foundation is widely shared, this commonality does not explain why people participate. Much of the social science research centers on the motivating factors of white nationalism. White groups struggling to access material resources often invoke the specters of strong racial identities and interracial conflict to define and identify potential constituents, allies, and threats. From this perspective, one joins a white nationalist organization via a conscious choice after recognizing a racial conflict over resources.[14] Other studies emphasize that people accept nationalism because of significant and increased "social strain."[15] From this vantage point, white nationalists are more likely to have experienced prior social, political, or economic marginalization. Another approach, called "framing,"[16] examines how a movement gains selective influence over members' perception of the world in such a way as to persuade and discourage certain interpretations.

In addition to these strands of work on white nationalism—those that fall under the rubrics of structural-functionalism and/or social movement approaches—recent years bear witness to a focus on identity construction and culture.[17] From this approach, white nationalists are doing much more than reacting to perceived changes in the economic, political, and social conditions of the United States or intentionally framing worldviews to encourage certain interpretations. Kathleen Blee found that people do not become white nationalists because of "strain," dwindling resources, or dominant "frames" of collective understanding.[18] Rather, positive social interactions with acquaintances, peers, friends, and family members involved in white nationalist organizations shape, structure, and even define a potential member's desire to join. The import of positive social interactions, rather than an explicit coherence of group-individual ideology or conflict over material resources, is paramount in understanding contemporary growth in white nationalism.[19]

Drawing from this research, white nationalism provides concrete settings in which to perform, in a supportive environment, a white racial identity that reforms specific understandings of race and resolves more abstract and existential questions about the nature of life. By examining recruitment, membership retention, membership styles, and objectives, we can observe white racial identity being constantly remade through shared white nationalist narratives. For example, the shared and familial memorization of musical lyrics and magazine articles or the collective wearing of a specific pin on one's coat lapel allows supporters to reiterate, rehearse, and reinforce various white nationalist beliefs with a feeling that their compatriots are doing likewise—thus leading to the solidification of a pan-Aryan or white diasporic "imagined community."[20]

Given the primacy of cultural influences, some scholars now investigate how white nationalist projects intertwine with other systems of meaning outside of race. Many white nationalist organizations meld with a religious that uses biblical authority to justify white superiority.[21] In addition to religious themes, several scholars show that conservative gender regimes—that naturalize a white, patriarchal, heterosexual masculinity—are embraced by nationalists.[22] Other research demonstrates how the genre of Western films attracts some to white nationalism because of the valorized performances of hypermasculinity and nostalgic maschismo constitutive of the genus.[23] By making meaning of specific religious, gendered, and aesthetic differences as primordially "natural" and "moral," white nationalists implicitly disarm social egalitarian messages unnatural "social engineering" that goes against either God's or nature's plan.[24]

By examining these beliefs and patterns of behavior as shared systems of meaning that serve as road maps for the navigation of a white nationalist life, the cultural logics and assumptions that undergird these frameworks are illumined as causal variables in the formation of particular white identities. Particular understandings of immigration, economic downturn, and changing social relations are not stable white nationalist positions but are constantly in flux as white members use them toward specific racial interests, while they are also constitutive of the white identities that wield them.[25]

White Antiracism

In broad strokes, white antiracism is a movement in which whites oppose laws, politics, and practices that promote negative treatment that creates racial inequality, especially against people of color. Writing in *Rethinking Anti-Racisms*, Lloyd makes the point that:

> A central feature of anti-racism is its diversity. Studies of anti-racism generally agree that it is a "difficult issue" which is not easily accommodated. . . . As a political movement anti-racism may be best understood as occupying different points on a continuum between well-organized, bureaucratic organizations,

pressure groups and protest or social movements which challenge dominant social practices and preconceptions.[26]

Bonnett writes that antiracism "refers to those forms of thought and/or practice that seek to confront, eradicate and/or ameliorate racism. Anti-racism implies the ability to identify a phenomenon—racism—and to do something about it."[27] White antiracism tends to promote the view that whites receive undeserved and unasked-for privileges and powers at the expense of people of color.

White antiracism formally organized around the slavery abolitionist movements in England and the United States.[28] Although many white abolitionists refused to see Africans as fully socially or theologically equal to Europeans, they generally believed in liberal notions of freedom. A few, like John Brown, asserted that freedom without a commensurate belief in the human equality of the races was contradictory. During the U.S. Civil War, white antiracism became much stronger and more widely disseminated.[29] However, much of the white antiracist movement collapsed after the Reconstruction era. The government was resegregated, and groups like the KKK grew in popularity and strength. The ideologies of past white antiracists were looked on as deeply misguided, and the antiracists themselves (as in the case of John Brown) were regarded as insane.[30] By the 1930s and 1940s, a handful of scholars began to rediscover the white antiracist movement.[31] They provided evidence of fundamental human equality and similarity. White socialist organizations adopted cooperative endeavors across the color line from the time of the Harlem Renaissance to the civil rights movements of the 1960s.

The modern white antiracist movement is composed of groups like the Southern Poverty Law Center, AWARE (Alliance of White Anti-Racists Everywhere), CURE (Caucasians United for Reparations and Emancipation), the White Anti-Racist Community Action Network and SHARP (Skin Heads Against Racial Prejudice). So, also, the past two decades witnessed an array of publications that speak to the white antiracist experience: *White Awareness*; *Uprooting Racism: How White People Can Work for Real Justice*; *Teaching / Learning Anti-Racism*; *A Promise and a Way of Life: White Antiracist Activism*; and *The Anti-Racist Cookbook*.[32]

Despite recent research, the study of antiracism is dwarfed in comparison to the literature on white nationalism. Only a handful of empirical studies attempt to map the field of white antiracism. Eileen O'Brien delineates various types of white antiracism: "selective race cognizance" (whereby whites acknowledge their privilege in the abstract but remain unable to analyze how socioracial privilege applies to them personally) and "reflexive race cognizance" (in which whites reflexively engage in both personal and abstract analysis).[33] In another typology, Mark George finds that some whites practice a "critical antiracism" that is underpinned by five belief systems: (1) Race is a social construct; (2) whites occupy a privileged social position; (3) racism is multiple in its dimensions; (4) whites must change themselves, not people of color; and (5) the purpose of antiracism is to alter power relationships, not to learn about "diversity" or "multiculturalism."[34]

Aside from categorizing types of antiracism, two distinct streams of thought divide the extant literature; most writing on antiracism is either celebratory or critical. In the former, writers emphasize that white antiracists actively make meaning of race and racism in ways that greatly influences their actions.[35] For example, Eichstedt applies various cultural sociological approaches to unpack how white antiracists negotiate their own "problematic identities."[36] She finds that, while white activism is complicated by a definition of racism that tends to essentialize whiteness, activists find ways to ways to reconceptualize their relationship to racism and antiracism activism in a less rigid ways. In the latter "critical" branch, writers and scholars accentuate the stumbling blocks to living an antiracist life. A few scholars now show that when whites do attempt to engage in antiracist work, they are often handicapped by their own guilt, anger, and denial, which facilitates a possible disengagement with an antiracist agenda.[37] For example, Marty and Zajicek find that white antiracists unintentionally reproduce racism by constantly apologizing for, and thus redeeming, problematic white behaviors.[38]

Across these two camps, much of writing on white antiracism unintentionally treats culture as epiphenomenal and/or refrains from asserting that cultures of white antiracism are at play. In addition, Niemonen's survey of the antiracist literature finds that the white antiracist movement is "not a sociologically grounded, empirically based account of the significance of race in American society. Rather, it is a morally based educational reform movement that embodies the confessional and redemptive modes common in evangelical Protestantism."[39] A large portion of the antiracist literature ignores cultural dynamics. That is, scant attention is paid to either the shared systems of meaning that actors consciously use to rationalize and build their activism or the unconscious frameworks that are constitutive of the identities that wield them. The missing cultural analysis is due, at least in part, to the specter of vulgar Marxist analysis that underpins most studies of white antiracism. Such an approach frames "culture" as secondary or tertiary to the more "real" material conditions of actors' social relationships, their participation in specific organizations, their use of specific resources, and actual encounters with racial discrimination.

For example, both Brown and Thompson examine how white antiracist activism contributes to members' participation in long-term intimate relationships with politically like-minded partners.[40] In so doing, they contend that antiracism serves to alleviate feelings of social isolation and psychological stress that white antiracists often describe.[41] For white antiracists uninvolved in intense, even romantic, partnerships with activist colleagues, their possession of extensive networks of friends and support is interpreted as the result of their activism, as members are described as searching out like-minded people "far beyond family and traditional friends to create a supportive antiracist network."[42] These studies frame such coping strategies as the result of resilient character traits of members, rather than stemming from patterned cultural strategies, practices, or external factors that constrain and enable members' lives. For example, Brown identified several qualities common to the white antiracists she studied: "a high degree of energy with less-than-usual need for sleep, good health, unusual optimism, and a pronounced capacity for independent thinking . . . [as well as] a relative lack of interest in material possessions and wealth."[43] In addition, Thompson found that white antiracists critically questioned "mainstream values about food, alcohol, and consumerism."[44]

Another strand of literature employs cultural analysis, albeit haphazardly, toward the illumination of ritualized interactions and performative expectations. Pramuk found that many white antiracists equate their racial privilege with a form of "original sin" and often engage in interactive rituals of expressive shame and regret for their possession of unearned resources.[45] Many white antiracists come to expect the performative display of guilt and believe that the evocation of such feelings enables part of the white "reconstructive process"[46] even if it is a "necessary and painful awakening."[47] Many white antiracist meetings and workshops serve as dramaturgical settings for expressions of profuse apology, relinquishment of claims to authority, and the confession of "bad deeds" to other whites.[48] A particularly fruitful example from the work of Sarita Srivastava shows that antiracist groups engage in a "song and dance" in which demands of racist disclosure are so dominant that "many people of color are dropping out of, rejecting, and refusing to participate in mixed antiracist workshops."[49] Hence, many antiracist groups become predominantly, if not entirely, white. Srivastava also found that expectations of emotional outpourings in antiracist settings actually constrains rather than enables antiracist practice:

> A predominant mode of discussion . . . is one that privileges the disclosure of personal experiences and emotion . . . which I refer to as the *"let's talk"* [emphasis in original] approach, also produces a tightly controlled space for the expression and suppression of knowledge and feelings about racism.[50]

Srivastava argues that antiracist debates often collapse into emotional and turbulent scenes characterized by anger and tears. The practices and discourses of emotional expression are shown to directly mold organizational and identity formation.[51]

Given the vast array of white antiracist organizations, it is difficult to speak of antiracism in broad strokes. Today's white antiracists support a variety of political and social agendas—from quasi-Marxist indictments of the white supremacist underpinnings of capitalism and more radical disruptions of white nationalist events to more mainstream counseling and training-focused organizations that operate within an array of educational and business communities. Because of the large breadth of the white antiracist movement, adherents come from a wide background. Generally, they possess some college education, range in age from their late teens into their mid-fifties, hold leftist political leanings, and are in the lower-middle to upper-middle class. Although diverse in their many manifestations and specific agenda, modern white antiracist thought can be generalized to five key trends.[52]

White antiracists understand racism as a central organizing principle of social life. White antiracists believe racism socially dysfunctional, unnatural, learned, sustentative of the ruling classes, intellectually unsound, and antiegalitarian.[53] They argue that racism is one of the most dangerous issues besetting the United States. Understanding how racism was purposefully and systematically engineered, what it is, from whence it comes, and why it is perpetuated remains essential to antiracist practice.[54]

Second, white antiracists focus on both the structural aspects of racism and on how racism is internalized to create feelings of superiority and inferiority. Ambalavaner Sivanandan, director of the antiracist organization Institute of Race Relations wrote that antiracists must "organise not for culture but against racism, against fascism, against the erosion of civil liberties, against injustice and inequality—against racism qua racism instead of particularising the racisms."[55] Using rather fixed, structural explanations, most antiracists view the average white person as someone who has internalized an understanding of him- or herself as racially superior. Simultaneously, antiracists generally view people of color as victims of internalized racial inferiority. The acceptance of an inferior identity, taught via oppression in de jure and de facto learning environments, perpetuates white supremacy. Many antiracists thus believe that, over generations, this process of disempowerment expresses itself in self-defeating and negative behaviors.[56]

Third, antiracists often believe that sharing diverse cultures help make a stronger and more cohesive community; "multiculturalism" and "diversity" are important principles. Many white antiracists believe that all people should have the right to speak for themselves and to live self-determined lives. Trying to understand multiple social identities has led to some anxieties among antiracists. The recognition of conflicting social pressures and identities destabilizes structural approaches to racism that view whites as winners and blacks as losers when other aspects of class, nationality, gender, and sexuality complicate that arrangement. Hence, antiracist organizing often struggles to understand the intersectional complexities of identity politics.[57]

Fourth, most antiracists are avid protectors of political correctness. They often contend that political correctness guards and defends against unfair labels and is a decidedly moral and respectful policy. By guarding against the use of certain terms or ideas, some believe that they can check the activation of peoples' unconscious biases. Such a restriction affords more freedom for people to act through reasoned and informed choices rather than through implicitly held stereotypes. By making certain labels and terms problematic, people are forced to consciously rethink the linkages of certain characteristics and traits with racial identity.[58]

Fifth, the most notable aspect of white antiracism is that it differs from multicultural or mixed antiracist organizations. The move to restrict membership to whites, rather than having an interracial membership, contains a strategic rationale. Many white antiracists feel that racial groups should have "safe spaces" in which they can come together, commiserate, problem-solve, and share in the common experiences of that racial group. For supporting evidence, white antiracists often point to Malcolm X, who stated that before blacks could unify with whites, they would have to first unify with themselves. Toward this end, many believe that whites should do the same and work with other whites in building a racially just society. They also refer to Dr. Huey P. Newton (cofounder of the Black Panther Party), who once stated that whites could not join the Black Panthers, but, if they sympathized with its goals, could form a "White Panther Party."[59] White antiracists also commonly refer to the infamous 1966 changing of the guard within SNCC (Student Non-Violent Coordinating Committee), whereby leadership changes effectively banned whites from membership so that blacks could possess an all-black political vehicle for the formulation and implementation of "black power." All-white antiracist organizations, many members believe, foster active consultation, cathartic emotional release, and practical guidance on how to live as "allies" of people of color.[60] Within such a homogenous group, their fundamental organizing principles are not understood as stylistic choices but as necessary moral imperatives.

Appendix B

Research Methodology

FROM MAY 2006 THROUGH JUNE 2007 I studied the members of National Equality for All (NEA) and Whites for Racial Justice (WRJ). I was careful not to rely on a solitary approach but cross-examined or triangulated the research. Triangulation facilitates the legitimacy of data collection and analysis by combining multiple points of observation, empirical materials, and/or theoretical frameworks so as to facilitate the intersubjectivity called for in reflexive science.[1] Specifically, I used "data triangulation" (time, location, and actors), "theory triangulation" (cultural sociology, critical sociology, and the sociology of race and ethnicity), and "methodological triangulation" (ethnography, interviews, and content analysis). To further explain about the latter: My research was composed of ethnographic fieldwork, thousands of hours of observation, semistructured and in-depth interviews, and content analysis inclusive of newsletter issues, flyers, and any textual information such as emails and office memos.[2] I detail each methodological approach in the following sections.

Ethnography

Michael Burawoy's "extended case method" influenced my method of ethnographic engagement. I did not approach the locales of NEA and WRJ as insulated from either history or extralocal social forces. Moreover, armed with the weapons of preexisting theory and prior observations on white racial identity, I deductively approached these field sites with a theoretical problem in mind and an informed approach to the fields. While collecting data, I was also informed by inductive methodology, à la Dorothy Smith's "institutional

ethnography" approach.[3] On leaving the field, I used the data collected to re-
fine and reconstruct the social theory of "hegemonic whiteness." In this sense,
my science is "reflexive." Burawoy writes:

> Reflexive science sets out from a dialogue between us and them, between so-
> cial scientists and the people we study. It does not spring from an Archime-
> dean point outside space and time; it does not create knowledge or theory
> tabula rasa. It starts out from a stock of academic theory on the one side and
> existent folk theory or indigenous narratives on the other. Both sides begin
> their interaction from real locations.[4]

In studying how white nationalists and white antiracists made meaning of
white racial identity, I traced the localized worldviews in both groups to discover similarities between them, or what Marjorie DeVault called "relevances
produced elsewhere."[5] Researchers who employ the approach direct their gaze
toward the ways that dominant ideology and dominant ways of practice are
established and negotiated among the local settings of everyday life. DeVault
writes:

> The point is to show how people in one place are aligning their activities with
> relevances produced elsewhere, in order to illuminate the forces that shape ex-
> perience at the point of entry. Many institutional ethnographers have adopted
> a rhetoric of "mapping" to highlight the analytic goal of explication rather
> than theory building; the analysis is meant to be "usable" in the way that a
> map can be used to find one's way.[6]

The slow aggregation of data makes generalizability a process rather than an
end point.[7] My data are not generalizable to all whites but build on existing
theory to illuminate particular interactions and meaning-making strategies
across diverse settings.

Shared Narratives and Symbolic Boundaries

As cursorily mentioned in Chapter 1, I consider whiteness a social classification constructed from, and guided by, shared narratives and symbolic boundaries. People interpret their lives through sets of recognizable storylines and
sequences of events. These shared narratives provide common accounts for
how the world works and where we fit within it; what Somers and Gibson call
"emplotment."[8] Through emplotment, people exchange and build on one another's narratives, as they become "part of a stream of sociocultural knowledge

about how structures work to distribute power and disadvantage."[9] Through aggregating the talk of NEA and WRJ actors over time, I was able to delineate: (1) a stable set of characters and (2) recognizable plots that connect actors and events through causal.[10] "Collective narratives can be said to emerge when regularly occurring plots connect to key characters in an empirically stable way."[11] Because narratives provide repeated and shared accounts of how people view themselves and others, they are central to the social construction of racial identity.[12] Shared narratives then direct the ongoing accomplishment of racial identity and people's actions because people tend to choose actions that are commensurate with their identities and personal narratives.

"Symbolic boundaries" are meaningful divisions that operate as a "system of rules that guide interaction by affecting who comes together to engage in what social act."[13] People engage in racial "boundary work" by drawing on supposedly common traits, experiences, and a shared sense of belonging.[14] "In short, symbolic boundaries constitute a system of classification that defines a hierarchy of groups and the similarities and differences between them. They typically imply and justify a hierarchy of moral worth across individuals and groups."[15] Not unlike narratives, symbolic boundaries remain central to the construction of racial identities. However, while shared narratives work to create linkages between racialized groups, defining them relationally to one another in a recognizable story, symbolic boundaries illuminate the cultural basis and meanings of inter- and intraracial categories.

Emphasizing Everyday Discourse

As deep generative structures of action and order, shared narratives and symbolic boundaries are not directly observable whole cloth. However, they do manifest empirically in the *discourse* and *interactions* of particular settings. As the preceding chapters demonstrate, I examine the everyday lives of NEA and WRJ members, and I pay particular attention to words. I take my cue from C. Wright Mills's attention to "vocabularies of motive" and Berger and Luckmann's focus on the language of everyday life.[16] Mills wrote that language is not merely an expression of "prior elements within the individual" but rather functions to coordinate diverse and future actions.[17] So, also, Berger and Luckmann contend:

> The language used in everyday life continuously provides me with the necessary objectifications and posits the order within which these make sense and within which everyday life has meaning for me. I live in a place that is

geographically designated; I employ tools, from can openers to sports cars, which are designated in the technical vocabulary of my society; I live within a web of human relationships, from my chess club to the United States of America, which are also ordered by means of vocabulary. In this manner language marks the co-ordinates of my life in society and fills that life with meaningful objects.[18]

Given this direction, we may focus on the discourse of actors in various ethnographic locales to grasp the role of shared narratives and symbolic boundaries in constantly reshaping the ongoing accomplishment of racial identity. Judith Howard makes the position quite obvious: "Identities are thus strategic social constructions created through interaction, with social and material consequences. . . . At the most basic level, the point is simply that people actively produce identity through their talk."[19]

Identifying the discourses by which actors make sense of their identity can be particularly challenging. Even among racially hyperconscious nationalists and antiracists, racial dynamics can hide in the seemingly mundane and neutral activities of everyday life. Monica McDermott faced similar problems in her attempt to tease out the meanings of race in two different neighborhoods in *Working Class White*. This difficulty is not limited to ethnographies of race; Paul Willis spoke of the trouble entailed in identifying the performance of British class identity in *Learning to Labour*, and Arlie Hochschild worked to portray the nuance of gender performance to reproduce or resist inequality in *The Second Shift*.[20] To identify important discourse, I followed in the footsteps of McDermott, Willis, and Hochschild: I paid particular attention to how actors spoke about their relative positioning vis-à-vis inter- and intragroup "others" and how that positioning entailed certain rules in the form of social expectations and accountabilities. While these rules of everyday conduct can differ from context to context, as they certainly did between NEA and WRJ, I soon recognized common patterns.

Racism

Given that I spend a great deal of time in *White Bound* showing how racism collides with white racial identity formation, I borrow from Laura Edles's definition of racism:

A specific kind of racialized system of meaning . . . in which (implicitly or explicitly) physical "racial" differences between groups are assumed to reflect internal (moral, personality, intellectual) differences, and that these differences are organized both biologically and hierarchically, i.e., racist systems of meaning suppose that on the basis of genetic inheritance, some groups are innately superior to others.[21]

I make an explicit cultural argument about racism in that I view the taken-for-granted narratives and boundaries in everyday life as enabling people to interpret, represent, and explain social life in ways that rationalize a certain distribution of material and symbolic resources along particular racial lines.

Gender

Ethnography does not aim for generalizable claims but aspires to gain explanatory power.[22] Hence, the preceding chapters explain how the dimensions of hegemonic whiteness are constantly pursued and how that pursuit binds these actors to a meaningful racial category replete with deeply felt and meaningful inter- and intraracial divisions. Yet, the reader will notice that both NEA and WRJ were decidedly male dominated (out of forty-five members I interviewed, forty-two, or 93 percent, were men). This introduces an obvious gender bias that should not be overlooked. Based on my intent to study the intersection of racism and ideal white identity, the overrepresentation of men becomes a strength. Claims to the normativity, superiority, and rationality of hegemonic whiteness pivot on the marginalization of nonwhite "others" and those whites thought "lesser" than the ideal—most often women.

David T. Goldberg asserts that as North America and Europe moved into the Enlightenment period, the standards of "reason in modernity arose against the backdrop of European domination and subjugation of nature, especially human nature."[23] "Rationality" and its opposites (irrationality, emotion, bias, loss of control, and so on) were defined through the (in)ability to "exhibit the values, metaphysical attitudes, epistemological principles or cognitive styles of 'whitemales.'"[24] Embodied departures from the hegemonic position of white masculinity, that is, select peoples' failures to demonstrate mastery of mind over body, rationality over carnality, and intellect over emotion, were bookended by two forms of deficiency: *women*—as corporeal embodiments of emotion and nature who were valued for little more than their reproductive capabilities—and enslaved and free *nonwhites*—who represented the deviant, dangerous, and demonic incarnate.

Accordingly, W. E. B. Du Bois makes prescient observations on the creation of white masculinity. He questions why claims to whiteness drove a racialized wedge between male laborers in the public sphere. Du Bois writes:

> It must be remembered that the white group of laborers, while they received a low wage, were compensated in part by a sort of public and psychological wage. They were given public deference and titles of courtesy because they were white. They admitted freely with all classes of white people to public functions, public parks and the best schools . . . The police were drawn from their ranks, and the courts, dependent upon their votes, treated them with such leniency as to encourage lawlessness. Their vote selected public officials, and while this had small effect on their economic situation, it had great effect upon their personal treatment and the deference shown them.[25]

Building explicitly on Du Bois, David Roediger's *Wages of Whiteness* demonstrates how the psychological wage did not just give cognitive benefits to those who were already understood as "white men" but was in fact constitutive of white masculinity.[26] Bret E. Carroll explicitly connects whiteness to an embattled form of masculinity: "White racial identity was a fundamental element of working-class manhood and provided an additional 'wage' for male workers."[27] In this vein, Jessie Daniels writes that white supremacist discourse often manifests the "conflation of 'whiteness' and masculinity [that demonstrates] . . . the inextricable connection between race and gender."[28]

By analyzing white men's discourse and behavior, I am afforded access to the "seat of power" within whiteness. This is not to suggest an essentialist connection between masculinity and white racial identity, but rather it highlights the historical connection in which men and whites share claims to power. By focusing on reconstructions of white masculinity in a white nationalist and white antiracist organization in our contemporary era, I zero in on the ways in which male constructions of white racial identity become hegemonic.

Participant Observation

My research began in May 2006 and lasted until June 2007. During that period, I spent at least one day a week almost every week with members of either or both the white nationalist organization National Equality for All and the white antiracist organization Whites for Racial Justice.[29] Observations were conducted in many locations, but the majority occurred at the two groups' headquarters.

There was a conscious effort on my part to minimize the problem of selectivity by gaining access to, and involving myself in, an array of wide-ranging activities, interpersonal relationships, and even office cliques. While positivist science might claim this as a form of bias that interferes with truth finding, reflexive science claims that such interventions:

> create perturbations that are not noise to be expurgated but music to be appreciated, transmitting the hidden secrets of the participant's world. Institutions reveal much about themselves when under stress or in crisis, when they face the unexpected as well as the routine. Instead of the prohibition against reactivity, which can never be realized, reflexive science prescribes and takes advantage of intervention.[30]

My immersion in more and more private settings added to my ability to ask in-depth and challenging questions, as well as for members (and even their family and friends) to sit around, asking me poignant and concerned questions about my research. As Lofland and Lofland point out:

> The researcher does not only (or mainly) wait for "significant" (sociologically or otherwise) events to occur or words to be said and then write them down. An enormous amount of information about the settings under observation or the interview in process can be apprehended in apparently trivial happenings or utterances, and these are indispensable grist for the logging mill.[31]

I construct this book from the double aggregation of these findings into (1) "social processes" and then into (2) "social forces."[32] These social forces are situated within the context of sociological theory. Hence, the ethnographic findings of this book should be regarded, as Mary Patillo-McCoy wrote of her ethnography of the black middle class, as "a conversation between the specificity of people's words and their actions . . . and the grand declarations of sociological theory."[33]

I approached my use of theory carefully and with concern. The use of theory is important because groups of people who cohere around specific agendas are often labeled "social movements" or "organizations." Both terms have a substantial sociological literature behind them, yet I am a sociologist of neither social movements nor organizations but of culture and race. I did not wish to approach either organization with such an a priori label in mind, looking at either group with a sociological lens that would transform it, in its representation in this book, into an object unrecognizable to itself. It was important not to impose an unchangeable theory on the people I studied. Simply, my concern was not to transform the white nationalists and white antiracists into sociological objects but to illuminate how these members constructed their white racial identity in everyday life.

Semistructured, In-depth Interviews

The members of both organizations were given the IRB-approved "Informed Consent Agreement," which provided extensive details on their rights as subjects. The semistructured, in-depth interviews with members of both organizations provided a deeper understanding of the role that their ideologies and logics played both as members and in their everyday lives. By employing a semistructured interview approach I engaged in a relatively free-flowing discussion, making sure to cover certain topics. This approach allowed for a realistic discussion with questions embedded naturalistically, thereby increasing the likelihood of candid and representative responses.

Extending Dorothy Smith's approach to interviewing, I combined two modes of inquiry. The first is the traditional hermeneutic method ensconced in ethnographic approaches that aim to understand how specific comments and situations countervail or complicate abstract generalizations. Such a technique allows examinations of how subjects make sense of situations, which then provides a glimpse of the forces that shape both the places they inhabit and the criteria that reflect people's perceptions of the meanings of those social forces. The second is what Hans-Georg Gadamer characterizes as the "hermeneutics of suspicion," whereby the researcher is geared toward revealing the meaningfulness of statements in an unexpected sense and "against the meaning of the author" in ways that challenge the validity of ideologies.[34] In the former, I listened for, and encouraged, more explanations so that I could obtain as much rich, detailed information as possible. In the latter, I began to challenge the validity of statements so that respondents had to expose the rationales, logics, and ideologies that underpinned and gave valid sense to their statements.

For each of the in-depth interviews, either an audio recording was made (and transcribed later for analysis), or extensive notes were taken during each interview period if the subjects did not consent to audio recording. The initial pass at data analysis took place during the interview period, whereby I used my notes to record initial thoughts regarding themes and patterns. When necessary, the interview schedule was amended to reflect newfound understandings.

From these interviews I gathered the demographic information about members (see Tables 2.1, 2.2, 3.1, and 3.2 in Chapters 2 and 3). On average, members of NEA are slightly more likely to own a home and have slightly higher education and income levels than members of WRJ. NEA members are more likely to hold no political party affiliation or identify with the Republican Party, whereas WRJ members are more likely to identity with the Democratic Party or consider themselves independent. The majority of both groups are quick to self-identify as religious, as being raised in the southern United States, and as either middle or upper-middle class. While both groups have members with high-status occupations, members of NEA are more likely to obtain jobs with higher status when compared with WRJ member jobs (for example, bankers, lawyers, accountants, and business managers as opposed to writers, car salesmen, teachers, and retail salespersons). On average, members of WRJ are slightly younger and more likely to be single (never married), while members of NEA are seven times more likely to be divorced. Indicators suggest that members of both groups are much better off than most white Americans.[35]

Interview Schedule

Section One: Organization and Ideology

1. Tell me about why you joined your organization.
2. In what ways does the organization meet, or fail to meet, your expectations?
3. What are the goals of the organization?
4. Tell me about the biggest strengths and weaknesses of the organization.
5. Did you ever want to quit? Did you, and why or why not?
6. In what ways do you think you are, and are not, living up the ideals of the organization?
7. Do any specific morals or ethics affect why you became or are a member? If so, which ones and why?
8. Why do you feel it is necessary for whites to work on your organization's goals?
9. How do whites differ from people of color who work on the same goals?
10. Do you feel there are any ways that you might unintentionally work against your goals?
11. How is your organization different than white [anti]racists?
12. How would you say that emotions and intellect come into what you do?

13. What does being white mean to you?

14. Do you think you were taught to be white or is it something you just are? Why?

15. Why is your organization all white? How does this help and/or hurt your goals?

16. What values do you think most whites hold?

17. How are whites different or similar to people of color?

18. Aside from being white, how else do you identify yourself?

19. How do other aspects of your identity (e.g., religion, class, gender, geographic upbringing) inform your beliefs about the work you do?

20. What would the world look like if the goals of your organization were accomplished? If your organization were defeated?

21. How would you describe your relationship to other whites? Other people of color?

22. What is racism to you?

23. Would you describe yourself as more traditional or more progressive? Why?

Section Two: Demographic Variables

24. In what age group are you:
    (1) Under 21   (2) 21–30   (3) 31–40   (4) 41–50   (5) 50+
    (6) DK/Refused

25. What is your yearly income?
    (1) Under 25,000   (2) Between 25,000 and 49,999
    (3) Between 50,000 and 74,999   (4) Between 75,000 and 99,999
    (5) Above 100,000

26. How would you describe your class status?
    (1) Lower   (2) Lower-middle   (3) Middle   (4) Upper-middle
    (5) Upper   (6) DK/Refused

27. Do you own your home, or are you renting?
    (1) Owns [or is buying]   (2) Rents   (3) Other _____
    (4) DK/Refused

28. In what kind of place are you living?
    (1) Single-family home   (2) A duplex or 2-family structure
    (3) An apartment   (4) A mobile home/trailer
    (5) Other _____   (6) DK/Refused

29. What is your occupation?

30. What are/were your parents'/guardians' occupations?
31. Do you have children?   (1) Yes   (2) No   If yes, how many?
32. In what geographic area of the country were you raised?
33. What is your current marital status?
    (1) Single   (2) Married   (3) Divorced   (4) Widowed
    (5) Separated   (6) Other   (7) DK/Refused
34. With what racial group do you identify?
35. What is the highest level of education you have attained:
    (1) Some high school   (2) High school diploma   (3) Some college
    (4) College degree   (5) Some graduate school
    (6) Graduate/professional degree   (7) Other   (8) DK/Refused
36. What is your religious affiliation?
37. Do you belong to a political party?   (1) Yes   (2) No   If yes, which one?
38. Gender?   M   F   Other

Content Analysis

My data for analysis in this component are inclusive of newsletters ($n = 7$), flyers ($n = 22$) and any textual information such as emails and office memos that were generated by the organization with which I came in contact ($n = 467$). Some were meant for public consumption, like flyers and newsletters. Generally, these fell into the categories of recruitment, advertisements for events, and the dissemination of the organizations' goals and purpose. Other documents were intraoffice communications, emails on which I was cc'd (carbon-copied), and various other documents. To analyze all relevant data, I used content analysis as formulated by Fairclough (2003) and Brown and Yule (1989). I employed four coding strategies: (1) identification of the target audiences; (2) classification of various formal features of the object; (3) causal effects of the object; and (4) ideological content.

Coding Schedule

1. General Information
   1.1 Title
   1.2 Time of publication
   1.3 Important precursors to publication
   1.4 Period of time publication in circulation
   1.5 Addressor
   1.6 Addressee

1.7 Audience

1.8 Topic

1.9 Setting

1.10 Channel (type of method)

1.11 Type of exchange (activity, knowledge)

1.12 Type of function (statement, question, demand, offer)

1.13 Tone (declarative, interrogative, imperative)

1.14 Style (pragmatic, metaphor, allegory, narrative)

1.15 Manifest and latent purpose

2. Target audiences

2.1 Demographics of audience

2.2 Producer's presupposed knowledge of the audience

2.3 Relation of audience to producer

2.4 Importance of publication in reaching audience

2.5 Context in which the publication is situated

2.6 Relevance of the information to audience

3. Classification of various formal features of the publication

3.1 Organization of knowledge in the object

3.2 Variation over time of publications (especially websites)

3.3 Usage of recognizable icons or forms

3.4 Point of view being represented

4. Causal effects of the publication

4.1 Producer's presupposed effect of the publication on the audience

4.2 Unintended consequences foreseen (negative or positive)

5. Ideological Content of the Publication

5.1 Openness, recognition of, exploration of, difference

5.2 Accentuation of power, conflict, or struggle

5.3 Tone of resolution

5.4 Tone of problematizing

5.5 Theme of individuality of community

5.6 Democratic or authoritative

5.7 Existential or value assumptions

5.8 Semantic relationships (causal, conditional, temporal, elaborative, additive, concessive, etc.)

5.9 Events/Actors/Object that are included/excluded

5.10 Abstract or concrete references

5.11 Processes represented (material, mental, verbal, relational, existential)

5.12 Classification of Events/Actors/Objects

5.13 Aesthetic references

Appendix C

Notes on Decisions, Difficulty, Development, and Dangers

> *I have no doubt you'll misrepresent us. I can hope that we got through to you somehow, and you can get our message out there to others, but I'm not holding my breath. . . . I remember when you first showed up here, and I didn't think highly of it, I've told you that. I mean, you want to make a book out of my heart. It's an emotional thing. . . . How could I just be a reserved quiet person you study any more than you could just be the same as a researcher?*
>
> **—Tim, National Equality for All**

> *Just do your best to tell our story right. You have to put your own spin on it, I guess, but try to see everything from our perspective, you know? You've been with us for a while, and I hope, at least, um, I feel like I know somehow that you get it, you understand us to a certain extent, yeah? . . . To you it's just words maybe, but to us, it's our lives.*
>
> **—Bret, Whites for Racial Justice**

Deciding to Compare "Racists" and "Antiracists"

"You're going to do what?" Such was the response I received from many a friend, colleague, and even the barely known acquaintance when they learned of my intention to study both a white nationalist and a white antiracist organization—and not just to study them from afar but to immerse myself in both. To many, this seemed not just a decision beset with difficulty but a foolhardy choice fraught with danger inclusive of access, my safety, and people's reception of my work. I was not without trepidation, but my reason for finally settling on this topic and approach was manifold.

First, my time at the University of Virginia (UVA) seemed inundated with the clash of differing forces: Its legacy as a haven for the inculcation of southern white male gentility was squarely met by various progressive campus movements to establish racial, gender, sexual, and class equality (once resulting in a three-day takeover of the university president's office); the classic pattern of "town versus gown" disputes; the overflow of nearby D.C. politics that left people torn over the George W. Bush administration, the meanings of the Patriot Acts, the two wars in Iraq and Afghanistan, and FEMA's (the

Federal Emergency Management Agency's) handling of Hurricane Katrina's devastation. These debates created an environment in which worldviews were often presented in the form of stark morality tales where everyone claimed the side of "good" and decried the other as "evil" . . . while real lives hung in the balance. It was against this backdrop that I gained a deepened familiarity with the sociology of race, inequality, culture, and knowledge. My intellectual curiosity was piqued when I considered how people construct dichotomous worlds of right and wrong and how that construction constrains and enables both identity formation and the practice of racism.

Second, the aforementioned milieu certainly influenced my students. My courses centered on the topics of race, inequality, and various "social problems." In teaching about these topics, I noticed how easily students flocked to the denunciation of overt forms of racism. Groups like the Klan, Neo-Nazis, and racists of this ilk were often anointed as evil incarnate while systematic and structural racism were matters not so easily grasped. So, too, many students—who were themselves active in many organizations geared to bringing on some form of social change—often interpreted good intentions as prima facie evidence that they were not a part of anything "racist." Such a rendering often resulted in their struggle to understand social life as becoming complex and rather sloppy. Many of the white students in my classroom especially often struggled to understand how "racism" could be reproduced without the presence of a "racist" in the picture.[1] To compound the issue, these students were constantly beset by messages that we live in a "postracial" world and that the remedy for racial inequality is to become "color-blind" in their personal lives as well as in public, legal, and policy stances. Teaching in these classrooms challenged me to think creatively about how to best present evidence and reasoning to that cohort of undergraduate students.

Third, not one to place myself above the fray, I was recruited to join an organization whose goal was to educate about, and try to eliminate, racism. Dominated by white members (seventy-three out of eighty-five), the group met weekly and frequently hosted activities, including lectures, workshops on problematizing racialized policies and laws, and movie nights in which a discussion of the film would follow. After a few weeks with the group, I noticed the tendency for members to treat racial "otherness" as an "exotic" or "authentic" feature of social life. I saw how members often reduced "racism" to the domain of individual bad intentions and prejudices. And I witnessed how structural explanations to racial inequality were easily labeled as "too abstract," as "engaging in theorizing," or as "uncaring about 'real things.'" That such a group would reproduce many of the things it sought to displace both saddened and intrigued me. I eventually studied this group formally.[2] After I interviewed members, observed their practices, and analyzed their official documents, it was clear to me that the white members, while holding seemingly sincere aspirations for racial equality, used this group for (1) their own credentialism and legitimation in part of the "good" (antiracist) corps of white people and (2) to up their "multicultural IQ" as they learned about racial "otherness." Activities that did confront policies and practices thought unfair were sparsely attended or spearheaded by the few members of color in the organization. From there, I started to wonder how it was that whites across the political spectrum—from "antiracist" to "racist"—actually made meaning of whiteness and its relation to racism, antiracism, and the material realities of racial inequality.

Fourth, with the aforementioned in mind, I turned to the sociological literature. In reading and teaching on race and ethnicity, particularly white racial identity, I noticed that scholarly discussions of whiteness were beset with a number of paradoxes. At one moment, whiteness was presented as an "invisible" norm, while at the next it was discussed in the context of the rising tide of explicitly marked white identity movements. In one instance it was framed as a heterogeneous cacophony of individuals, while in other places whiteness was discussed as a cohesive group of privileged actors. Scholars spoke of how whites often implicitly think of themselves as superior to nonwhites, while they also highlighted the tendency of whites to claim unfair victimhood in a "politically correct" world. And in reference to white racists and antiracists, studies seemed to presuppose these groups to be the dominant bookends of whiteness; adherents supposedly possessed by different political leanings, resources, and ideological worldviews. Sociological discourse seemed to fall short on explaining how supposedly distinct and antagonistic forms of whiteness—under both the best and worst of intentions—drew on and reproduced the logics and rationales for maintaining white privilege and supremacy. This realization coalesced for me the day I read an *Annual Review of Sociology* article in which Monica McDermott and Frank Samson wrote, "Navigating between the long-term staying power of white privilege and the multifarious manifestations of the experience of whiteness remains the task of the next era of research on white racial and ethnic identity."[3] "That's it!" I thought. I was off and running . . . or so I thought.

The Difficulties of Entrance

My initial belief that I would get not just one, but two, ethnographies off the ground without too much trouble was a result of either my naïveté or my enthusiasm or perhaps a combination of both. Don't get me wrong: I certainly did not think such groups would afford access with open arms, but I was unprepared for how difficult Institutional Review Board (IRB) approval would become. Before I submitted my initial paperwork to study white nationalists and white antiracists, I thought of myself as an "old hat" at IRB protocol. Prior to this study, I had worked on a number of projects with mentors and colleagues and had familiarized myself with the nuances of ethics protocol. Moreover, I was already seduced by the promise of critical and cultural theory to unmask the power and meanings of everyday life.[4] I saw IRBs as predictable enough via their authoritative function to safeguard both subjects from harm and institutions of higher learning from lawsuits. I knew I had to present a thorough case grounded in the extant literature on studying activist groups and proper methodology conforming to institutional and American Sociological Association (ASA) standards and to perform a docile humility in my interactions with the board. And so I set my course.

My first idea was to study both groups as an "undisclosed participant observer" (meaning that I would use deception and not disclose my identity as a sociologist until the end of the study). I submitted two separate IRB research proposals (one for each group) and waited. My first contact with the IRB was one of flat refusal. They declined further consideration of my project on the grounds that deception was "unethical."[5] I had no desire to reproduce any research debacles, and thanks to their curt dismissal of my proposed research, recollections of studies like Humphries' *Tearoom Trade*, the Milgram research at Yale University, and the Zimbardo prison experiments at Stanford University all ran through my head.[6] I neither wished for any duplication of their unethical studies, nor did I want to use deception for its own sake. But I was concerned that no politicized racial group—especially a white nationalist or supremacist organization—would receive an intruding sociologist with open arms. Still, the IRB rejection of deception in my proposal was adamant, so I revised my methodology to reflect disclosed research, inclusive of all language and forms that would enable others to give their "informed consent" to participate in the research. Still my proposal was rejected.

For the weeks that followed, revision after revision seemed to bring new concerns to the fore. Weeks later, the board escalated their requests for revisions and began contradicting their own instructions. In one version, the board questioned my desire to use audio recording equipment (this had never been an issue in any prior IRB proposals) and maintained that I use "anonymous notes" rather than audio. A later response told me that I could not "legally" rely on notes or oral consent, so I revised my proposal accordingly and resubmitted it. In the next response letter, I was told that that oral consent would protect participants better than written consent. Such flip-flops disturbed my equilibrium. As the gymnastics went on for months, I began to feel that the routine would never end. In another response—and even though I was not investigating a group with any ties to my university—my proposal was rejected under the rationale that "racism is a heated issue at the university right now." In another letter the board began to undermine the entire platform of my research. They questioned the scientific merit of my study by either insinuating or outright stating that interviews or surveys would more than suffice in the place of ethnographic methods.

After nearly ten months of this back-and-forth on both IRB proposals, I was at wits' end. One of my mentors was also at a loss. "I've never seen anything like this," he told me. As a last resort, he suggested I appeal directly to the director of the IRB. In December 2005, armed with all the revisions to both proposals, I sent a mountain of paperwork to IRB office, requesting a meeting with the director to discuss my research. By early January 2006, I received a response. Without much explanation, both of my much-revised proposals, inclusive of ethnographic methodology, were approved given that the research was "minimal risk."[7] Suddenly, my research seemed to present little to no danger. The only information I planned to withhold was that I would not inform either group that I was studying their "enemy."[8] As these were two separate cases with separate IRB protocols, it was my theoretical goal only to compare one with the other at the conclusion of the study. To wit, I chose not to disclose my interest in comparison for fear of radically altering how each group perceived me and how they would portray themselves. While my presence certainly changed the setting (what ethnographic procedure does not?), my goal was not so much seeing how one group dealt with, or thought about, the other but how racialized talk and practice emerged in everyday life with the members of two different groups.[9]

Although my research could be considered sensitive, my experiences illustrate the escalating difficulty some scholars have in not only implementing "reflexive" science (currently unaligned with the National Research Council's interpretation of "science") but also in studying politicized groups and people. Contemporary research gatekeepers like the IRB possess a necessary function in protecting people. This is an ethical concern of utmost import with which I wholeheartedly agree. At the same time, IRBs exhibit a disciplinary function: "the ability to discipline (and punish) members of the social science research community who choose to exercise alternative methodological (e.g., qualitative), framework (e.g., critical theorist positions), or design (e.g., emergent) choices for their studies."[10] IRBs were formed to review biomedical and psychological research involving high risk to human participants. As they expanded to review other branches of the social sciences, they inscribed the peculiarities of medical and psychometric traditions of inquiry, effectively imposing moral and ethical standards inappropriate to some theoretical and methodological frameworks.[11] Given this mismatch, during my quest for approval, I often felt that "the stances of IRBs have shifted from assuring that human subjects' rights are protected toward monitoring, censuring, and outright disapproval of projects that use qualitative research, phenomenological approaches, and other alternative frameworks for knowing and knowledge."[12] I battled tooth and nail to keep my ethnographic procedures intact. Even though I was finally granted approval, my research was delayed nearly a year, and I would venture to say that perhaps my own welfare was not exactly protected. Still, some might consider I was lucky given that many researchers have not suffered such a kind fate.[13]

With the unexplained IRB approval in hand, I was now tasked with convincing a white nationalist and an antiracist group to allow my ethnographic entrance. This too tested my mettle. Months passed as I approached groups by letter, telephone, email, and in person and was rejected. Generally, groups were initially receptive about my interest in them, but, after learning that I wanted to study how their members understood whiteness, many seemed unsettled or puzzled. "What is there to study?" I was often asked. "You're either white or you're not," many stated. I kept at it, searching for groups up and down the U.S. East Coast. Finally, in March and April 2006 the stars seemed to align, and the leadership of two separate groups agreed to meet with me. Both were skeptical of my intentions, but, after a series of meetings, anxieties were laid to rest with the assurance that all identifying names, places, and actions would be disguised with pseudonyms. By May 2006 I was meeting regularly with members of both National Equality for All and Whites for Racial Justice.

A Developing Acceptance

Gaining entry and negotiating a continued acceptance should not be conflated. Attending public meetings and meeting skeptical members characterized my first few weeks with NEA and WRJ. While the time I spent with members of WRJ helped to generate trust and rapport, I faced a significant challenge with the membership of NEA—they repeatedly turned me down for interviews. While no one took issue with my attendance of meetings and reading NEA literature, they seemed distrustful of my presence. After my first few weeks, one member pulled me aside to tell me why others seemed hesitant to talk to me. In the past, another social scientist had interviewed members of the organization and published the findings in an unflattering manner. The organization, many of its members, and its goals were not disguised, and while members all agreed to the terms of that research, they felt as though the researcher's portrayal was inaccurate and defamatory. "You're here because your work might publicize white nationalism," one member told me. Continuing, she said: "But I'm not sure I trust talking to you about my life."

Building trust with research informants is difficult business and remains a central focus of ethnographic inquiry. For example, in both *Dude You're a Fag: Masculinity and Sexuality in High School* and *Heaven's Kitchen: Living Religion at God's Love We Deliver*, authors C. J. Pascoe and Courtney Bender, respectively, recounted the trials and tribulations of engendering trust.[14] In these studies, both high school boys and volunteers in a nonprofit organization were incredibly defensive and highly cognizant of how others saw them. Accordingly, they had great difficulty in creating an affinity between the "researcher" and the "researched." In taking cues from studies such as these, I learned that trust was sometimes gained when I consented to my *informants interviewing me*. In choosing whether to open up their lives, the men and women of NEA (and to a lesser degree, WRJ) possessed a litany of questions about my study, my professional training, my mentors, and even my personal life—from personal queries about my family to my taste in music—to assess my ethics, politics, and ability to tell their story correctly. These types of questions never stopped throughout the research, but I was quite receptive to them at the beginning of my research as they generated a rapport of sharing as a crucial baseline.

Another tactic was emphasizing my status as a "social scientist" (emphasis on word *scientist*) at the University of Virginia. This was counterintuitive to me, as I thought such Jeffersonian accoutrements would only cement the insider/outsider distinction. However, the cachet of a credentialed person writing down one's words and actions signaled scholarly import, and seeing oneself as worthy of such scrutiny can be an attractive proposition. This meant that some became quite excited for me to ask them questions. In more than one instance—and with slight braggadocio—I heard one member say to another, "He asked *me* for a follow-up interview tomorrow."

As much as these approaches did work, I don't want to overstate the case. These tactics were context dependent. My emphasis on, and the ratio between, personal exposure and professional expertise was neither a simple function of time spent with both organizations nor a rational and conscious decision on my part. I emphasize that these interactions were decidedly social arrangements that were constantly navigated. I never controlled them. Some details about my professional life never came up, I consciously hid some personal information, and on a few occasions I destroyed trust rather than created it. In one instance, my attempt to wield "sociological expertise" backfired when my knowledge of segregation differed from one of my informants. In another, my easy familiarity with one participant led him to question the seriousness by which I undertook my research.

This tension forced me to reflect even more on how my own identity was perceived by subjects. I was determined not to fall into a pattern all too endemic to social science. Reflexivity concerns the entire research process. It is more than how sociologists write up their results, as if the ethnographic process can be left unaltered and the only things that change are the post hoc narratives. Throughout the research, I aimed for awareness of the conditions of my own knowledge production and my cultural and social location within the academy and in the field. I speak only to my own status as a white male researcher with humility because I can analyze only the processes and positions of which I am aware. After all, "some of the influences arising from aspects of social identity remain beyond the reflexive grasp."[15] Hence, I followed the suggestions of Charles Gallagher: "While the majority of whites enjoy many privileges relative to other racial groups, one must nevertheless critically access where one's social location, political orientation, religious training, and attitudes on race fit in with the research process."[16]

The question of racial reflexivity between researcher and subjects often boils down to an overly simplistic assumption. "Closeness of identity and, in particular shared racial identity is generally presumed to promote effective communication between researcher and subject and, conversely, disparate identity to inhibit it."[17] While I am confident that only a white researcher could gain the access that I did, I remain unconvinced that my racial (and gender) alignment with most of my subjects guaranteed closeness. As a white male with working- and middle-class dispositions that I performed via clothing, language and intonation, and various aesthetic tastes, I was often "read" by members of both groups as similar to them but not "radical" enough in ideology. My identity, not just in terms of race, had to occupy a space that was just right. To open up, people had to feel I was open to "recruitment" as either a nationalist or antiracist, while I had to simultaneously perform the "rationality," "objectivity," and "logic" that a competent white man was supposed to embody.

To overcome this hurdle, I created spaces in which the subjects and I could meditate on the similarities of our lived experiences with white masculinity. Concentrating on these similarities proved crucial starting places for the research. As I emphasized our commonalities and portrayed a "possessive investment in whiteness,"[18] members slowly changed their tone. Members began to say, "I used to be like you," or that I might one day "become one of us." Soon thereafter, I received increased requests to visit members' homes to meet their families, had my choice of daily lunch dates, and was given numerous invitations to join both their organizations at the conclusion of my research. With such permission and under the condition that the members' identities would be kept confidential, my research site suddenly expanded to local coffee shops, trips to the store in members' cars, and conversations in their homes as their children sat on my lap and cats roamed about (causing a great deal of members' sympathy for my feline allergies).

Yet just as much as attention to differences can silently privilege common experiences, I was concerned that focus on our apparent similarities, and its generated closeness, might result in my unintentional objectification of our social dynamics. Accentuating sameness could generate an affective pull that might lead me to miss particular representations of power dynamics and dominant ideologies at work. Yasmin Gunaratnam writes:

> Interpretations of commonality and difference, and the constructed opposition between these identifications need to be viewed with caution. They are most productively seen as emotional, discursive, interactional and inconclusive movements that test out and push at the boundaries, entanglements and contradictions of the production of identifications.[19]

I focused on what generated both closeness and alienation, namely patterned feelings of empathy and repulsion that generated affect on my or my subjects' part. As Sara Ahmed writes, "A politics of encountering gets closer in order to allow the differences between us, as differences that involve power and antagonism, to make a difference to the very encounter itself."[20]

Attention to my own reflexivity in these settings required that I also question my subjects' presentation of selves. Both groups labored extensively to appeal to the abstract principles of individual liberty and equality. I wondered whether the acknowledgment of these principles was more a condition of impression management rather than a genuine attitude. There is a great deal of research that examines the strategic moves one makes—through appeals to widely shared cultural principles—to present a favorable image to others.[21] I have tried throughout the preceding chapters to show that the people portrayed felt comfortable with me to speak honestly enough. I then "triangulated" that data with other instances in which they spoke, wrote, or acted. For the white antiracists, this should be more or less believable, as they dedicated their lives to the principles and practices of a racially just and equal society. For the nationalists—and this might be a stretch to some—many of them truly believed that equal treatment was an important and necessary component of modernity and one to which all people were entitled. For others, they rationalized the presence of inequality through other mechanisms . . . just as the antiracists did.

One of the ways I validated these assertions was by exploring how race operated with and through narratives not directly related to race. For example, Caroline Knowles found that one should "deconstruct" the meanings of race by highlighting the seemingly nonracial narratives that people use. Racial dynamics need

> to be broken down into concepts which can be applied in the task of making sense of lives. The concept race itself may or may not be used in individual narratives. Whether or not race features *directly* depends on the political culture and individuals experiences within it. . . . There *are* ready-worked narratives of collective suffering which some people use to make sense of what has happened to them individually.[22]

Through members' shared comfort in talking about suffering, victories, hard work, citizenship, music, and a plethora of "nonracial" objects, ideas, and practices, these members demonstrated their own understandings of whiteness. It was during these discussions that I observed how, when, and why they became (un)conscious of their whiteness in relation to those things.

After the six-month mark of my research, I gained a preliminary sense of the common patterns and logics employed in these members' lives. I tested my observations by engaging in what both Paul Ricoeur and Hans-Georg Gadamer called the "hermeneutics of suspicion"—whereby I overtly questioned the logic or assumptions of informants' statements and asked them repeatedly to clarify and defend their rationales. Such a technique created an interesting space in which dialog, rather than monolog, was the order of the day. Fieldwork with nationalists and antiracists transformed from passive observation and defined schedules of interview questions to lively debates, lengthy conversations, and sometimes (although usually civil) arguments.

My trust in the authenticity of their words was further deepened as both groups tested how I saw them. As the members of both groups, but especially NEA, coded me as a "liberal sociologist," they constantly questioned what I was writing down, what I thought, and how I would convey what I saw to colleagues. These queries were not stumbling, but building, blocks from which I constructed hypothesizes and tested them. The "data" generated from such back-and-forth were eye-opening. My field notes and preliminary reports were subject to scrutiny and refinement by members who commented passionately on what they thought I got both wrong and right. This book is better for that, and I thank them for their attentive labor. I learned much from these conversations. At times, they turned quite personal, so I refrain from sharing those dialogs in their totality. And while I chose not to turn some of those precise moments into fodder for the sociological can[n]on, these conversations certainly better informed my sociological imagination.

My ingratiation with nationalists and antiracists, the attempt to create honest and repeatedly scrutinized data, and the considerable attention paid to the nuance of my and their racialized facework led to a tangle of research in which the line between insider and outsider was blurred, if not drastically disfigured. Nancy Naples writes:

> By acknowledging the fluidity of outsiderness/insiderness, we also acknowledge three key methodological points: as ethnographers we are never fully outside or inside the "community"; our relationship to the community is never expressed in general terms but is constantly being negotiated and renegotiated in particular, everyday interactions; and these interactions are themselves located in shifting relationships among community residents.[23]

The shifting "locations" (in both an ontological and epistemological sense) were intertwined with my attempt to retain a critical sociological perspective and my worry that I relay accurate interpretations of how white nationalists and antiracists feel similarly about, and "perform," whiteness. Together, this led me to another concern: How you, the reader, will interpret them and me.

The Dangers of Reception

While the promise of confidentiality vis-à-vis pseudonyms and disguise was both an ethical component of these two ethnographies and a crucial passport that kept me in good graces, the richness of my experiences with NEA and WRJ was double edged. From the onset of the research, I was blessed and cursed by access to the incredible practices of white nationalists and white antiracists. My field notes ran wild, and my journals exploded with data that, in at least one instance, would make a court case really worth watching. This left me in a predicament. If I disguised the data enough, I would significantly blunt the power of these members' stories. Conversely, if I told the specificities of what was going on, I would compromise their confidentiality. The fallout over Arlene Stein's study *The Stranger Next Door*, in which the identity of the small Oregon "Timbertown" and many of its residents was exposed in a regional newspaper, came to mind.[24] The identity of her subjects was laid bare, leaving many whom she interviewed feeling betrayed and embittered. I decided to err on the side of reining in my data to protect my subjects. For that, I pay the price of not presenting a considerable number of details worthy, in their own right, of telling. In consideration of the limitations inherent in ethical ethnographic accounts, this book does resemble a "controlled fiction of difference and similitude."[25] And because of the inherent difficulties in ethnographic inquiry, I hold a three-pronged concern for this book's reception.

A core tenet of ethnography is that one should take a sympathetic stance toward one's subjects. Stemming from Weber's and Simmel's concept of *verstehen* (one might call it "interpretive understanding"), the ethnographer attempts an empathic or participatory understanding of social phenomena. Under this logic, ethnographic inquiry should illumine, perhaps in a soft light, the worldviews of others. When the "other" is a Trobriand Islander (as in Malinowski's *Argonauts of the Western Pacific*) or an isolated Brazilian community (as in Lévi-Strauss's *Tristes Tropiques*) this posture is generally received as straightforward and relatively problem free.[26] However, when the "other" is close to home, the sympathetic identification with subjects is much, much trickier. I take great pains in this book to explain the cultural logic behind both the nationalist and antiracist movements, how these logics intertwine with the meanings of white racial identity, and how actors' ongoing racial identity formation is enabled and constrained by these worldviews. Each member, regardless of orientation, took pains to present his or her understanding of race as fairly "natural" and self-evident. They believed in the legitimacy of their positions and attempted to make the other side seem immoral and false. Importantly, members lived these positions; they were not just talking points for impression management. I felt compelled to portray how these logics are sensible and common sense to their adherents. In turn, I worry that some will think I have either "gone native" or lost my critical perspective. In so doing, I find myself in a camp with other scholars who study "politically incorrect" groups. Kathleen M. Blee has been accused of being too empathetic in her treatment of women in the Klan, and Faye Ginsburg has taken significant heat for her portrayal of right-to-life women's movements.[27] In fact, Ginsburg herself wrote that scholars "inevitably find it difficult to suspend judgment, particularly when they disagree with those represented. . . . the people I studied are considered by most of my colleagues to be their enemies."[28] The people I studied are considered both enemies and endeared friends. I have labored mightily not to place my own opinions in my subjects' mouths and then "discover" them as unique and vital data. And it is because of my critical stance that I felt incumbent to tell a story, at least in key places, that allows them the benefit of the doubt.

Second, I worry about a converse reading. Some may think my analysis too hard edged and critical. I find similarities between racists and antiracists. This will upset quite a few. For example, after I gave a talk on this research to an academic audience in Canada, several attendees disputed my findings by saying such similarities between racist and antiracist whites were flatly impossible. Furthermore, they asserted that I was really studying "American-ness" rather than "whiteness" (the subtext a denial that liberal, antiracist Canadians would ever subscribe to the kinds of racism I show in this book).[29] In another instance, I blogged about my research on RacismReview.com, and I received a message from a prominent antiracist (not one whom I studied in my research) who accused me of a personal "attack" on her/him and said that my blog entry was a "pretty gross insult." In other informal settings, I have been flatly told that my research is either untrue or ideologically biased. What is one to do? I did my utmost to write with a sympathetic pen while refusing to compromise my sociological chops. In either case, some will find fault. It is my hope that the strengths of my analysis will outweigh the missteps.

Third, I worry that the subjects I studied will think ill of my work and of me. I have tried my best to present accurate worldviews of both the white nationalists and white antiracists I met. As an antiracist would not want anyone to think there would be overlap with a nationalist, and vice versa, my project of comparing for similarities puts me between a rock and a hard place. I doubt that either will like my evaluation of similarity. Still, I stand by that assessment. I can say it no better than Kristin Luker did in her approach to prolife and prochoice activists in *Abortion and the Politics of Motherhood*: "If I have done my job well, both sides will soon conclude that I have been unduly generous with the opposition and unfairly critical of themselves. They will become annoyed and perhaps outraged as they read things that they know to be simply and completely wrong."[30] I am relieved that many subjects did agree with some of my appraisals during the fieldwork, just as I am happy that many did not agree (I would hope others would find a work suspect if those studied agreed with every one of the researcher's evaluations). In the end, I believe that sociologically informed thinking can grind a lens that allows us to see previously invisible and mystified patterns of social activity.

I take this position not because I believe sociology affords a "view from nowhere" but because I believe in a rather a highly disciplined and rigorous intersubjectivity. I argue that this approach mitigates one of ethnography's primary difficulties: As hard as we try, in the end, ethnography is a tale about many told by one. Accordingly, James Clifford acknowledges that the ethnographic representation of different voices ends up "confirming the final virtuoso orchestration by a single author of all the discourses in his or her text."[31] Simply put, writing means authoring, when all is said and done. I know some of my subjects will pick up this book, see themselves on the pages, and disagree with my words. To that, I can only say that I offer a mirror that will, on a profound level, refuse to flatter.

Despite some people's unwillingness to see similarities between NEA and WRJ, my research claims are quite humble. The correspondence between these two groups exists where they together hold up an ideal form of white racial identity. By destabilizing the bifurcated narrative of "good" and "evil" whites, I don't mean to reinstall another essentialist claim that these whites are all the same. One-dimensional narratives are tempting when dealing with the complexity of controversial subjects, even more so here in my comparison of two radical groups. There were many forms of white identity expressed during my research, but many of these were subordinate, and measured as wanting, in relation to that ideal. My concentration on the similarities invites us to consider the ways in which racist scripts underlie an array of whitenesses today and that we must be careful to avoid political or moralizing judgments in deciding who is who or where one really stands. My concentration on the hegemonic ideal serves as a heuristic that can assist us to make sense of one aspect of social life. After all, life is messy, complex, and contradictory.

In deciphering the meanings of whiteness, it was important to examine NEA and WRJ members in that messiness—in their everyday lives. I saw not just formalized "activists" but people navigating the mundane—just as we all do. When approached in this way, there was no magnetic attraction that neatly pulled people to their corresponding activist community. Neither NEA nor WRJ held a static ideology that fit members' already preconceived notions of race. Their attitudes and identities constantly evolved as they both settled their gaze on the same world to which we all awake. Members of both sides voice a scathing critique of a society that embodies a litany of inconsistencies in relation to democracy, freedom, rights, and privileges. Both groups' members see the nation's attempt to deal with racial difference as fraught with mishaps, inconsistencies, and lies. Members of both groups were anxious about the future, and they worried about their children's lives. Like many a dialectic, NEA and WRJ have a kind of equivalence. They both draw on a predominant understanding of race that prevails in our contemporary moment, and they use that understanding to chase after a common racial identity. And so I chose to weave that common thread throughout this book, and I remain confident that it will hold the pages together.

Notes

Chapter 1

1. For an analogous and apt discussion of the construction of gendered identities, see Ridgeway, 2011.

2. Omi and Winant, 1994 [1986]: 56.

3. Lamont and Fournier, 1992: 12.

4. Bryson, 2005.

5. Lamont and Molnár, 2002: 168–169.

6. Croll, 2007: 634–635.

7. Zerubavel, 2002.

8. Aptheker, 1992.

9. White supremacist ideologies and practices (and their opposition) do not always—or even often—fall along the conventional and expected lines of white "racists" like neo-Nazis or white "antiracists" like the Alliance of White Anti-Racists Everywhere. This is not to say that such distinctions are meaningless or false. Rather, I emphasize that bigoted, chauvinistic, or xenophobic worldviews do not exclusively belong to those we already understand as "racist." By looking for white racism and white antiracism as neatly defined and oppositional categories, we may blind ourselves to the ways that white supremacist practices manifest in more subtle and complex forms of white racial identity to produce profound consequences.

10. Feagin and Vera, 1995: xi.

11. Southern Poverty Law Center (SPLC), 2011.

12. See "James W. Von Brunn: Holocaust Museum Shooting Suspect Is White Supremacist," retrieved on September 17, 2011, from www.huffingtonpost.com/2009/06/10/james-w-von-brunn-holocau_n_213864.html; "KTLA Gets Davenport Scoop. Racist Orange County Republican Email: President Obama and His Parents

Are Apes," retrieved on September 10, 2011, from http://blogs.ocweekly.com/
navelgazing/2011/04/racist_orange_county_republica.php; "Mayor Is Criticized for
White House Watermelon Patch E-Mail," retrieved on September 10, 2010, from
www.ocregister.com/news/mail-140877-price-public.html; Kanazawa, 2011.

13. Hughey, 2011b.

14. Wilson, 1860.

15. Hughes, 1971 [1934]; Du Bois, 1976 [1920]; Baldwin, 1998.

16. Frankenberg, 1993.

17. Terry, 1981: 119; Feagin and Vera, 1995: 139; Tatum, 1997: 93; Doane, 2003: 7.

18. Dyer, 1988: 44.

19. Gallagher, 1995.

20. Daniels, 1997; Dobratz and Shanks-Meile, 1997.

21. Frankenberg, 2001. In this essay, Frankenberg revises her earlier contention
that whiteness is little more than unmarked privilege.

22. Doane and Bonilla-Silva, 2003.

23. Bonilla-Silva, 2010 [2003].

24. *Gratz v. Bollinger* found the University of Michigan undergraduate affirma-
tive action admissions policy to be too mechanistic and therefore unconstitutional.
Conversely, *Grutter v. Bollinger* upheld the affirmative action admissions policy of the
University of Michigan Law School by a 5–4 decision. *Meredith v. Jefferson County
Board of Education* concerned racial segregation in public education. The U.S. Su-
preme Court rejected the use of a student's race in student assignment plans.

25. Gallagher, 1995: 169.

26. Ferber, 2000: 31.

27. Winant, 2004: 12.

28. Winant, 1997: 105.

29. Winant, 2004: 3.

30. Bonnett, 2000a: 10.

31. Niemonen, 2007: 166–167.

32. Bonilla-Silva, 2010 [2003]: 15.

33. Wise, 2009: 84.

34. Duster, 2001: 115.

35. Cleaver, 1989 [1968]: 80.

36. Kenny, 2000; Morris, 2006.

37. Lewis, 2004: 634.

38. Gramsci, 1971. Gramsci described cultural conflict as a "war of position." In
this sense, hegemony is never total or final. At any moment there are always competing racial logics circulating that hold the possibility of undermining, if not challenging, hegemonic "common sense."

39. Marcuse, 1964.

40. Hall, 1981. "Cultural dupes" is a well-known phrase in cultural theory that posits that actors are easily tricked or duped by ideology to mindlessly act as ideology would tell them to do.

41. Weber, 2002 [1905]. The exaltation of free will from a "rational actor" position—whereby actors maximize gain and reduce cost through focused calculation of efficiency and probable advantage—seems nearly controlled by the external structure of (un)available resources that Weber might call an "iron cage."

42. See Hays, 1994, for a larger discussion of the complex relationship of culture to both "structure" and "agency."

43. Berger and Luckmann, 1966; Garfinkel, 1967; Goffman, 1974; Giddens, 1984; Alexander, 1987.

44. Hughey, 2011b.

Chapter 2

1. Bonilla-Silva, 2010 [2003]: 3.

2. Blee, 2002: 167.

3. Charles refered to an oft-quoted phrase by Jefferson: "Nothing is more certainly written in the book of fate than that these people [blacks] are to be free. Nor is it less certain that the two races, equally free, cannot live in the same government. Nature, habit, opinion has drawn indelible lines of distinction between them." See Jefferson, 1904 [1853]; Lincoln, 1996 [1862].

4. They referred to the September 8, 2006, trial of a Pennville, NJ, man named Gabriel Carafa (age twenty-five) who was sentenced to eighty months in federal prison on charges of selling rifles, shotguns, and handguns without the required federal license to deal in firearms and for being a previously convicted felon in possession of a firearm. U.S. District Judge Robert B. Kugler also sentenced Carafa to pay a $2,000 fine and to serve three years of supervised release on the completion of his prison sentence. At his plea hearing Carafa admitted that he was a member of a white supremacist group known as "The Hated." See "Carafa, Gabriel, Guilty Plea, News Release"; retrieved on March 14, 2009 from www.usdoj.gov/usao/nj/press/files/cara0504_r.htm.

5. Daniel referred to a 2005 lawsuit brought against Macon, Mississippi, local Democratic Party Chairman Ike Brown by the U.S. Justice Department. Using the 1965 Voting Rights Act, the government alleged that Brown and local elections officials discriminated against whites. It is the first time the Justice Department has ever claimed that whites suffered voting discrimination because of race. See Nossiter, 2006.

6. Bonilla-Silva, 2010 [2003].

7. See Walsh, 2004.

8. Bonilla-Silva, 2010 [2003].

9. This section raises a particular concern regarding the betrayal of anonymity promised to my subjects. I aim to be as specific as possible without revealing details

that could jeopardize anonymity. Therefore, I am intentionally vague about certain details.

10. Hochschild, 1983, 2003.

11. See Myers and Williamson, 2001; Myers, 2005.

12. Bonilla-Silva, 2010 [2003].

13. I am unsure as to the precise words the NEA member used at this moment. I did not have my audio recorder with me, and I did not feel it would be appropriate or appreciated to suddenly pull out my notepad and start writing. Shortly after this interaction, I excused myself to the bathroom and wrote down as much of what I could remember on a notepad. I recommend this strategy for recording such unexpected yet important social interactions that will undoubtedly occur for every ethnographer in the field.

14. Building on Lewis (2004), I first advanced the theory of "hegemonic whiteness" in 2010 (Hughey 2010). I then have expanded on the theory elsewhere. See Hughey 2012a, 2012b, 2011a.

Chapter 3

1. Andersen, 2003: 30.

2. O'Brien, 2001: 4–5.

3. Thompson, 2001: 329.

4. Thompson, 2001; Brown, 2002.

5. Scott, 2001: 126.

Chapter 4

1. Labaton, 2008; Keller, 2009.

2. Reed, 1989.

3. Ferber, 2007.

4. Limbaugh, 2007, 2009.

5. Bennett, 2005.

6. Hunt-Grubbe, 2007.

7. Moynihan, 1965.

8. Massey and Denton, 1993: 8.

9. Many cite Lewis (1966) as the argument that propelled the "culture of poverty" perspective into the mainstream

10. Collins, 2005: 56–57.

11. Ferber, 2007: 15.

12. In a review of NYPD's "stop-and-frisk" policy, Lani Guinier found that 89 percent of the 575,000 New Yorkers stopped in 2009 were black or Latino, but those stop-and-frisks found no more contraband or illegal activity among blacks or Latinos than among whites. See Guinier, 2010; Parks and Hughey, 2010; Baker, 2010.

13. By the time of this research in 2007, serious violent crimes (homicide, rape, robbery, and aggravated assault) had dropped from 37.3 per 1,000 blacks in 1973 to 10.3 per 1,000 blacks by 2007, a reduction of over 3.6 times. See Bureau of Justice Statistics, Office of Justice Programs, 2010.

14.

After reviewing 22 recent studies estimating sentencing severity based on federal-level data, . . . more than two-thirds of the estimates reveal that blacks were sentenced more harshly than whites . . . Black and Hispanic offenders—particularly those who are young, male, or unemployed—are more likely than their white counterparts to be sentenced to prison; they also may receive longer sentences than similarly situated white offenders. Most striking perhaps is that, in 2001, 46 percent of inmates in state and federal prisons were black and 40.6 percent of inmates in jails were black, whereas blacks make up only 32.9 percent of those arrested for serious (FBI Index) crimes.

See Reiman and Leighton, 2004: 134.

15. Swain, 2002: 173.

16. Daniels, 1997: 99.

17. Ferber, 1999: 77.

18. Montagu, 1942; Gossett, 1963.

19. Frankenberg, 1993: 198.

20. Frazier, 1939.

21. While Lewis (1966) was a formative "culture of poverty" text, other manuscripts preceded Lewis's study to make a similar point: Material deprivation led to pathological and dysfunctional values and habits that, once normalized within a particular subculture, functioned to hold people in poverty. See Elkins, 1959; Clarke, 1965.

22. Moynihan, 1965.

23. Grier and Cobbs, 1968.

24. Fanon, 1967 [1952]: 7.

25. Staples, 1982.

26. Many influential studies framed black men as "feminized." See Franklin, 1984, 1985; Oliver, 1989a, 1989b.

26. Wilson, 1987.

27. Glassner, 1999.

28. Majors and Billson, 1992; Hunter and Davis, 1992.

29. Bernard, 1966. Of note, the American Sociological Association gives the annual "Jessie Bernard Award" in recognition of "scholarly work that has enlarged the horizons of sociology to encompass fully the role of women in society. The contribution may be in empirical research, theory, or methodology. It is presented for significant cumulative work done throughout a professional career."

30. hooks, 1992: 94.

31. Hill, 2005: 83.

32. Wray, 2006.

33. Collins, 2005.

34. Kelley, 1997: 19.

35. Portions of this chapter were revised from Hughey, 2012a.

Chapter 5

1. Blake, 2011; Norton and Sommers, 2011: 215.

2. Jones and Cox, 2010: 6.

3. See "Only 4 in 10 Americans Satisfied with Treatment of Immigrants"; retrieved on August 10, 2011, from www.gallup.com/poll/28405/only-americans-satisfied-treatment-immigrants.aspx.

4. See: AP-GfK Poll, GfK Roper Public Affairs & Corporate Communications, PollingReport.com; retrieved on September 4, 2011, from www.pollingreport.com/race.htm.

5. Gallagher, 2011.

6. Wise, 2009.

7. Bonilla-Silva, Goar, and Embrick. 2006; Lewis, 2004.

8. I have reworded some of the newspaper and media quotes throughout to maintain the anonymity of WRJ, NEA, and their members. I have done my best to retain the overall message and tone.

9. Daniels, 1997: 38. This text provides one of the most thorough treatments of the major principles and contradictions that underpin white supremacist discourse.

10. McKinney, 2005: 116.

11. Forman and Lewis, 2006: 193.

12. Eichstedt, 2001.

13. I remind the reader that Lisa was the only regular full-time female member of NEA. However, during the two months in which NEA attempted to mitigate the negative press brought about by their conference planning, six additional female members worked in The Office. They effectively became a temporary public face of NEA, whereby they marshaled a demure femininity to convince vendors and the media that NEA held an innocuous social agenda.

14. Daniels, 1997: 40–42. Daniels continues this trenchant discussion in reference to white nationalism's use of online and virtual forms of interaction and communication: See Daniels, 2009.

15. "Emotion work" is a phrase popularized by sociologist Arlie Hochschild. See Hochschild, 1983.

16. I was ill at ease during these outings with Colin and Andre. As a researcher bound by ethical obligations, the combination of alcoholic drinks, sexually charged

encounters, and the potential for betraying anonymity together created an environment in which one could too easily cross a line. As a result, I often distanced myself from Colin and Andre during these nights out. I made do with observing from afar or frequently excusing myself from situations I thought improper. This technique also enabled me to easily retire to the bathroom to take notes, and many of the quotations in this section are constructed from these notes and/or from the best of my recollection.

17. Horace refers to the well-known article on white privilege. See McIntosh, 1988.

18. According to the Bureau of Labor Statistics, by January 2011 there were approximately 112,754,000 employed white people and 2,938,000 unemployed black people. Hence, even if every single unemployed black worker displaced a white worker, less than 3 percent of whites would be affected. "Furthermore, affirmative action pertains only to job-qualified applicants, so the actual percentage of affected Whites would be a fraction of 1%. The main sources of job loss among White workers have to do with factory relocations and labor contracting outside the United States, computerization and automation, and corporate downsizing" (Plous, 2003). If affirmative action were displacing white workers, one would not see such disparity in actual unemployment rates (calculated by dividing the number of group unemployed workers by the total group labor force): By January of 2011 the white unemployment rate was 8.8 percent compared to an almost double black rate of 16.5 percent.

19. Woodson, 1990 [1933].

20. The members of NEA are much like what cultural sociologist Bethany Bryson described in *Making Multiculturalism*:

> Defenders of traditional education . . . worried that de-emphasizing Western culture might be dangerous. The ideas contained in those classic works of literature are, they argued, "the glue that binds together our pluralistic nation" . . . Soon, pundits such as Dinesh D'Souza and Roger Kimball jumped into the fray and escalated the rhetoric of cultural preservation to the point of frenzy, charging that multiculturalism would disintegrate U.S. national culture. (Bryson, 2005: 2)

21. Berbrier, 2000: 178.

22. The philosopher Alain Badiou suggests that people are often categorized in one of two ways: "On the one hand, a passive, pathetic [pathétique], or reflexive subject—he who suffers—and, on the other, the active, determining, subject of judgment—he who, in identifying suffering, knows that it must be stopped by all available means." Here, NEA seems to attempt a synthesis of these two categories as a crucial dimension of the ideal white self. See Badiou, 2002: 9.

23. Goffman, 1983: 4.

24. Goffman, 1983: 14.

25. Wallace, 2011.

26. *White Reference*, 2011.

27. Hartigan, 2010: x.

28. For example, between 1934 and 1962, the federal government backed $120 billion in home loans, of which 98 percent went to whites—further entrenching white housing segregation so that today whites are more segregated than any other racial group. Moreover, home ownership is a major determinate in wealth accumulation and reproduction between generations. Such programs enabled the white retention of wealth; while, comparatively, blacks held only 0.5 percent of the total wealth in the United States in 1865, only 1 percent by 1990, and only 2.5 percent by 2001. See Bullard, 2007: 7.

29. The following works hold thorough overviews of racialized inequality over an array of social structures and settings. See Oliver and Shapiro, 1995; Conley, 1999; Smedley, Stith, and Nelson, 2003; Bertrand and Mullainathan, 2004; Chesler, Lewis, and Crowfoot, 2005; Pager, 2007; Moore, 2008; Wacquant, 2009; Attewell and Newman, 2010; Freund, 2010; Parks and Hughey, 2010.

30. I remind the reader of Alastair Bonnett's poignant prose: "Whiteness has often been experienced as something very vulnerable, as an identity under threat. . . . the fragility of whiteness is a direct product of the extraordinary claims of superiority made on its behalf" (Bonnett, 2000b: 39).

Chapter 6

1. Associated Press, June 13, 2007.

2. Associated Press, October 15, 2007.

3. Associated Press, October 27, 2007.

4. Bennett, 2008.

5. Hamacher, 2011.

6. Cauvin, 2006.

7. Erikson, 2001: xii.

8. Sullivan, 2006: 149.

9. Foucault, 1984: 252.

10. Each of these techniques was observed in various settings and was coded (1 = present, 0 = absent) for each unit of analysis for each mode of observation. The units of analysis were: a paragraph of field notes, an observed interaction between two or more actors (ethnographic observations), a paragraph of transcribed interview data (in-depth interviews), and a paragraph of text from written communications (content analysis).

11. At times throughout the text I refrain from identifying NEA or WRJ members. I throw down this extra layer of anonymity when discussing particular examples that may be perceived as particularly unflattering. I do so because I feel, beyond the formal requirements of IRB and ethnographic ethics, a responsibility to protect their identities not only from outsiders but also from fellow members.

12. Like all names, this is a pseudonym.

13. In the landmark book *The Velvet Glove*, Mary Jackman draws attention to how paternalism is easily overlooked or misrecognized as friendly cooperation. See Jackman, 1994: 10–11.

14. Coontz, 2000; Cott, 2000.

15. Hill, 2005: 8.

16. Fraiman, 1994: 71.

17. Schwalbe, 2008: 182.

18. Ridgeway, 1990: 19.

19. When arriving at members' homes for the first time, I was often asked about my research, my intentions, and my findings. This was often a challenge, as speaking in both honest and tactful language was a necessary step in continuing my stay in their homes. On one home visit such a talk lasted five minutes, and I was told to make myself at home, while another meeting lasted hours during which each member of the family scrutinized my intentions. In the end, I was able to observe five NEA daughters and their living arrangements. So, too, families allowed me to roam their homes while I jotted notes and even permitted me to interrupt their daily activities to ask questions about the arcane details of their homes, from questions about their ownership and display of pictures, posters, books, and various kitsch to questions as to why they had decided to live in their particular neighborhood.

20. Kipling, 1908.

21. Spivak, 1985.

22. Bush, 2001.

23. Abu-Lughod, 2002: 784. See also Cooke, 2001.

24. Schwalbe, 2008: 182.

25. Like all names, this is a pseudonym.

26. It is possible that such logic found resonance with WRJ members because of its historical embeddings in antiracist activism. In discussing the gendered dynamics of the civil rights movement for racial equality, Ferree and Hess write:

> Much of the African American male leadership, and *virtually all of their white male sympathizers* [my emphasis], believed that the costs of racism were borne primarily by black men, "emasculated" by their lack of economic power. They claimed that without the power that comes from earning, black men "lost" control over their families, and without the ability to dominate their wives and children they lost self-respect. The ideal that men should be sole providers for their families was accepted uncritically, so that poverty was seen as a blow to the male ego, the only ego that counted. (Ferree and Hess, 1994: 55)

27. As the (Product)Red website (www.joinred.com/red/) maintains:

> What's the meaning of the parentheses or brackets? Well, we call them "the embrace." Each company that becomes (RED) places its logo in this embrace and is

then elevated to the power of red. Thus the name—(PRODUCT)RED. You, the consumer, can take your purchase to the power of (RED) simply by upgrading your choice. Thus the proposition: (YOU)RED. Be embraced, take your own fine self to the power of (RED). What better way to become a good-looking samaritan?!

The Gap Red website (www.gapinc.com/red/) states: "Gap (PRODUCT) RED is about great products that can help make a difference for Africa. As a global partner of (PRODUCT) RED, we're contributing half the profits from Gap (PRODUCT) RED sales to the Global Fund to help women and children affected by HIV/AIDS in Africa."

28. Trepagnier, 2006: 40.

29. Bhabha, 1994: 85–86.

30. Vallely, 2006.

31. Shepherd, 2006: 20.

32. Cooley, 1964 [1902]: 184.

33. Schwalbe, 2008: 171.

34. Jackson, 2008. See in particular chapter 2, "The Birth of Political Correctness and the White Man's Newest Burden."

35. Ibid: 68.

36. Schwalbe, 2008: 171.

37. Portions of this chapter were revised from Hughey, 2011a.

Chapter 7

1. Du Bois, 1976 [1920]: 22.

2. Du Bois, 1999 [1935]: 700.

3. Du Bois, 1899: 322.

4. Du Bois, 1924.

5. Du Bois, 1903: 159–160.

6. Sullivan, 2006: 145.

7. Lott, 1993.

8. Deloria, 1998.

9. Grazian, 2003: 20.

10. Mailer, 1957.

11. Nemoto, 2006.

12. Nakamura, 2002.

13. Nagel, 2003.

14. Savishinsky, 1994.

15. *The Washington Post* outlined how white youths in New York City are throwing "Kill Whitey" parties in which "it has something to do with young white hipsters believing they can shed white privilege by parodying the black hip-hop life. In this way, they hope to escape their uptight conditioning and get in touch with the looser soul within them." *The Post* reports that one Kill Whitey partygoer named Casady

"tried the conventional (that is, non-hipster) hip-hop clubs but found the men 'really hard-core,' and in this vastly different scene, Casady said that 'it's a safe environment to be freaky'"(Garcia, 2005: A03).

16. Cose, 1992; Takaki, 1993; Daniels, 2002; Vickerman, 2007.

17. Blazak, 2008: 172.

18. Omi, 2001.

19. Gordon, 1964.

20. Guglielmo, 2003.

21. Pratt, 1892.

22. Ignatiev, 1995; Roediger, 1996; Brodkin, 1998; Jacobson, 1998.

23. Takaki, 1993.

24. Goldberg, 1993.

25. Feuer, 1991.

26. The term *melting pot* came into common parlance after it was used in the 1908 play by Israel Zangwill entitled *The Melting Pot*, first performed in Washington, D.C. See Hirschman, 1983: 397; Gerstle, 2001: 51.

27. Trotman, 2002: ix.

28. Schlesinger, 1998 [1991]: 125.

29. Lieberson, 1980; Higham, 1988; Vickerman, 2007.

30. Eller and Coughlin, 1983.

31. Ferber, 1999.

32. In the January 28, 1974, issue of *The New York Times* Gene Maeroff wrote: "America's white ethnic groups, apparently stirred by the rise of black consciousness and a heightened sense of their own group identities, have begun pressing for programs to help young people of European extraction explore their heritage and the immigrant experience of their forebears" (Maeroff, 1974, p. 11). The federal act funded development of curriculum materials that introduced and supported ethnic studies in public school and college curricula. Projects were developed throughout the country and were collected initially by the Social Science Education Consortium at Boulder, Colorado, at which there are over two thousand reports, print and audiovisual materials, instruction kits, and scholarly monographs covering more than sixty-five different ethnic groups. See also Jacobson, 2006: 19.

33. hooks, 1992: 21–22.

34. Eliasoph and Lichterman, 2003.

35. Benjamin, 1999 [1936]. The notion of racial authenticity is examined further by Bonnie Urciuoli, who writes,

> The authenticity generated by the context in which the objects are displayed, performed, or used becomes a property of objects themselves . . . because authenticity must be linked to a high national culture, racialized [in this context, nonwhite] people are at a disadvantage. They are seen as people from colonized places so

they [and others] must seek their authenticity in a past before or beyond colonial status. (Urciuoli, 1996: 34)

36. Barth, 1969.

37. Hochschild, 2003.

38. Bourdieu, 1977, 1984.

39. Jackson, 2005.

40. Ibid.: 15.

41. Goldberg, 1993; Mills, 1997.

42. Fanon, 1967 [1952]: 8.

43. My analysis of mimicry involved in color capital appropriation does not reveal a harmonious interracial unification but rather the masking of racial conflict and white domination. I recall Jacques Lacan's comments on mimicry: "The effect of mimicry is camouflage . . . It is not a question of harmonizing with the background, but against a mottled background, of becoming mottled—exactly like the technique of camouflage practised in human warfare" (Lacan, 1998: 99).

44. Portions of this chapter were revised from Hughey, 2012b.

Chapter 8

1. Foucault, 1995 [1979].

2. Althusser, 1971.

3. Ibid.: 174–175.

4. Goldberg, 1993.

5. Chuck D, lead vocalist for the rap group Public Enemy, supposedly said that rap music is the "CNN of the streets" because it expressed topics, points, and news that mainstream media does not carry. See Jones, 2001: 285.

6. I became a member of the BGLO, Phi Beta Sigma Fraternity in the fall of 1996.

7. Hughey, 2007.

8. Ibid.: 88.

9. Garfinkel, 1967.

10. Althusser, 1971.

Chapter 9

1. Nietzsche, 1907 [1886]: 7.

2. Winant, 2004: 5.

3. Stuart Hall once wrote,

It is a highly unstable theory about the world which has to assume that vast numbers of ordinary people, mentally equipped in much the same way as you or I, can simply be thoroughly and systematically duped into misrecognizing entirely where their real interests lie. Even less acceptable is the position that, whereas "they"—the masses—are the dupes of history, "we"—the privileged—are some-

how without a trace or illusion and can see, transitively, right through into the truth, the essence, of a situation.
See Hall, 1988: 44.

4. McDermott and Samson, 2005: 256.

5. Lewis, 2004.

6. Shirley, 2010.

7. Banton, 1983: 6.

8. Ridgeway, 2011.

9. Bonilla-Silva and Embrick, 2007: 341.

10. Ridgeway, 2011: 37–38.

11. Sewell, 1992: 17–18.

12. Bonilla-Silva writes, "Although processes of racialization are always embedded in other structurations . . . they acquire autonomy and have 'pertinent effects' . . . in the social system. This implies that the phenomenon which is coded as racism and is regarded as a free-floating ideology in fact has a structural foundation" (Bonilla-Silva, 1997: 469).

13. Erving Goffman made this point when he wrote that situational meanings have a "loose coupling" to dominant understandings of "age-grade, gender, class, and race, [which] constitute a cross-cutting grid" (Goffman, 1983: 14).

14. "The power to hold others accountable in one setting depends upon relationships—that is, a larger *net of accountability*—with actors outside the setting" (Schwalbe et al. 2000: 442).

15. Lewis, 2004.

16. Schwalbe, 2008: 171.

17. Lewis, 2004: 634.

18. Mills, 1997: 14.

19. Gliebe, 2011.

20. Accordingly, this study answers the call posed by Eduardo Bonilla-Silva: "We must perform comparative work on racialization . . . One of the main objectives of this comparative work should be to determine whether societies have specific mechanisms, practices, and social relations that produce and reproduce racial inequality at all levels—that is, whether they possess a racial structure" (Bonilla-Silva, 1997: 476).

21.

Color-blind racial attitudes reflect aspects of contemporary racism. Unlike more overt forms of racism, the color-blind perspective does not necessarily make explicit claims about White superiority. Rather, color-blind attitudes reflect the seemingly benign position that race should not and does not matter. Included in this stance, however, is a denial that racism continues to benefit White individuals . . . The color-blind perspective maintains that all people today do, in fact, have equal access to economic and social success, regardless of race. (Gushue and Constantine, 2007: 323)

22. "We have met the enemy and he is us" comes from the comic strip *Pogo*. See Kelly, 1971. Social problems are not so much the cause of some immoral or evil "bad apple" but are begot from our own tacit acceptance and participation in the social order as constituted.

23. Butler, 1993; Dyer, 1997; Dyson, 2002; Birt, 2004; Lewis, 2004; Morris, 2006; Shirley, 2010.

24. Burawoy, 1998: 16.

25. This point owes to Ruth Frankenberg's contention that "whiteness changes over time and space and is in no way a transhistorical essence . . . Thus, the range of possible ways of living whiteness . . . *is delimited by the relations of racism at that moment and in that place* [my emphasis]" (Frankenberg, 1993: 236).

26. Madden, 2008: 35.

Appendix A

1. Swain and Nieli, 2003: 6.

2. Daniels, 1997; Dobratz and Shanks-Meile, 1997; Gallagher, 2003; Simi and Futrell, 2010.

3. These numbers are presented with the caveat that "hate groups" also encompass some (although a small minority) groups with no explicit racial agenda (for example, antigay organizations). In addition, a portion of the "rise" in hate groups as reported by the Southern Poverty Law Center (SPLC) from 1992 to 2000 could result from the SPLC changing their classification system in 1996, the same year in which such groups supposedly increased in number. With that possible methodological bias acknowledged, there still seems to be a steady growth in white nationalist groups if we take into account that the SPLC uses informants, tracks how groups splinter off and grow, and uses digital technology, as well as considering the techniques these groups use to enter "mainstream" discourse. See Southern Poverty Law Center (SPLC), 2011.

4. Jefferson, 1904 [1853]: 49.

5. Chen, 2009.

6. Dobratz and Shanks-Meile, 1997; Zeskind, 2009.

7. Swain, 2002: 21–22.

8. U.S. Census Bureau, 2000.

9. Daniels, 2009; Simi and Futrell, 2010.

10. Kaplan and Weinber, 1998.

11. Berbrier, 2000, 2002.

12. Ibid.

13. Ibid; Dobratz and Shanks-Meile, 1997; Zeskind, 2009.

14. Ferree and Miller, 1994.

15. Hamm, 1994; Ezekiel, 1995.

16. Berbrier, 1999; Arena and Arrigo, 2000; Balch, 2006.

17. Barkun, 1994; Daniels, 1997; Dobratz and Shanks-Meile, 1997; Blee, 2004; Ferber and Kimmel, 2004; Hughey, 2006, 2007.

18. Blee, 2002.

19. O'Brien, 2000.

20. Anderson, 1991.

21. Barkun, 1994; Sharpe, 2000; Burlein, 2002; Balch, 2006.

22. Dobratz and Shanks-Meile, 1997; Blee, 2002, 2004; Ferber and Kimmel, 2004; Blazak, 2008.

23. Ferber and Kimmel, 2004.

24. Daniels, 1997; Dobratz and Shanks-Meile, 1997.

25. Horsman, 1981; Higham, 1988.

26. Lloyd, 2002: 62.

27. Bonnett, 2000a: 4.

28. Aptheker, 1992.

29. Bonnett, 2000a.

30. Aptheker, 1992.

31. Ibid.

32. Kivel, 1995; Derman-Sparks and Phillips, 1997; Thompson, 2001; Katz, 2003 [1978]; Parker and Chambers, 2005.

33. O'Brien, 2007, 2009.

34. George, 2004.

35. Frankenberg, 1993; Carvery and Bishop, 1994; O'Brien, 2001; Thompson, Schaefer, and Brod, 2003.

36. Eichstedt, 2001.

37. McIntosh, 1988; Kivel, 1995; Winant, 2001.

38. Marty, 1999; Zajicek, 2002.

39. Niemonen, 2007: 159.

40. Brown, 2002; Thompson, 2001.

41. Aptheker, 1992; Segrest, 1994; Thompson, 2001; Brown, 2002.

42. Brown, 2002: 142.

43. Ibid.

44. Thompson, 2001: 348.

45. Pramuk, 2006: 362–363.

46. Niemonen, 2007: 164.

47. Moulder, 1997: 120.

48. Berlak, 1999; Schacht, 2001; Srivastava and Francis, 2006.

49. Srivastava, 1996.

50. Srivastava, 2005: 55.

51. Srivastava, 1996; 2005; 2006.

52. Thompson, 2001.

53. Bonnett, 2000a.

54. Thompson, Schaefer, and Brod, 2003.

55. Sivanandan, 1995: 75.

56. Bonnett, 2000a; Thompson, Schaefer, and Brod, 2003.

57. Hartigan, 2000.

58. Carvery and Bishop, 1994; Kivel, 1995; Bonnett, 2000b; Eichstedt, 2001.

59. Such a group, the White Panther Party, was founded in 1968 by Lawrence Pla-mondon, Leni Sinclair, and John Sinclair. They advocated a "cultural revolution" and a "full endorsement and support of Black Panther Party's 10-Point Program."

60. Tatum, 1997; Marty, 1999; Bonnett, 2000a.

Appendix B

1. Burawoy, 1998.

2. My research was composed of: (1) ethnographic fieldwork (I attended NEA and WRJ meetings: fifty-eight meetings in total; $n = 31$ with NEA, $n = 27$ with WRJ) and nearly countless hours of observation; (2) semistructured, in-depth interviews ($n = 24$ with NEA, $n = 21$ with WRJ); and (3) content analysis inclusive of newsletter issues ($n = 7$), flyers ($n = 22$) and any textual information such as emails and office memos ($n = 467$).

3. Smith, 2005.

4. Burawoy, 1998: 7.

5. DeVault, 2006: 294.

6. Ibid.

7. Vaughan, 2009.

8. Somers and Gibson, 1994.

9. Ewick and Silbey, 2003: 1328.

10. Jacobs, 1996; Gerteis, 2002.

11. Gerteis, 2002: 593.

12. Small, Harding, and Lamont, 2010.

13. Lamont and Fournier, 1992: 12; Lamont and Molnár, 2002.

14. Bryson, 2005.

15. Small, Harding, and Lamont, 2010: 17.

16. Mills, 1940; Berger and Luckmann, 1966.

17. Mills, 1940: 904.

18. Berger and Luckmann, 1966: 22.

19. Howard, 2000.

20. McDermott, 2006; Willis, 1977; Hochschild, 1989.

21. Edles, 2002: 101.

22. Homans, 1967.

23. Goldberg, 1993: 119.

24. Ibid.

25. Du Bois, 1999 [1935]: 700–701.

26. Roediger, 1996.

27. Carroll, 2003: 381.

28. Daniels, 1997: 36.

29. I attended fifty-eight meetings in total; $n = 31$ with NEA, $n = 27$ with WRJ.

30. Burawoy, 1998: 14.

31. Lofland and Lofland, 1994: 46.

32.

In this instance the reduction is an aggregation—the aggregation of *situational knowledge into social process.* Just as survey research aggregates data points from a large number of cases into statistical distributions from which causal inferences can be made, reflexive science collects multiple readings of a single case and aggregates them into social processes. . . . This wider field of relations cannot be bracketed or suspended, yet it is also beyond the purview of participant observation. We therefore look upon the external field as the conditions of existence of the locale within which research occurs. We therefore move beyond *social processes to delineate the social forces* that impress themselves on the ethnographic locale [emphasis in original]. (Burawoy, 1998: 15)

33. Pattillo-McCoy, 1999: 223–224.

34. Gadamer, 1984: 64.

35. At the time of data collection (2006–2007), the median individual income of a white American (age twenty-five or older) was $33,030, compared with both the NEA and WRJ median income range of $50,000 to $74,999. Most white Americans overlap in middle- to working-class status, whereas both NEA and WRJ hold middle- to upper-middle-class status indicators, and while approximately 33 percent of white Americans held a bachelor's degree, 79 percent of NEA members and 81 percent of WRJ members held a bachelor's or advanced degree.

Appendix C

1. Bonilla-Silva, 2010 [2003].

2. Hughey, 2006, 2007.

3. McDermott and Samson, 2005: 256.

4. Johnson, 2008.

5. Some hold that undisclosed participant research is both unlawful and unethical. The American Sociological Association's "Code of Ethics" maintains that deception can be used, as a last resort, if (1) it will not harm the research participants, it is justified by the scientific value of the study, and equally effective procedures are not

available; and (2) the researcher has the approval of an IRB. Furthermore, deception can be used if it will not disturb subjects' willingness to participate through physical risks, discomfort, or unpleasant emotional experiences; if the deception is revealed to the research participants no later than the conclusion of the research; if there is not more than minimal risk for participants in a study that could only be carried out through disguising identity. See American Sociological Association (ASA) 1999: 14; Marzano, 2007.

6. Milgram, 1963; Humphreys, 1970; Zimbardo, 1973.

7.

Traditionally, unless research procedures seemed to indicate close supervision to assure the protection of research participants, student dissertations were frequently remanded to the "Exempt" category—that is, highly unlikely to require more than cursory review and unlikely to cause any damage or psychological harm to individual human subjects (even as they are equally unlikely to do any good)—and given review by a subcommittee rather than the full IRB committee. This process was swift, expeditious, and thorough, even though completed by fewer IRB committee members. At this point in time, reviews are taking far longer than the usual 6 weeks; dissertation work that is qualitative is undergoing full-committee review; and at some institutions, qualitative, phenomenological, critical theorist, feminist, action research, and participatory action research projects have been summarily rejected as "unscientific," "ungeneralizable," and/or inadequately theorized (even though they maybe descriptive, historical, or exploratory projects and therefore, unable to be theorized at the moment). A variety of strategies have been devised by researchers to overcome persistent rejection by IRBs, including several that actually undermine the work but that have the effect of permitting graduate students to complete their doctorates. (Lincoln and Tierney, 2004: 223)

8. I was also careful not to share information gleaned in one group with the other. Moreover, I was vigilant in showing respect to the members of both groups, no matter how much I disagreed in any given moment or with an overall goal or method of the organization.

9. While this story may risk offending certain authorities, I follow Richardson, who wrote, "For the most part, I have found no ethical problem in publishing stories that reflect the abuse of power by administrators; I consider the damage done by them far greater than any discomfort my stories might cause them" (Richardson, 2000: 932).

10. Lincoln and Cannella, 2004: 8.

11. Nelson, 2004; Tierney and Corwin, 2007.

12. Lincoln and Tierney, 2004: 220.

13. Boser, 2007; Rambo, 2007; Johnson, 2008.

14. Bender, 2003; Pascoe, 2007.

15. Reay, 1996: 443.

16. Gallagher, 2000: 69.

17. Rhodes, 1994: 550.

18. Lipsitz, 1995.

19. Gunaratnam, 2003: 101.

20. Ahmed, 2000: 180.

21. Goffman, 1959; Wetherell and Potter, 1992; Bonilla-Silva and Forman 2000; Myers, 2005.

22. Knowles, 1999: 123.

23. Naples, 2003: 49.

24. Stein, 2001.

25. Clifford and Marcus, 1986: 101.

26. Malinowski, 1984[1922]; Lévi-Strauss, 1992 [1955].

27. Ginsburg, 1989; Blee, 1991, 2002.

28. Ginsburg, 1997: 285.

29. I was taken aback that my academic audience would conflate whiteness with Americanness to avoid any association of Canadian whiteness and racism. Just months after my talk, the prime minister of Canada evidenced the same tendency to disconnect Canadian white identity from racism: "We also have no history of colonialism. So we have all of the things that many people admire about the great powers but none of the things that threaten or bother them" (Reuters, 2009).

30. Luker, 1985: xiii.

31. Clifford, 1988: 50–51.

Works Cited

Abu-Lughod, Lila. 2002. "Do Muslim Women Really Need Saving? Anthropological Reflections on Cultural Relativism and Its Others." *American Anthropologist* 104(3): 783–790.

Ahmed, Leila. 1992. *Women and Gender in Islam*. New Haven, CT: Yale University Press.

Ahmed, Sara. 2000. *Strange Encounters: Embodied Others in Post-Coloniality*. London: Routledge.

Alexander, Jeffrey C. 1987. *Twenty Lectures*. New York: Columbia University Press.

Althusser, Louis. 1971. *Lenin and Philosophy*, translated by B. Brewster. New York: Monthly Review Press.

American Sociological Association (ASA). 1999. *Code of Ethics and Policies and Procedures of the ASA Committee on Professional Ethics*. "(12.05) Use of Deception in Research." Washington, DC: American Sociological Association.

Andersen, Margaret L. 2003. "Whitewashing Race: A Critical Perspective on Whiteness." In *White Out: The Continuing Significance of Racism*, edited by A. W. Doane Jr. and E. Bonilla-Silva, pp. 21–34. New York: Routledge.

Anderson, Benedict. 1991. *Imagined Communities*. London and New York: Verso.

Aptheker, Herbert. 1992. *Anti-Racism in the United States: The First Two Hundred Years*. Westport, CT: Praeger Publishers.

Arena, Michael P., and Bruce A. Arrigo. 2000. "White Supremacist Behavior: Toward an Integrated Social Psychological Model." *Deviant Behavior* 21: 213–244.

Associated Press. June 13, 2007. "Cajun Town Bans Saggy Pants in Bid to Cover Up 'Private Parts.'" Foxness.com. Retrieved on March 15, 2009, from www.foxnews.com/story/0,2933,281932,00.html.

Associated Press. October 15, 2007. "Several U.S. Cities Snapping over Baggy Pants." USAToday.com. Retrieved on March 15, 2009, from www.usatoday.com/news/nation/2007-10-14-Baggy_N.htm.

Associated Press. October 27, 2007. "Song Links Saggy Pants to Being Gay." NPR .org. Retrieved on March 15, 2011, from www.npr.org/templates/story/story.php?storyId=15654565.

Attewell, Paul, and Katherine S. Newman. 2010. *Growing Gaps: Educational Inequality Around the World*. New York: Oxford University Press

Badiou, Alain. 2002. *Ethics: An Essay on the Understanding of Evil*. New York: Verso Press.

Baker, Al. May 19, 2010. "Police Accused of Ignoring Law on Sealing Stop-and-Frisk Records." *The New York Times*, p. A22.

Balch, Robert W. Summer 2006. "The Rise and Fall of Aryan Nations: A Resource Mobilizations Perspective." *Journal of Political and Military Sociology* 34(1): 81–113.

Baldwin, James. 1998. "On Being 'White' and Other Lies." In *Black on White: Black Writers on What It Means to Be* White, edited by D. R. Roediger, pp. 177–180. New York: Schocken Books.

Banton, Michael. 1983. *Racial and Ethnic Competition*. Cambridge, UK: Cambridge University Press.

Barkun, Michael. 1994. *Religion and the Racist Right: The Origins of the Christian Identity Movement*. Chapel Hill: University of North Carolina Press.

Barth, Fredrik. 1969. *Ethnic Groups and Boundaries: The Social Organization of Culture Difference*. Oslo: Universitetsforlaget.

Bender, Courtney. 2003. *Heaven's Kitchen: Living Religion at God's Love We Deliver*. Chicago: University of Chicago Press.

Benjamin, Walter. 1999 [1936]. "The Work of Art in the Age of Mechanical Reproduction." In *Illuminations*, translated by H. Zohn, pp. 219–253. London: Pimlico.

Bennett, Jessica. July 18, 2008. "Fashion Police: Flint Cracks Down on Sagging." *Newsweek*. Retrieved on May 10, 2011, from www.newsweek.com/2008/07/17/fashion-police-flint-cracks-down-on-sagging.html.

Bennett, William. September 28, 2005. "Bill Bennett's Morning in America." *Media Matters for America*. Retrieved on May 9, 2011, from http://mediamatters.org/mmtv/200509280006.

Berbrier, Mitch. 2002. "Making Minorities: Cultural Space, Stigma Transformation Frames, and the Categorical Status Claims of Deaf, Gay, and White Supremacist Activists in the Late Twentieth Century America." *Sociological Forum* 17(4): 553–591.

Berbrier, Mitch. 2000. "The Victim Ideology of White Supremacists and White Separatists in the United States." *Sociological Focus* 33: 175–191.

Berbrier, Mitch. 1999. "Impression Management for the Thinking Racist: A Case Study of Intellectualization as Stigma Transformation in Contemporary White Supremacist Discourse." *Sociological Quarterly* 40(8): 411–433.

Berger, Peter L., and Thomas Luckmann. 1966. *The Social Construction of Reality: A Treatise in the Sociology of Knowledge*. New York: Doubleday.

Berlak, Ann 1999. "Teaching and Testimony: Witnessing and Bearing Witness to Racisms in Culturally Diverse Classrooms." *Curriculum Inquiry* 29(1): 99–127.

Bernard, Jessie. 1966. *Marriage and Family among Negroes*. Englewood Cliffs, NJ: Prentice Hall.

Bertrand, Marianne, and Sendhil Mullainathan. 2004. "Are Emily and Greg More Employable Than Lakisha and Jamal? A Field Experiment on Labor Market Discrimination." *American Economic Review* 94(4): 991–1013.

Bhabha, Homi. 1994. *The Location of Culture*. New York: Routledge.

Birt, Robert. 2004. "The Bad Faith of Whiteness." In *What White Looks Like: African-American Philosophers on the Whiteness Question*, edited by G. Yancy, pp. 55–64. New York: Routledge.

Blake, John. March 4, 2011. "Are Whites Racially Oppressed?" CNN. Retrieved on March 5, 2011, from www.cnn.com/2010/US/12/21/white.persecution/index.html?hpt=T2.

Blazak, Randy. 2008. "Ethnic Envy: How Teens Construct Whiteness in Globalized America." In *Globalizing the Streets; Cross-Cultural Perspectives on Youth, Social Control, and Empowerment*, edited by Michael Flynn and David C. Brotherton, pp. 169–184. New York: Columbia University Press.

Blee, Kathleen M. 2004. "Women and Organized Racism." In *Home-Grown Hate: Gender and Organized Racism*, edited by A. L. Ferber, pp. 49–74. New York: Routledge.

Blee, Kathleen M. 2002. *Inside Organized Racism: Women in the Hate Movement*. Berkeley: University of California Press.

Blee, Kathleen M. 1991. *Women of the Klan: Racism and Gender in the 1920s*. Berkeley: University of California Press.

Bonilla-Silva, Eduardo. 2010 [2003]. *Racism without Racists: Color-Blind Racism and the Persistence of Racial Inequality in the United States*. Lanham, MD: Rowman and Littlefield.

Bonilla-Silva, Eduardo. 1997. "Rethinking Racism: Toward a Structural Interpretation." *American Sociological Review* 62(3): 465–480.

Bonilla-Silva, Eduardo, and David D. Embrick. 2007. "'Every Place Has a Ghetto . . .' The Significance of Whites' Social and Residential Segregation." *Symbolic Interaction* 30(3): 323–345.

Bonilla-Silva, Eduardo, and Tyrone A. Forman. 2000. "I Am Not a Racist, but . . . : Mapping White College Students' Racial Ideology in the U.S.A." *Discourse & Society* 11: 50–85.

Bonilla-Silva, Eduardo, Carla Goar, and David D. Embrick. 2006. "When Whites Flock Together: The Social Psychology of White Habitus." *Critical Sociology* 32 (2–3): 229–253.

Bonnett, Alastair. 2000a. *Anti-Racism*. New York: Routledge.

Bonnett, Alastair. 2000b. "Whiteness in Crisis." *History Today* 50(12): 38–43.

Boser, Susan. 2007. "Power, Ethics, and the IRB: Dissonance over Human Participant Review of Participatory Research." *Qualitative Inquiry* 13(8): 1060–1074.

Bourdieu, Pierre. 1984 [1979]. *Distinction: A Social Critique of Taste*. London: Routledge and Kegan Paul.

Bourdieu, Pierre. 1977. *Outline of a Theory of Practice*. Cambridge, UK: Cambridge University Press.

Brodkin, Karen. 1998. *How Jews Became White Folks and What That Says about Race in America*. New Brunswick, NJ: Rutgers University Press.

Brown, Cynthia Stokes. 2002. *Refusing Racism: White Allies and the Struggle for Civil Rights*. New York: Teachers College Press.

Brown, Gillian, and George Yule. 1989. *Discourse Analysis*. Cambridge, UK: Cambridge University Press.

Bryson, Bethany. 2005. *Making Multiculturalism: Boundaries and Meaning in U.S. English Departments*. Stanford, CA: Stanford University Press.

Bullard, Robert Doyle. 2007. *The Black Metropolis in the Twenty-First Century: Race, Power, and Politics of Place*. Landham, MD: Rowman & Littlefield.

Burawoy, Michael. 1998. "The Extended Case Method." *Sociological Theory* 16(1): 4–33.

Bureau of Justice Statistics, Office of Justice Programs. 2010. "Key Facts At A Glance." Retrieved on December 20, 2010, from http://bjs.ojp.usdoj.gov/content/glance/race.cfm.

Burlein, Ann. 2002. *Lift High the Cross: Where White Supremacy and the Christian Right Converge*. Durham, NC: Duke University Press.

Bush, Laura. 2001. "Radio Address by Laura Bush to the Nation." Retrieved on July 7, 2011, from www.whitehouse.gov/news/releases/2001/11/20011117.html.

Butler, Judith. 1993. *Bodies That Matter: On the Discursive Limits of "Sex."* New York: Routledge.

Carroll, Bret W. 2003. *American Masculinities: A Historical Encyclopedia*. Thousand Oaks, CA: Sage Publications.

Carvery, Valerie, and Anne Bishop. 1994. *Unlearning Racism: A Workshop Guide to Unlearning Racism*. Halifax: Oxfam/Deveric.

Cauvin, Henri E. August 5, 2006. "Debating Race in Cyberspace." *The Washington Post*.

Chen, Stephanie. February 26, 2009. "Growing Hate Groups Blame Obama, Economy." *Cable News Network.* Retrieved on March 4, 2009, from www.cnn.com/2009/US/02/26/hate.groups.report/index.html.

Chesler, Mark A., Amanda E. Lewis, and James E. Crowfoot. 2005. *Challenging Racism in Higher Education: Promoting Justice.* Lanham, MD: Rowman and Littlefield.

Clarke, Kenneth B. 1965. *Dark Ghetto: Dilemmas of Social Power.* New York: Harper & Row.

Cleaver, Eldridge. 1989 [1968]. *Soul on Ice.* New York: Ramparts Press.

Clifford, James. 1988. *The Predicament of Culture: Twentieth-Century Ethnography, Literature, and Art.* Cambridge, MA: Harvard University Press.

Clifford, James, and George E. Marcus. 1986. *Writing Culture: The Poetics and Politics of Ethnography.* Berkeley: University of California Press.

Collins, Patricia Hill. 2005. *Black Sexual Politics: African Americans, Gender, and the New Racism.* New York: Routledge.

Conley, Dalton. 1999. *Being Black, Living in the Red: Race, Wealth, and Social Policy in the America.* Berkeley: University of California Press.

Cooke, Miriam. 2001. *Women Claim Islam: Creating Islamic Feminism through Literature.* New York: Routledge.

Cooley, Charles M. 1964 [1902]. *Human Nature and the Social Order.* St. Louis, MO: Transaction Publishers.

Coontz, Stephanie. 2000. *The Way We Never Were: American Families and the Nostalgia Trap.* New York: Basic Books.

Cose, Ellis. 1992. *A Nation of Strangers.* New York: William Morrow and Company.

Cott, Nancy. 2000. *Public Vows: A History of Marriage and the Nation.* Cambridge, MA: Harvard University Press.

Croll, Paul. 2007. "Modeling Determinants of White Racial Identity: Results from a New National Survey." *Social Forces* 86(2): 613–642.

Daniels, Jessie. 2009. *Cyber Racism: White Supremacy Online and the New Attack on Civil Rights.* Lanham, MD: Rowman & Littlefield.

Daniels, Jessie. 1997. *White Lies: Race, Class, Gender and Sexuality in White Supremacist Discourse.* New York: Routledge.

Daniels, Roger. 2002. *Coming to America.* New York: HarperCollins.

Deloria, Philip J. 1998. *Playing Indian.* New Haven, CT: Yale University Press.

Derman-Sparks, Louise, and Carol Brunson Phillips 1997. *Teaching / Learning Anti-Racism: A Developmental Approach.* New York: Teachers College.

DeVault, Marjorie L. 2006. "Introduction: What Is Institutional Ethnography?" *Social Problems* 53(3): 294–298.

Doane, Ashley W. Jr. 2003. "Rethinking Whiteness Studies." In *White Out: The Continuing Significance of Racism,* edited by A. W. Doane Jr. and E. Bonilla-Silva, pp. 3–18. New York: Routledge.

Doane, Ashley W. Jr., and Eduardo Bonilla-Silva. 2003. *White Out: The Continuing Significance of Racism*. New York: Routledge.

Dobratz, Betty A., and Stephanie L. Shanks-Meile. 1997. *White Power, White Pride: The White Separatist Movement in the United States*. New York: Twain.

Du Bois, W. E. B. 1999 [1935]. *Black Reconstruction in America, 1860–1880*. New York: Simon & Schuster.

Du Bois, W. E. B. 1924. *The Gift of Black Folk*. Boston: Stratford Co.

Du Bois, W. E. B. 1976 [1920]. *Darkwater: Voices from within the Veil*. Millwood, NY: Kraus-Thomson Organization.

Du Bois, W. E. B. 1903. *The Souls of Black Folk*. Chicago: A. C. McClurg & Co.

Du Bois, W. E. B. 1899. *The Philadelphia Negro: A Social Study*. Philadelphia: University of Pennsylvania Press.

Duster, Troy. 2001. "The 'Morphing' Properties of Whiteness." In *The Making and Unmaking of Whiteness*, edited by E. B. Rasmussen, E. Klinenberg, I. J. Nexica, and M. Wray, pp. 113–133. Durham, NC: Duke University Press.

Dyer, Richard. 1997. *White: Essays on Race and Culture*. New York: Routledge.

Dyer, Richard. 1988. "White." *Screen* 29(4): 44–65.

Dyson, Michael Eric. 2002. *Open Mic: Reflections on Philosophy, Race, Sex, Culture and Religion*. New York: Basic Civitas Books.

Edles, Laura. 2002. *Cultural Sociology in Practice*. Malden, MA: Blackwell.

Eichstedt, Jennifer L. 2001. "Problematic White Identities and a Search for Racial Justice." *Sociological Forum* 16: 445–470.

Eliasoph, Nina, and Paul Lichterman. 2003. "Culture in Interaction." *American Journal of Sociology* 108(4): 735–794.

Elkins, Stanley. 1959. *Slavery: A Problem in American Institutional and Intellectual Life*. Chicago: University of Chicago Press.

Eller, Jack, and Reed Coughlin. 1983. "The Poverty of Primordialism—The Demystification of Ethnic Attachments." *Ethnic and Racial Studies* 16(2): 183–202.

Erikson, Kai. 2001. "Foreword." In *Red Lines, Black Spaces: The Politics of Race and Space in a Black Middle-Class Suburb*, edited by B. D Haynes, pp. ix–xii. New Haven, CT: Yale University Press.

Ewick, Patricia, and Susan S. Silbey. 2003. "Narrating Social Structure: Stories of Resistance to Law." *American Journal of Sociology* 108(6):1328–1372.

Ezekiel, Raphael S. 1995. *The Racist Mind: Portraits of Neo-Nazis and Klansmen*. New York: Viking.

Fairclough, Norman. 2003, *Analysing Discourse*. London: Routledge.

Fanon, Frantz. 1967 [1952]. *Black Skin, White Masks*. New York: Grove Press.

Feagin, Joe R., and Hernán Vera. 1995. *White Racism: The Basics*. New York: Routledge.

Ferber, Abby. 2007. "The Construction of Black Masculinity: White Supremacy Now and Then." *Journal of Sport and Social Issues*, 31: 11–24.

Ferber, Abby. 2000. "Racial Warriors and Weekend Warriors: The Construction of Masculinity in Mythopoetic and White Supremacist Discourse." *Men and Masculinities* 3(1): 30–56.

Ferber, Abby. 1999. "The White Supremacist Movement in the United States Today." In *Race and Ethnic Conflict: Contending Views on Prejudice, Discrimination, and Ethnoviolence*, edited by F. L. Pincus and H. J. Ehrlich, pp. 346–354. Boulder, CO: Westview Press.

Ferber, Abby L., and Michael S. Kimmel. 2004. "'White Men are This Nation': Right-Wing Militias and the Restoration of Rural American Masculinity." In *Home-Grown Hate: Gender and Organized Racism*, edited by A. L. Ferber, pp. 143–160. New York: Routledge.

Ferree, Myra Marx, and Beth B. Hess. 1994. *Controversy and Coalition: Three Decades of the Feminist Movement*, New York: Twayne.

Ferree, Myra Marx, and Frederick D. Miller. 1994. "Mobilization and Meaning: Toward an Integration of Social Psychological and Resource Mobilization Perspectives on Social Movements." *Sociological Inquiry* 55: 38–51.

Feuer, Lewis S. 1991. "From Pluralism to Multiculturalism." *Society* 29(1): 19–22.

Forman, Tyrone, and Amanda E. Lewis. 2006. "Racial Apathy and Hurricane Katrina: The Social Anatomy of Prejudice in the Post-Civil Rights Era." *Du Bois Review* 3(1): 175–202.

Foucault, Michel. 1995 [1979]. *Discipline and Punish: The Birth of the Prison*, translated by A. Sheridan. New York, NY: Vintage Books.

Foucault, Michel. 1984. "Space, Knowledge, and Power." In *The Foucault Reader*, edited by P. Rabinow, pp. 239–256. New York: Pantheon Books.

Fraiman, S. 1994. "Geometries of Race and Gender: Eve Sedgwick, Spike Lee, Charlayne Hunter-Gault." *Feminist Studies* 20: 67–84.

Frankenberg, Ruth. 2001. "The Mirage of an Unmarked Whiteness." in *The Making and Unmaking of Whiteness*, edited by B. B. Rasmussen, E. Klinenberg, I. J. Nexica, and M. Wray, pp. 72–96. Durham, NC: Duke University Press.

Frankenberg, Ruth. 1993. *The Social Construction of Whiteness*. London: Routledge.

Franklin, Clyde W. 1985. "The Black Male Urban Barbershop as Sex-Role Socialization Setting." *Sex Roles* 12: 965–979.

Franklin, Clyde W. 1984. *The Changing Definition of Masculinity*. New York: Plenum.

Frazier, E. Franklin. 1939. *The Negro Family in the United States*. Chicago: University of Chicago Press.

Freund, David M. P. 2010. *Colored Property: State Policy and White Racial Politics in Suburban America*. Chicago: University of Chicago Press.

Gadamer, Hans-Georg. 1984. "The Hermeneutics of Suspicion." In *Hermeneutics: Questions and Prospects*, edited by G. Shapiro and A. Sica, pp. 58–65. Amherst: University of Massachusetts Press.

Gallagher, Charles. March 3, 2011. Op-Ed. "Living in Fictional Land of Color-Blind America." *The Philadelphia Inquirer.*

Gallagher, Charles A. 2003. *On the Fault Line: Race, Class and the American Patriot Movement.* Lanham, MD: Rowman & Littlefield

Gallagher, Charles A. 2000. "White Like Me? Methods, Meaning, and Manipulation in the Field of White Studies." In *Racing Research, Researching Race*, edited by F. W. Twine and J. Warren, pp. 67–99. New York: New York University Press.

Gallagher, Charles A. 1995. "White Reconstruction in the University." *Socialist Review* 24(1–2): 165–187.

Garcia, Michelle. August 26, 2005. "Deejay's Appeal: 'Kill The Whiteness Inside.'" *The Washington Post.* A03.

Garfinkel, Harold. 1967. *Studies in Ethnomethodology.* Englewood Cliffs, NJ: Prentice Hall.

George, Mark P. 2004. Race Traitors: Exploring the Motivation and Action of White Antiracists. Ph.D. dissertation. Albuquerque: The University of New Mexico

Gerstle, Gary. 2001. *American Crucible: Race and Nation in the Twentieth Century.* Princeton, NJ: Princeton University Press.

Gerteis, Joseph. 2002. "The Possession of Civic Virtue: Movement Narratives of Race and Class in the Knights of Labor." *American Journal of Sociology* 108(3): 580–615.

Giddens, Anthony. 1984. *The Constitution of Society.* Berkeley: University of California Press.

Ginsburg, Faye. 1997. "The Case of Mistaken Identity: Problems in Representing Women on the Right." In *Reflexivity and Voice*, edited by R. Hertz, pp. 283–299. Thousand Oaks, CA: Sage.

Ginsburg, Faye. 1989. *Contested Lives: The Abortion Debate in an American Community.* Berkeley: University of California Press.

Glassner, Barry. 1999. The *Culture of Fear: Why Americans Are Afraid of the Wrong Things.* New York: Basic Books.

Gliebe, Erich. 2011. "Erich Gliebe, National Alliance Neo-Nazi Leader: 'Most White Americans Agree With Our Message.'" *The Seattle Weekly.* Retrieved March 10, 2011, from http://blogs.seattleweekly.com/dailyweekly/2011/03/erich_gliebe_national_alliance.php.

Goffman, Erving. 1983. "The Interaction Order." *American Sociological Review* 48: 1–17.

Goffman, Erving. 1974. *Frame Analysis.* New York: Harper and Row

Goffman, Erving. 1959. *The Presentation of Self in Everyday Life.* Garden City, NY: Doubleday.

Goldberg, David T. 1993. *Racist Culture: Politics and the Philosophy of Meaning.* Oxford, UK: Blackwell.

Gordon, Milton. 1964. *Assimilation in American Life: The Role of Race, Religion, and National Origins*. New York: Oxford University Press.

Gossett, Thomas F. 1963. *Race: The History of an Idea in America*. Dallas, TX: Southern Methodist University Press.

Gramsci, Antonio. 1971. *Selections from the Prison Notebooks*, translated and edited by Q. Hoare and G. Nowell-Smith. London: Lawrence and Wishart.

Grazian, David. 2008. *On The Make: The Hustle of Urban Nightlife*. Chicago: University of Chicago Press.

Grier, William H., and Price M. Cobbs. 1968. *Black Rage*. New York: Basic Books.

Guglielmo, Thomas A. 2003. *White on Arrival: Italians, Race, Color, and Power in Chicago, 1890–1945*. New York: Oxford University Press.

Guinier, Lani. 2010. "From Racial Profiling to Racial Literacy: Lessons of 12 Angry Men." In *12 Angry Men: True Stories of Being a Black Man in America Today*, edited by G. S. Parks and M. W. Hughey, pp. xi–xliv. New York: The New Press.

Gunaratnam, Yasmin. 2003. *Researching Race and Ethnicity: Methods, Knowledge, and Power*. London: Sage.

Gushue, George V., and Madonna G. Constantine. 2007. "Color-Blind Racial Attitudes and White Racial Identity Attitudes in Psychology Trainees." *Professional Psychology: Research and Practice* 38(3): 321–328.

Hall, Stuart. 1988. "The Toad in the Garden: Thatcherism amongst the Theorists." In *Marxism and the Interpretation of Culture*, edited by C. Nelson and L. Grossberg. London: Macmillan.

Hall, Stuart. 1981. "Notes on Deconstructing the Popular." In *People's History and Socialist Theory*, edited by R. Samuel, pp. 227–239. London: Routledge & Kegan Paul.

Hamacher, Brian. May 5, 2011. "Bills Banning Bestiality, Baggy Pants Pass in Fla." *MSNBC*. Retrieved on May 10, 2011,from www.msnbc.msn.com/id/42920080/ns/local_news-miami_fl/.

Hamm, Mark S. 1994. *American Skinheads: The Criminology and Control of Hate Crime*. Westport, CT: Praeger.

Hartigan, John Jr. 2010. *What Can You Say? America's National Conversation on Race*. Stanford, CA: Stanford University Press.

Hartigan, John Jr.. 2000. "Object Lessons in Whiteness: Antiracism and the Study of White Folks." *Identities* 7(3): 373–406.

Hays, Sharon. 1994. "Structure and Agency and the Sticky Problem of Culture." *Sociological Theory* 12(1): 57–72.

Higham, John. 1988. *Strangers in the Land: Patterns of American Nativism, 1860–1925*, 2nd ed. New Brunswick, NJ: Rutgers University Press.

Hill, Shirley A. 2005. *Black Intimacies: A Gender Perspective on Families and Relationships*. New York: AltaMira Press.

Hirschman, C. 1983. "America's Melting Pot Policy Reconsidered." *Annual Review of Sociology* 9: 397–423.

Hochschild, Arlie Russell. 2003. *The Commercialization of Intimate Life: Notes from Home and Work*. Berkeley: University of California Press.

Hochschild, Arlie Russell (with Anne Machung). 1989. *The Second Shift: Working Parents and the Revolution at Home*. New York: Viking.

Hochschild, Arlie Russell. 1983. *The Managed Heart: Commercialization of Human Feeling*. Berkeley: University of California Press.

Homans, George C. 1967. *The Nature of Social Science*. New York: Harcourt, Brace and World.

hooks, bell. 1992. *Black Looks: Race and Representation*. Boston: South End Press.

Horsman, Reginald. 1981. *Race and Manifest Destiny: The Origins of American Racial Anglo-Saxonism*. Cambridge, MA: Harvard University Press.

Howard, Judith. 2000. "Social Psychology of Identities." *Annual Review of Sociology* 26: 367–393.

Hughes, Langston. 1971 [1934]. *The Ways of White Folks*. New York: Vintage Books.

Hughey, Matthew W. 2012a. "Black Guys and White Guise: The Discursive Construction of White Masculinity." *Journal of Contemporary Ethnography*. In press.

Hughey, Matthew W. 2012b. "Color Capital, White Debt, and the Paradox of Strong White Racial Identities." *Du Bois Review: Social Science Research on Race*. 41(1): 96–125.

Hughey, Matthew W. 2011a. "Backstage Discourse and the Reproduction of White Masculinities." *The Sociological Quarterly* 52(1): 132–153.

Hughey, Matthew W. 2011b. "Measuring Racial Progress in America: The Tangled Path." In *The Obamas and a (Post) Racial America?*, edited by G. S. Parks and M. W. Hughey, 1–26 . New York: Oxford University Press.

Hughey, Matthew W. 2010. "Navigating the (Dis)similarities of White Racial Identities: The Conceptual Framework of 'Hegemonic Whiteness.'" *Ethnic and Racial Studies* 33(8): 1289–1309.

Hughey, Matthew W. 2007. "Racism with Antiracists: Color-Conscious Racism and the Unintentional Persistence of Inequality." *Social Thought and Research* 28: 67–108.

Hughey, Matthew W. 2006. "Specters of Whiteness: The (Mis)Educational Reproduction of 'Anti-Racist' Racism." In *Ethnographic and Qualitative Research in Education*, edited by P. Brewer and M. Firmin, pp. 21–43. New Castle, UK: Cambridge Scholars Press.

Humphries, Laud. 1970. *Tearoom Trade: A Study of Homosexual Encounters in Public Places*. London: Duckworth.

Hunt-Grubbe, Charlotte. October 14, 2007. "The Elementary DNA of Dr. Watson." *The Sunday Times*. Retrieved on November 5, 2011, from http://entertainment .timesonline.co.uk/tol/arts_and_entertainment/books/article2630748.ece.

Hunter, Andrea G., and James Earl Davis. September 1992. "Constructing Gender: An Exploration of Afro-American Men's Conceptualization of Manhood." *Gender and Society* 6(3): 464–479.

Ignatiev, Noel. 1995. *How the Irish Became White*. New York: Routledge.

Jackman, Mary. 1994. *The Velvet Glove: Paternalism and Conflict in Gender, Class, and Race Relations*. Berkeley: University of California Press

Jackson, John L. Jr. 2008. *Racial Paranoia: The Unintended Consequences of Political Correctness*. New York: Basic Books

Jackson, John L. Jr. 2005. *Real Black: Adventures in Racial Sincerity*. Chicago: University of Chicago Press.

Jacobs, Ronald N. 1996. "Civil Society and Crisis: Culture, Discourse and the Rodney King Beating." *American Journal of Sociology* 101(5): 1238–1272.

Jacobson, Matthew Frye. 2006. *Roots Too: White Ethnic Revival in Post–Civil Rights America*. Cambridge, MA: Harvard University Press.

Jacobson, Matthew Frye. 1998. *Whiteness of a Different Color: European Immigrants and the Alchemy of Race*. Cambridge, MA: Harvard University Press.

Jefferson, Thomas. 1904 [1853]. *Writings of Thomas Jefferson, Vol. 1*, edited by A. A. Lipscomb. Washington, DC: Thomas Jefferson Memorial Association.

Johnson, Tara Star. 2008. "Qualitative Research in Question: A Narrative of Disciplinary Power with/in the IRB." *Qualitative Inquiry* 14(2): 212–232.

Jones, Quincy. 2001. *The Autobiography of Quincy Jones*. New York: Random House Digital.

Jones, Robert P., and Daniel Cox. 2010. "Old Alignments, Emerging Fault Lines: Religion in the 2010 Election and Beyond." Washington, DC: Public Religion Research Institute.

Kanazawa, Satoshi. May 15, 2011. "Why Are Black Women Less Physically Attractive Than Other Women?" *Psychology Today*.

Kaplan, Jeffrey, and Leonard Weinber. 1998. *The Emergence of a Euro-American Radical Right*. New Brunswick, NJ: Rutgers University Press.

Katz, Judy H. 2003 [1978]. *White Awareness: Handbook for Anti-Racism Training*. Norman: University of Oklahoma Press.

Keller, Larry. 2009. "Minority Meltdown: Immigrants Blamed for Mortgage Crisis." Intelligence Report 133. Retrieved on 25 April 25, 2010, from www.splcenter .org/get-informed/intelligence-report/browse-all-issues/2009/spring/minority-meltdown.

Kelley, Robin D. B. 1997. *Yo' Mama's DisFunktional! Fighting the Culture Wars in Urban America*. Boston: Beacon Press.

Kelly, Walt. 1971. "Pogo" daily strip.

Kenny, Lorraine Delia. 2000. *Daughters of Suburbia: Growing Up White, Middle Class and Female*. New Brunswick, NJ: Rutgers University Press.

Kipling, Rudyard. April 1908. "The Stranger." *Morning Post.*

Kivel, Paul. 1995. *Uprooting Racism: How White People Can Work for Racial Justice.* Philadelphia: New Society Publishers.

Knowles, Caroline. 1999. "Race, Identities and Lives." *The Sociological Review* 47(1): 110–135.

Labaton, Stephen. October 3, 2008. "Agency's '04 Rule Let Banks Pile Up New Debt." *The New York Times.* Retrieved on April 17, 2010, from www.nytimes.com/2008/ 10/03/business/03sec.html?_r=2&em&oref=slogin.

Lacan, Jacques. 1998. *The Four Fundamental Concepts of Psycho-analysis,* translated by A. Sheridan. New York: W. W. Norton & Co.

Lamont, Michèle, and Marcel Fournier. 1992. *Cultivating Differences.* Chicago: University of Chicago Press.

Lamont, Michèle, and Virag Molnár. 2002. "The Study of Boundaries in the Social Sciences." *Annual Review of Sociology* 28: 167–195.

Lévi-Strauss, Claude. 1992 [1955]. *Tristes Tropiques.* New York: Penguin Books.

Lewis, Amanda E. 2004. "What Group? Studying Whites and Whiteness in the Era of Colorblindness." *Sociological Theory* 22(4): 623–646.

Lewis, Oscar. 1966. *La Vida: A Puerto Rican Family in the Culture of Poverty—San Juan and New York.* London: Secker & Warburg.

Lieberson, Stanley. 1980. *A Piece of the Pie: Blacks and White Immigrants since 1880.* Berkeley: University of California Press.

Limbaugh, Rush. December 8, 2009. "Reverend Jackson Slams Obama." *The Rush Limbaugh Show.* Retrieved on 28 January 28, 2011, from http://img.rushlimbaugh .com/home/daily/site_120809/content/01125107.guest.html.

Limbaugh, Rush. January 19, 2007. "The Classless NFL Culture." *The Rush Limbaugh Show.* Retrieved on January 28, 2011, from http://www.rushlimbaugh.com/home/ estack_12_13_06/the_classless_nfl_culture_.guest.html.

Lincoln, Abraham. 1996 [14 August 1862]. "Address on Colonization to a Deputation of Colored Men." In *Classical Black Nationalism: From the American Revolution to Marcus Garvey,* edited by W. J. Moses, pp. 209–214. New York: New York University Press.

Lincoln, Y. S., and G. Cannella 2004. "Qualitative Research, Power, and the Radical Right." *Qualitative Inquiry* 10(1): 5–14.

Lincoln, Y. S., and W. G. Tierney. 2004. "Qualitative Research and Institutional Review Boards (IRBs)." *Qualitative Inquiry* 10(2), 219–234.

Lipsitz, George. 1995. "The Possessive Investment in Whiteness: Racialized Social Democracy and the 'White' Problem in American Studies." *American Quarterly* 47(3): 369–387.

Lloyd, Cathie. 2002. "Anti-Racism, Social Movements, and Civil Society." In *Rethinking Anti-Racisms: From Theory to Practice*, edited by F. Anthias, pp. 60–77. New York: Routledge.

Lofland, John, and Lyn H. Lofland. 1994. *Analyzing Social Settings: A Guide to Qualitative Observation and Analysis*. New York: Wadsworth.

Lott, Eric. 1993. *Love and Theft*. New York: Oxford University Press.

Luker, Kristin. 1985. *Abortion and the Politics of Motherhood*. Berkeley: University of California Press.

Madden, Ed. 2008. *Signals*. Columbia: University of South Carolina Press.

Maeroff, Gene. January 28, 1974. "White Ethnic Groups in Nation Are Encouraging Heritage in a Trend toward Self-Awareness." *The New York Times*.

Mailer, Norman. Summer 1957. "The White Negro: Superficial Reflections on the Hipster." *Dissent*.

Majors, Richard, and Janet Mancini Billson. 1992. *Cool Pose: The Dilemmas of Black Manhood in America*. New York: Lexington Books.

Malinowski, Bronislaw. 1984[1922]. *Argonauts of the Western Pacific*. Long Grove, IL: Waveland Press.

Marcuse, Herbert. 1964. *One-Dimensional Man: Studies in the Ideology of Advanced Industrial Society*. London: Routledge.

Marty, Debian. 1999. "White Antiracist Rhetoric as Apologia: Wendell Berry's *The Hidden Wound*." In *Whiteness: The Communication of Social Identity*, edited by T. K Nakayama and J. N. Martin, pp. 51–68. Thousand Oaks, CA: Sage.

Marzano, Marco. 2007. "Informed Consent, Deception, and Research Freedom in Qualitative Research." *Qualitative Inquiry* 13(3): 417–436.

Massey, Douglass S., and Nancy A. Denton. 1993. *American Apartheid: Segregation and the Making of the Underclass*. Cambridge, MA: Harvard University Press.

McDermott, Monica. 1996. *Working-Class White: The Making and Unmaking of Race Relations*. Berkeley: University of California Press.

McDermott, Monica, and Frank L. Samson. 2005. "White Racial and Ethnic Identity in the United States." *Annual Review of Sociology* 31: 245–261.

McIntosh, Peggy. 1988. White Privilege and Male Privilege: A Personal Account of Coming to See Correspondences through Work in Women's Studies. Wellesley, MA: Center for Research on Women.

McKinney, Karyn D. 2005. *Being White: Stories of Race and Racism*. New York: Routledge.

Mills, C. Wright. 1940. "Situated Actions and Vocabularies of Motive." *American Sociological Review* 5: 904–913.

Mills, Charles W. 1997. *The Racial Contract*. Ithaca, NY: Cornell University Press.

Milgram, Stanley. 1963. "Behavioral Study of Obedience." *The Journal of Abnormal and Social Psychology* 67(4): 371–378.

Montagu, M. F. Ashley. 1942. *Man's Most Dangerous Myth: The Fallacy of Race.* New York: Columbia University Press.

Moore, Wendy Leo. 2008. *Reproducing Racism: White Space, Elite Law Schools, and Racial Inequality.* Lanham, MD: Rowman and Littlefield.

Morris, Edward. 2006. *An Unexpected Minority: White Kids in an Urban School.* New Brunswick, NJ: Rutgers University Press.

Moulder, F. V. 1997. "Teaching about Race and Ethnicity: A Message of Despair or a Message of Hope?" *Teaching Sociology* 25(2): 120–127.

Moynihan, Daniel Patrick. March 1965. *The Negro Family: The Case For National Action.* Washington, DC: U.S. Department of Labor, Office of Policy Planning and Research.

Myers, Kristen. 2005. *Racetalk: Racism Hiding in Plain Sight.* Lanham, MD: Rowman and Littlefield.

Myers, Kristen, and Passion Williamson. 2001. "Race Talk: The Perpetuation of Racism Through Private Discourse." *Race & Society* 4: 3–26.

Nagel, Joan. 2003. *Race, Ethnicity, and Sexuality. Intimate Intersections, Forbidden Frontiers.* New York: Oxford University Press.

Nakamura, Lisa. 2002. *Cybertypes: Race, Ethnicity, and Identity on the Internet.* New York: Routledge.

Naples, Nancy. 2003. *Feminism and Method: Ethnography, Discourse Analysis, and Activist Research.* New York: Routledge.

Nelson, C. 2004. "The Brave New World of Research Surveillance." *Qualitative Inquiry* 10(2): 207–218.

Nemoto, Kumiko. 2006. "Intimacy, Desire, and the Construction of Self in Relationships between Asian American Women and White American Men." *Journal of Asian American Studies* 9(1): 27–54.

Niemonen, Jack. 2007. "Antiracist Education in Theory and Practice: A Critical Assessment." *The American Sociologist* 38(2): 159–177.

Nietzsche, Friedrich W. 1907 [1886]. *Beyond Good and Evil: Prelude to a Philosophy of the Future*, translated by H. Zimmern. New York: The Macmillan Company.

Norton, M. I., and S. R. Sommers. 2011. "Whites See Racism as a Zero-Sum Game That They Are Now Losing." *Perspectives on Psychological Science* 6: 215–218.

Nossiter, Adam. October 11, 2006. "U.S. Says Blacks in Mississippi Suppress White Vote." *The New York Times.* Retrieved on January 20, 2007, from www.nytimes.com/2006/10/11/us/politics/11voting.html.

O'Brien, Eileen. 2009. "From Antiracism to Antiracisms." *Sociology Compass* 3(3): 501–512.

O'Brien, Eileen. 2007. "Antiracism." In *Handbooks of the Sociology of Racial and Ethnic Relations*, edited by Hernan Vera and Joe R. Feagin, pp. 427–440. New York: Springer Press.

O'Brien, Eileen. 2001. *Whites Confront Racism: Antiracists and Their Paths to Action.* Lanham, MD: Roman and Littlefield.

O'Brien, Eileen. 2000. "Are We Supposed to Be Colorblind or Not? Competing Frames Used by Whites against Racism." *Race and Society* 31: 41–59.

Oliver, William. 1989a. "Black Males and Social Problems: Prevention through Afrocentric Socialization." *Journal of Black Studies* 20: 15–39.

Oliver, William. 1989b. "Sexual Conquest and Patterns of Black-on-Black Violence: A Structural-Cultural Perspective." *Violence and Victims* 4: 257-273.

Oliver, Melvin, and Thomas M. Shapiro. 1995. *Black Wealth/White Wealth: A New Perspective on Racial Inequality.* New York: Routledge.

Omi, Michael. 2001. "The Changing Meaning of Race." In *America Becoming: Racial Trends and Their Consequences*, edited by Neil Smelser, William Julius Wilson, and Faith Mitchell, pp. 243–263. Washington, DC: National Academy Press.

Omi, Michael, and Howard Winant. 1994. [1986]. *Racial Formation in the United States: From the 1960s to the 1980s.* New York: Routledge.

Pager, Devah. 2007. *Marked: Race, Crime, and Finding Work in an Era of Mass Incarceration.* Chicago: University Of Chicago Press.

Parker, R., and P. S. Chambers. 2005. *The Anti-Racist Cookbook: A Recipe Guide for Conversations about Race That Goes Beyond Covered Dishes and "Kum-Bah-Ya."* Roselle, NJ: Crandall, Dosties & Douglass Books.

Parks, Gregory S., and Matthew W. Hughey. 2010. *12 Angry Men: True Stories of Being a Black Man in America Today.* New York: The New Press.

Pascoe, C. J. 2007. *Dude You're a Fag: Masculinity and Sexuality in High School.* Berkeley: University of California Press.

Pattillo-McCoy, Mary. 1999. *Black Picket Fences: Privilege and Peril among the Black Middle Class.* Chicago: University of Chicago Press.

Plous, S. 2003. *Understanding Prejudice and Discrimination.* New York: McGraw-Hill.

Pramuk, Christopher. 2006. "'Strange Fruit': Black Suffering/White Revelation." *Theological Studies* 67(2): 345–377.

Pratt, Richard H. 1892. *Official Report of the Nineteenth Annual Conference of Charities and Correction*, pp. 46–59. Reprinted in Richard H. Pratt. 1973. "The Advantages of Mingling Indians with Whites." In *Americanizing the American Indians: Writings by the "Friends of the Indian" 1880–1900*, pp. 260–271. Cambridge, MA: Harvard University Press.

Rambo, Carol. 2007. "Handing IRB an Unloaded Gun." *Qualitative Inquiry* 13(3): 353–367.

Reay, Diane. 1996. "Dealing with Difficult Differences: Reflexivity and Social Class in Feminist Research." *Feminism and Psychology* 6(3): 443–456.

Reed, Ishmael. November 20, 1989. "The Black Pathology Biz." *The Nation*. Retrieved on January 21, 2011, from www.thenation.com/article/black-pathology-biz.

Reiman, Jeffrey, and Paul Leighton. 2004. *The Rich Get Richer and the Poor Get Prison*. Boston, MA: Allyn and Bacon.

Reuters. September 25, 2009: "Every G20 Nation Wants to be Canada, Insists PM." Retrieved on May 15, 2010, from www.reuters.com/article/2009/09/26/columns-us-g20-canada-advantages-idUSTRE58P05Z20090926.

Rhodes, P. J. 1994. "Race-of-Interviewer Effects: A Brief Comment." *Sociology* 28(2): 547–558.

Richardson, L. 2000. "Writing: A Method of Inquiry." In *Handbook of Qualitative Research*, edited by N. K. Denzin & Y. S. Lincoln, pp. 923–948. Thousand Oaks, CA: Sage.

Ridgeway, Cecelia. 2011. *Framed By Gender: How Gender Inequality Persists in the Modern World*. New York: Oxford University Press.

Ridgeway, James. 1990. *Blood in the Face: The Ku Klux Klan, Aryan Nations, Nazi Skinheads, and the Rise of a New White Culture*. New York: Thunder's Mouth.

Roediger, David R. 1996. *The Wages of Whiteness: Race and the Making of the American Working Class*. New York: Verso.

Savishinsky, Neil J. 1994. "Transational Popular Culture and the Global Spread of the Jamaican Rastafarian Movement." *New West Indian Guide/Nieuwe West-Indische Gids* 68(3/4): 259–281.

Schacht, S. P. 2001. "Teaching about Being an Oppressor." *Men and Masculinities* 4(2): 201–208.

Schlesinger, Arthur M. Jr. 1998 [1991]. *The Disuniting of America: Reflections on a Multicultural Society*. New York: W. W. Norton and Co.

Schwalbe, Michael. 2008. *Rigging the Game*. New York: Oxford University Press.

Schwalbe, Michael, Sandra Godwin, Daphne Holden, Douglas Schrock, Shealy Thompson, and Michele Wolkomir. 2000. "Generic Processes in the Reproduction of Inequality: An Interactionist Analysis." *Social Forces* 79(2): 419–452.

Scott, Ellen K. 2001. "From Race Cognizance to Racism Cognizance: Dilemmas in Antiracist Activism in California." In *Feminism and Antiracism: International Struggles for Justice*, edited by Kathleen Blee and France Winddance Twine, pp. 125–149. New York: New York University Press.

Segrest, Mab. 1994. *Memoir of a Race Traitor*. Boston: South End Press.

Sewell, William H., Jr. July 1992. "A Theory of Structure: Duality, Agency, and Transformation." *American Journal of Sociology* 98(1): 1–29.

Sharpe, Tanya Telfair. 2000. "The Identity Christian Movement: Ideology of Domestic Terrorism." *Journal of Black Studies* 30(4): 604–623.

Shepherd, Laura J. 2006. "Constructions of Gender in the Bush Administration Discourse on the Attacks on Afghanistan Post 9/11." *International Feminist Journal of Politics* 8(1): 19–41.

Shirley, Carla D. 2010. "'You Might Be a Redneck if . . .': Boundary Work among Rural, Southern Whites." *Social Forces* 89(1): 35–62.

Simi, Pete, and Robert Futrell. 2010. *American Swastika: Inside the White Power Movement's Hidden Spaces of Hate.* Landham, MD: Rowman and Littlefield.

Sivanandan, Ambalavaner. 1995. "Fighting our Fundamentalisms: An Interview with A. Sivanandan." *Race & Class* 36(3): 73–81.

Small, Mario Luis, David J. Harding, and Michèle Lamont. 2010. "Reconsidering Culture and Poverty." *Annals of the American Academy of Political and Social Science* 629: 6–27.

Smedley, Brian D., Adrienne Y. Stith, and Alan R. Nelson. 2003. *Unequal Treatment: Confronting Racial and Ethnic Disparities in Health Care.* Washington, DC: Institute of Medicine of the National Academies.

Smith, Dorothy. 2005. *Institutional Ethnography: A Sociology for People.* Walnut Creek, CA: AltaMira Press.

Somers, Margaret, and Gloria Gibson. 1994. "Reclaiming the Epistemological 'Other': Narrative and the Social Constitution of Identity." In *Social Theory and the Politics of Identity,* edited by C. Calhoun. Cambridge, MA: Blackwell.

Southern Poverty Law Center (SPLC). 2011. "U.S. Hate Groups Top 1,000." *Intelligence Report* 141, edited by M. Potok. Montgomery, AL: Southern Poverty Law Center. Available at www.splcenter.org/get-informed/intelligence-report/browse-all-issues/2011/spring

Spivak, Gayatri Chakravorty. Winter–Spring 1985. "Can the Subaltern Speak? Speculations on Widow-Sacrifice." *Wedge* 7–8: 120–130.

Srivastava, Sarita. 2006. "Tears, Fears and Careers: Anti-Racism and Emotion in Social Movement Organizations." *The Canadian Journal of Sociology* 31(1): 55–90.

Srivastava, Sarita. 2005. "You're Calling Me a Racist? The Moral and Emotional Regulation of Antiracism and Feminism." *Signs: Journal of Women in Culture and Society* 31(1): 29–62.

Srivastava, Sarita. 1996. "Song and Dance? The Performance of Antiracist Workshops." *The Canadian Review of Sociology and Anthropology* 33(3): 291–315.

Srivastava, Sarita, and Margot Francis. 2006. "The Problem of 'Authentic Experience': Storytelling in Anti-Racist and Anti-Homophobic Education." *Critical Sociology* 32(2/3): 275–307.

Staples, Robert. 1982. *Black Masculinity: The Black Male's Role in American Society.* San Francisco: The Black Scholar Press.

Stein, Arlene. 2001. *The Stranger Next Door: The Story of a Small Community's Battle over Sex, Faith, and Civil Rights.* Boston: Beacon Press.

Sullivan, Shannon. 2006. *Revealing Whiteness: The Unconscious Habits of Racial Privilege*. Bloomington: Indiana University Press.

Swain, Carol M. 2002. *The New White Nationalism in America: Its Challenge to Integration*. New York: Cambridge University Press.

Swain, Carol, and Russ Nieli. 2003. *Contemporary Voices of White Nationalism in America*. Cambridge, UK: Cambridge University Press.

Takaki, Ronald. 1993. *A Different Mirror: A History of Multicultural America*. Boston: Little, Brown and Company.

Tatum, Beverly. 1997. *Why Are All the Black Kids Sitting Together in the Cafeteria? And Other Conversations about Race*. New York: Basic Books.

Terry, Robert W. 1981. "The Negative Impact on White Values." In *Impacts of Racism on White Americans*, edited by B. P. Bowser and R. G. Hunt, pp. 119–151. Beverly Hills, CA: Sage.

Thompson, Becky. 2001. *A Promise and a Way of Life: White Antiracist Activism*. Minneapolis: University of Minnesota Press.

Thompson, Cooper, Emmett Schaefer, and Harry Brod. 2003. *White Men Challenging Racism: 35 Personal Stories*. Durham, NC: Duke University Press.

Tierney, William G., and Zoë Blumberg Corwin. 2007. "The Tensions between Academic Freedom and Institutional Review Boards." *Qualitative Inquiry* 13(3): 388–398.

Trepagnier, Barbara. 2006. *Silent Racism: How Well-Meaning White People Perpetuate the Racial Divide*. New York: Paradigm Publishers.

Trotman, C. James. 2002. *Multiculturalism: Roots and Realities*. Bloomington: Indiana University Press.

U.S. Census Bureau. 2000. Retrieved on June 19, 2008, from www.census.gov/main/www/cen2000.html.

Urciuoli, Bonnie. 1996. *Exposing Prejudice: Puerto Rican Experiences of Language, Race, and Class*. Boulder, CO: Westview Press.

Vallely, Paul. September 21, 2006. "Kate Moss Goes 'African' for The Independent's Red Issue." *The Huffington Post*. Retrieved on March 15, 2009, from www.huffingtonpost.com/2006/09/21/kate-moss-goes-african-_n_29934.html

Vaughan, Diane. 2009. "Analytic Ethnography." In *The Oxford Handbook of Analytical Sociology*, edited by P. Hedstrom and P. Bearman, pp. 688–711. Oxford, UK: Oxford University Press.

Vickerman, Milton. 2007. "Recent Immigration and Race: Continuity and Change." *The Du Bois Review* 4(1): 141–165.

Wacquant, Loic. 2009. *Prisons of Poverty*. Minneapolis: University of Minnesota Press.

Wallace, Alexandra. "Asians in the Library." Cited in *The Huffington Post*. March 14, 2011. "Alexandra Wallace, UCLA Student, Films Racist Rant." Retrieved on

March 15, 2011, from www.huffingtonpost.com/2011/03/14/alexandra-wallace-racist-video_n_835505.html.

Walsh, Keith R. 2004. "Book Review: Color-Blind Racism in Grutter and Gratz: Racism without Racists: Color-Blind Racism and the Persistence of Racial Inequality in the United States, by Eduardo Bonilla-Silva." 24 *Boston Third World Law Journal* 443.

Weber, Max. 2002 [1905]. *The Protestant Ethic and the Spirit of Capitalism*. New York: Penguin Classics.

Wetherell, Margaret, and Jonathan Potter. 1992. *Mapping the Language of Racism: Discourse and the Legitimation of Exploitation*. New York: Columbia University Press.

White Reference. March 14, 2011. "Backlash against Forced Diversity: White UCLA Coed Alexandra Wallace Pressured to Apologize after Video Rant against 'Asians In The Library.'" Retrieved on March 18, 2011, from http://whitereference.blogspot.com/2011/03/backlash-against-forced-diversity-white.html.

Willis, Paul. 1977. *Learning to Labor: How Working Class Kids Get Working Class Jobs*. Farnborough, UK: Saxon House.

Wilson, William J. (aka "Ethiop"). 1860. "What Shall We Do with the White People?" *Anglo-African Magazine*.

Wilson, William Julius. 1987. *The Truly Disadvantaged: The Inner City, the Underclass, and Public Policy*. Chicago: University of Chicago Press.

Winant, Howard. 2004. "Behind Blue Eyes: Whiteness and Contemporary U.S. Racial Politics." In *Off White: Readings on Power, Privilege, and Resistance* (2nd ed.), edited by M. Fine, L. Weis, L. P. Pruitt, and A. Burns, pp. 3–16. New York: Routledge.

Winant, Howard. 2001. *The World Is Ghetto: Race and Democracy since World War II*. New York: Basic Books.

Winant, Howard. 1997. "Racial Dualism at Century's End." in *The House That Race Built*, edited by W. Lubiano, pp. 87–115. New York: Random House.

Wise, Tim. 2009. *Between Barack and a Hard Place: Racism and White Denial in the Age of Obama*. San Francisco: City Lights Books.

Woodson, Carter G. 1990 [1933]. *The Mis-Education of the Negro*. Trenton, NJ: Africa World Press.

Wray, Matt. 2006. *Not Quite White: White Trash and the Boundaries of Whiteness*. Durham, NC: Duke University Press.

Zajicek, Anna 2002. "Race Discourses and Antiracist Practices in a Local Women's Movement." *Gender & Society* 16(2): 155–174.

Zerubavel, Evitar. 2002. "The Elephant in the Room: Notes on the Social Organization of Denial." In *Culture in Mind: Toward a Sociology of Culture and Cognition*, edited by K. A. Cerulo, pp. 21–27. New York: Routledge.

Zeskind, Leonard. 2009. *Blood and Politics: The History of the White Nationalist Movement from the Margins to the Mainstream.* New York: Farrar Straus Giroux.

Zimbardo, Philip G. 1973. "On the Ethics of Intervention in Human Psychological Research: With Special Reference to the Stanford Prison Experiment." *Cognition* 2(2): 243–256.

Index